ECONOMIC REFORMS AND WELFARE SYSTEMS IN THE USSR, POLAND AND HUNGARY

Also by Jan Adam

WAGE, PRICE AND TAXATION POLICY IN CZECHOSLOVAKIA, 1948–70
*WAGE CONTROL AND INFLATION IN THE SOVIET BLOC COUNTRIES
*EMPLOYMENT AND WAGE POLICIES IN POLAND, CZECHOSLOVAKIA AND HUNGARY SINCE 1950
*ECONOMIC REFORMS IN THE SOVIET UNION AND EASTERN EUROPE SINCE THE 1960s
*EMPLOYMENT POLICIES IN THE SOVIET UNION AND EASTERN EUROPE (*editor*)

**Also published by Macmillan*

Economic Reforms and Welfare Systems in the USSR, Poland and Hungary

Social Contract in Transformation

Edited by

Jan Adam

Professor Emeritus of Economics
The University of Calgary, Canada

M

MACMILLAN

First published 1991

Published by
MACMILLAN ACADEMIC AND PROFESSIONAL LTD
Houndmills, Basingstoke, Hampshire RG21 2XS
and London
Companies and representatives
throughout the world

Printed in Hong Kong

British Library Cataloguing in Publication Data
Economic reforms and welfare systems in the USSR, Poland and Hungary: social contract in transformation.
1. Eastern Europe. Governments. Social policies
I. Adam, Jan
361.610947
ISBN 0–333–52685–6

Contents

List of Tables

List of Figures

Acknowledgements

I would like to express my appreciation to the University of Calgary Research Grants Committee for the financial contribution which enabled the work on the book to be carried out. I would also like to thank Professor Merlin B. Brinkerhoff, Associate Vice President for Research, whose help and encouragement contributed to the realisation of the volume.

Finally, I would like to express thanks to Mrs E. Blackman for improving the English of some of the contributions, and to Mrs S. Langan for her care in typing a number of the chapters.

JAN ADAM

Notes on the Contributors

Jan Adam, the editor, is Professor Emeritus of Economics at the University of Calgary, Canada. Born in Czechoslovakia, he received his doctorate and candidacy of economic sciences from Charles University, Prague, where he was Dozent up to 1968. He is the author of several books, inter alia, *Wage Control and Inflation in the Soviet Bloc Countries* and *Economic Reforms in the Soviet Union and Eastern Europe since the 1960s*.

Janet G. Chapman is Professor of Economics at the University of Pittsburgh, where she has also served as Chair of the Economics Department (1978–85) and Director of the Russian and East European Studies Programme (1970–83). Her Ph.D. is in Economics from Columbia University, 1963. Her publications include *Real Wages in Soviet Russia since 1928*, *Wage Variation in Soviet Industry*, 'Gorbachev's Wage Reform', *Soviet Economy*, vol. 4, 1988, 'Income Distribution and Socialist Justice in the Soviet Union', *Comparative Economic Studies*, vol. XXXI, no. 1.

Elizabeth Clayton is Professor of Economics and Associate Vice Chancellor for Research at the University of Missouri, St Louis. She is president elect of the Association for Comparative Economic Studies and former president of the Midwest Economics Association. She has published numerous articles on the contemporary Soviet economy.

Zbigniew M. Fallenbuchl is Professor of Economics and Dean of Social Sciences at the University of Windsor, Canada. Born in Poland, he received his B.Sc. from the University of London, an M.A. from the University of Montreal, his Ph.D. from McGill University, and D. honoris causa from the Université de Droit, d'Economie et des Sciences d'Aix-Marseille in 1979. He has published extensively on Soviet and East European economics, particularly on the Polish economy.

Zsuzsa Ferge was born in 1931 in Budapest, worked first in social statistics, then turned to sociology and social policy. She is currently

Professor of Sociology at Eötvös University where she is Head of the Department of Social Policy. She has published eight books (one in English: *A Society in the Making: Hungarian Social and Societal Policy, 1945–1975*), edited six (one in English), and published over fifty papers.

Murray Feshbach has been Research Professor since 1981 at Georgetown University Washington. Previously he was the Chief of the USSR Population, Employment and Research in the USA Bureau of the Census. He was a member of working groups under the US–USSR Agreement on Science and Technology. His M.A. is from Columbia University and his Ph.D. from the American University. He has published extensively on the Soviet population situation and on trends in employment, manpower management, health care, and the environment.

Henryk Flakierski is Professor of Economics at the University of York (Canada). He has published several books and numerous articles about income distribution in East European countries. He is now involved in a broad project about Gorbachev's Economic Reform and Income Distribution.

Ann Rubin received her B.A. in Russian Studies from William Smith College in 1983 and has an M.A. in Russian Area Studies from Georgetown University, Washington. Since completion of her graduate work in 1988, she has worked as a Research Associate with Dr. Murray Feshbach at Georgetown University, with whom she has published jointly.

János Timár is Professor at the Department of Labour and Education Economics of the Karl Marx University of Economics in Budapest. He specialises primarily in employment and educational aspects of the Hungarian economy, and is the author of many publications in Hungary and abroad. His book *Planning the Labour Force in Hungary* was published in the United States. His latest major book deals with time and work time.

Preface

The social welfare system which was gradually built up in the post-NEP era in the USSR and later embraced by East European countries (as they were called until recently) was an integral part of the building of socialism in those countries.* This system has been regarded as socialist for two reasons. On the one hand, programmes, aimed to ensuring incomes and health care for aged, ill, weak, and disadvantaged people, at protecting people against possible unemployment and at mitigating income inequalities stemming from different incomes and number of children, were first advocated by socialists and are often associated with socialism. On the other hand, the way in which most of the programmes have been organised and implemented, mainly the fact that some of them have been so conceived that social aspects have been given priority over economic and market rationality, and thus has definitely separated them from social programmes in capitalist countries, has made them distinctively socialist.

The welfare system built up in this way can be regarded as part of a package deal – a social contract – between the regime and the people. The latter accept the regime, though it is not the result of democractic will, and in return the government vows to provide a welfare system containing – to mention some important components – social security, health care, and subsidised prices for important consumer goods, utilities and housing. The social contract also promises the right to a job and more equal distribution of incomes. The latter can be regarded as a manifestation of social justice rather than as social welfare, while the classification of the right to a job is surely controversial. Some argue that it is also a matter of welfare, others that it is a human rights issue. For simplification, I will call all the mentioned components of the social contract social welfare in the broad sense, whereas welfare in the narrow sense does not include the right to a job or more equal distribution of incomes. If not otherwise indicated, the term 'welfare system' is always meant in its broader sense.

* NEP stands for New Economic Policy; it is used as a name for the phase of development in the USSR from 1921 to 1930. In this phase, market forces were allowed to play an important role after they had been eliminated during War Communism, a period which preceded NEP.

In the second half of the 1980s, Poland and Hungary committed themselves to establishing market economies. In 1989, Czechoslovakia joined these two countries. It seems that the USSR will go in the same direction. Once it is decided drastically to overhaul the economic system, especially if this means the transition to a market economy, then questions arise about the social contract and the welfare system. Some of its components, such as the right to a job, the use of prices to solve social problems and excessive narrowing of wage differentials for skill are contrary to the traditional working of a market economy. The transition period will necessarily make deep inroads in these programmes, all the more because the change will also involve a restructuring of the economy. The right to a job will be the first victim; the needed restructuring of the economy can hardly be achieved without unemployment. The political forces which are at the helm nowadays in the countries under review are no longer genuinely committed to full employment. Some believe that unemployment is an integral part of a working market economy, others see it as an important instrument for disciplining workers. A market economy, which is based to a great extent on private ownership, needs and creates more powerful incentives than exist under a socialist system. Private enterprise and competition, especially if they are combined with the elimination of income controls, necessarily lead to a widening of income differentials, which in turn may act as strong incentives. A properly working economy needs a rational price system, a system which, among other things, is more or less neutral to social problems.

The Soviet Union and East European countries are, in addition, in a precarious economic situation, *inter alia* because of the budget deficit. Under such conditions, the welfare system even considered in its narrow sense, presents a burden. Regardless of the budget deficit, some believe that the social programmes are excessive and should be substantially scaled down, and that the state should be less involved in taking care of social problems. If people are forced to care more about their own well-being, it is argued, this will encourage them to have greater initiative and perform better.

There are, of course, other reasons why the welfare system has been given considerable attention recently. With the political changes and a relatively free press, it has become possible to write openly and it transpires, as was always clear to close observers, that apart from its good points – understandably stressed excessively by politicians of the old regime – the welfare system in its existing form has many dark aspects. Indeed, the broadly designed welfare system on the one hand together with the great stress laid on the production sphere, especially heavy industry and armaments, have led to the neglect of some of the important components of the welfare system mainly the delivery of health care services (in the USSR in particular the health situation is unsatisfactory and all the countries under review have remained far behind in the great revolution in health technology). There has been a gap between the promises and their implementation, notably with regard to equity. In the design of some programmes, economic rationality was largely disregarded, *inter alia* priority was given to solutions which in the short run did not cost much but were used at the expense of solving long-term problems and hardships. The approach to the housing problem is a good example. As already mentioned, some programmes constitute obstacles to marketisation of the economy. The design and organisation of the welfare system, for instance, was determined from above in the USSR and later embraced in East European countries with few modifications. Ordinary people had little say in its design format or implementation.

The attention given to the welfare system at present is an integral part of the ongoing criticism of the old regime. Some believe, however, that this is also aimed at blackening the welfare system in order to soften public resistance to impending cuts in welfare programmes.

Being aware of the importance of the welfare system and its possible development, five of the present contributors to this volume decided, in 1988, to organise a roundtable discussion at the annual meeting of the American Association for the Advancement of Slavic Studies which took place in Chicago, in November 1989, on *Economic Reforms and the Welfare System: Social Contract in Crisis*. Since we felt that this topic might be of interest to a larger economic community, we subsequently decided to publish our revised papers in the form of a book. To this end, we held detailed discussions in Chicago after the public debate and invited Professors Zs. Ferge, M. Feshbach and J. Timár to join us in contributions to the volume.

The purpose of the book is to examine how recent systemic changes in Poland and Hungary, and expected changes in the USSR, affect and will affect the welfare system. This means examining what impact the transition to a market economy, and a democratisation of the political system have and will have on the social contract. The old *quid pro quo* is no longer valid. The public's part of the contract, to accept the regime although it is not the result of the popular will, is no longer an issue; the two smaller countries have committed themselves to democracy and even in the USSR, where democratic institutions are weakest, tremendous progress in democratisation has been achieved, compared to the pre-Gorbachev era. Does this mean that the new regimes are no longer bound by their part of the contract? The welfare system in the narrow sense is mostly applied in developed capitalist countries and has become an integral part of modern society. It is doubtful whether the new regimes, even in Poland and Hungary where the neo-liberals and conservatives respectively hold power, can disregard this fact. Even if they wanted to, they could not do so, since the public has already become used to certain programmes and will not tolerate their elimination or excessive scaling down. This does not mean that the organisation of the welfare system, in the narrow sense, and its financing will not change. As will be shown in the country studies, some provisions have already been made in Poland and Hungary, and many, more substantial ones will follow in order to bring the welfare system, or some of its parts, closer to the rationality of the market, as the new regimes understand it. In addition, price (including rent) subsidies will certainly be restricted. The right to a job and wage differentials policy, which I have defined as part of the welfare system in the broader sense, will surely also be affected.

As previously mentioned, the systemic changes are going on in precarious economic conditions, and these necessarily have an impact on the changes in the welfare system – a fact that will not be overlooked in a volume such as this.

To understand the ongoing and impending changes in the welfare institutions, it is necessary to examine their rise, development and connection with the building of the socialist system, as an economic as well as a political system. And this is also one of the purposes of this book.

In addition, the evolution of views on the welfare system is discussed, though this is by no means the main purpose of these studies.

There is no study on Czechoslovakia, though it is discussed in the first chapter, since, at the time the papers were discussed, no important movement was noticeable in the welfare system there.

When it comes to a contributed volume, there is always the question of the usefulness of coordination and its extent. Two dangers are always present. First, there may be excessive coordination, which is tantamount to putting constraints on the creativity and imagination of the authors, a phenomenon which must adversely affect the end product. Secondly, no coordination at all may produce a product which is not in line with what the title promises. As editor, I have tried to follow a middle road. I have encouraged the authors to stick to the topic, but I have not tried to influence their approaches to the subject matter. Therefore, this volume is marked by different approaches and, of course, by a variety of views on the same problems.

Of the eight chapters, the first, written by the editor, can be regarded as an introduction, in which all the components of the welfare system, as they developed in the smaller countries after the Communists took power and in the USSR in the post-NEP era, are discussed. Of the remaining seven chapters which deal with recent developments in the welfare system, three are devoted to the USSR and two each to Poland and Hungary. The structure of country studies is not the same in each case. The specialisation and interest of the authors has naturally had an imprint on structure. As a result, some topics are discussed more than others. On the whole, it is possible to say that social welfare in the narrow sense takes a central role in most country studies.

In Chapter 2, J. Chapman deals with most of the topics arising in the book as far as they refer to the USSR. E. Clayton, the author of the third chapter, analyses food prices as well as housing policy in rural areas. Housing in urban areas is discussed by J. Chapman in her chapter. Chapter 4, which deals with health care in the USSR, is discussed by M. Feshbach and A. Rubin.

The chapters on Polish welfare (5 and 6) are written by H. Flakierski and Z. Fallenbuchl. The former covers the debates on the welfare system in Poland as well as price subsidies and wage differentials, whereas the latter discusses all other problems pertinent to the welfare system in the broader sense, including employment policy.

Zs. Ferge and J. Timár are the authors of the Hungarian studies. Zs. Ferge discusses the welfare system in the narrow sense with the exception of price subsidies, which are briefly discussed by J. Timár, whose contribution is primarily devoted to employment policies.

November 1990 JAN ADAM

1 Social Contract

Jan Adam*

1.1 INTRODUCTION

This chapter deals with the common and contrasting features of the social welfare system in the USSR, Poland, Czechoslovakia and Hungary. It focuses on the welfare system as it developed after the seizure of political power by the Communists (in the USSR in the post-NEP era). Recent developments in the welfare system in the countries under review are the topic of other chapters.

The Stalinist system did not end with Stalin's death. His rule was marked by tyranny and the worst possible repression. The dictator did not hesitate to abuse the fundamental rights of his real or assumed opponents; the slightest dissent was punished mercilessly. Stalin's successors eliminated the worst excesses of his regime but still did not restore human rights. (Gorbachev's administration is disregarded here). The Stalinist system also used propaganda in its worst form in the service of its objectives, the most important being to maintain its rule.

It would, however, be wrong to assume that Stalin's dictatorship survived only due to terror, intimidation and propaganda. No dictatorial system can survive for long if it relies on such methods alone.

Stalinism had some popular support because of its appeal to various segments of the population. The latter accepted the system because they liked many of its policies. Undoubtedly, sympathy for the system was influenced by propaganda, but this is of no relevance here.

We may say that a social contract was established between the Soviet leaders and a great part of the population, mainly ordinary people. It evolved gradually with the rise of the Stalinist system in the economy and took on a more or less final form in the 1950s, developing later in East European countries.

* I would like to thank Professors J. Chapman, E. Clayton, Z. Fallenbuchl, H. Flakierski and J. Timár, co-contributors to this volume, for valuable comments to my original paper which has helped to improve the final draft.

The idea of a social contract is not new. It was formulated by philosophers in the course of the seventeenth to nineteenth centuries. The two best known works on this topic are *Leviathan* by Thomas Hobbes (1588–1679) and *Du contrat social* by J.- J. Rousseau (1712–78). In a nutshell, the two philosophers argued that the people enter voluntarily into a contract with their rulers. They give up certain rights and, in return, the rulers vow to ensure security, safety and certain freedoms.

The understanding of the relationship between the regime and the population in socialist countries as a social contract appeared in the literature for the first time not long ago (see Hauslohner 1987). Since the social contract in socialist countries is, of course, not a written but a tacit one, there may be disagreements among scholars as to exactly what such a contract contains. In my opinion, people have committed themselves to accept the regime and not to revolt against it, though it (the regime) is not the result of a democratic will. Furthermore, they have agreed to accept low wages and not to strike against the government. In return, the government offers a package of rights and benefits which can be denoted as socialist.

More concretely, the social contract (meaning henceforth the social welfare package promised by the government to the public) included:

1. A right to a job.
2. A series of social programmes which can be called social security and which include, to mention the most important, protection of people against loss of income because of ill health, disability or old age, provisions for health care.
3. Stable and low prices for basic food, services and shelter.
4. A more egalitarian distribution of income.
5. Accessibility of education (including university) to segments of the population which, in the past, could not take much advantage of it. Extensive subsidising of culture.

In brief, it can be said that the social contract has promised to ensure full employment, social justice, solidarity with the weak and disadvantaged, and equal opportunity for all. Points 2 and 3 of the social contract are clearly of a welfare nature; the classification of the others is controversial (see p. xi). For simplification I will refer to the whole package as welfare in the broader sense. If not otherwise indicated, the term welfare is always meant to be understood in this way.

The introduction of the welfare system was the result of the old socialist credo that it was the task of a socialist government to be deeply involved in curing various social problems. Of course, it followed other aims too, one of them being to achieve social peace. Maybe a more important aim was to attain legitimacy for the regime. The Communist leaders hoped that by showing the public that the regime cared about the weak, the underprivileged, the sick and the aged, and was able to settle social problems which the capitalist system could not or did not want to solve, such as unemployment and large inequalities in wealth and incomes, they would get the needed popular support. And this, in turn, would not only contribute to the stabilisation of the regime, but also favourably affect people's attitude to performance.

It should be stressed right away that not all promises have been turned into deeds to the same extent; as will be shown later, the implementation of some of the components was from the beginning not fully consistent with the declared principles, others could not be properly developed because of insufficient funding or because low priority was attached to them.

In this chapter, I am going to discuss how the individual components or their parts (with the exception of point 5) of the social contract came into being and developed for some time in the countries under review, together with their role in and consequences for the economy. While some of the components – such as social security – are an integral part of a progressive and humane society, others, or at least their implementation, can be questioned.

1.2 THE RIGHT TO A JOB

The right to a job is one of the most important elements of the social contract. If it becomes a fact, then full employment exists. Indeed, until recently all the countries under review had more or less full employment.[1] This came about gradually mainly as a result of two factors: the strategy of economic development and the way it was implemented, and the system of management of the economy, which is to a great degree the product of the strategy of economic development.

In the 1930s, the Soviets embarked on an ambitious industrialisation programme whose focus was on heavy industry. Its purpose was to overcome backwardness in the shortest possible time and also to create the foundation of a powerful armament industry. It can be assumed that the architects of the strategy also pursued the goal of eliminating open and disguised unemployment. The first goal was undoubtedly of greater urgency than the second (unemployment liquidation), but in order to achieve it, a strategy was chosen which made it possible to achieve the second goal as well.

The Soviets were short of capital but had an abundance of jobless workers, mainly unskilled. Therefore, they followed a policy of applying the most advanced production techniques available to the basic production processes, and labour-intensive methods to auxiliary production processes and administration (see also Ellman 1979). The Soviet planners apparently believed that this strategy would enable output to be maximised.

The demand for labour was strengthened by the fact that most of the investment funds were channelled into the construction of new factories rather than into the modernisation of existing ones, a policy which was strengthened in the further process of industrialisation. This strategy, adopted in the 1930s in the USSR, survived until recently; after the Second World War it was embraced by East European countries.

The adopted system of management has pushed the economy to the full employment of non-human and human resources. J. Kornai (1980), who can be credited with developing a theory of shortages, argues that the centralised system must sooner or later absorb all the people willing to work. The primary mover of this process is the '*expansion drive and closely related almost insatiable investment hunger*' (ibid., p. 260). Shortages are a permanent accompaniment of the system; they cannot '*be eliminated by an increase in supply – as long as the inner regularities of the economy make demand almost insatiable*. Increased supply is also *finite* – while the demand facing it is always driven by insurmountable inner tendencies towards *infinity*' (ibid., p. 264).

In another book, Kornai (1983, p. 29) explicitly states that full employment 'is not brought about by specific economic policy measures aimed at increasing employment'.

Kornai's conclusions are on the whole correct. Two comments, one supplementary and one quasi-critical, are in order. That the system works in the way Kornai describes is also due to the fact that the central planners view economic efficiency as a macroeconomic concept and, therefore, do not mind if enterprises do not exercise the employment constraint characteristic of a capitalist firm. As long as a socialist enterprise grows, managers may expand employment beyond the point at which the contribution of newly hired workers is equal at least to the labour cost involved, provided that they add to the output of the enterprise.

In my opinion, he underestimates the role that economic policy played in the course of the last decades in achieving full employment. He is generally correct in maintaining that the system of management will sooner or later bring about full employment. However, without economic-policy measures, the economies of certain countries and in certain periods would have been marked by unemployment (Cf. Granick, 1987, p. 69).

The right to a job, which is incorporated in the constitution of the USSR and East European countries,[2] was not always the case. It was included when the socialist countries achieved a stage in employment which can be denoted as 'full'. In practice it means that new entrants to the labour force are helped by the authorities to find jobs,[3] if they themselves are not successful in their search. Since, until recently, all the countries under review had labour shortages, finding a job was not difficult. In addition, employment considerations played a very important role in the decisions about allocation of investment projects. The right to a job also means job security; once a worker acquires a job, and the enterprise where he works is not in a critical situation in terms of output assignments or orders, he can be more or less sure that he will not be fired unless he grossly violates the labour code.

The full employment policy apparently has both positive and negative aspects. The positive aspect lies in the full employment idea itself. Some economists, with certain qualification including the author, believe that the right to a job is an important component of human rights, and people without jobs cannot view and feel themselves as fullyfledged citizens. In addition, unemployment is not without costs to society. These include not only the lost output and state revenues, but also social and psychological costs which cannot be quantified.

The negative side of the full employment policy is that the socialist environment in which it has been carried out and the way it has been implemented have made it an important factor of underutilisation of labour and lack of labour discipline, and an obstacle to a restructuring of the economy. Under conditions of full employment, when it is easy to find jobs, a segment of the labour force which works hard and behaves according to the set rules of employment, including the ones concerning quality only under economic pressure, abuses the system. This abuse is like a contagious disease which spreads quickly and affects great segments of the population. The underutilisation of labour and lax labour discipline are also due to the lack of adequate incentives and to the fact that the position of the managers depends to a great degree on the good will of the workers. Had the political system been democratically based, the authorities would not be reluctant to take unpopular actions, including strengthening the position of managers, needed in order to reduce abuses.

With the development of the economy, some sectors (branches) grow fast and others lag behind, some new lines of production arise and others disappear. The continuous restructuring of the economy also requires a restructuring of the labour force. The growing sectors (branches) need more labour and new skills, and the lagging sectors have redundant labour. A smooth restructuring of the economy presupposes a continuous mobility, but this is hampered in a socialist economy. The full employment policy makes management reluctant to dismiss redundant workers because of the fear of not getting new workers if the need arises, and because this is very often resisted by trade unions. The authorities' fear of the political consequences produced by violating the principle of job security (which has often been understood to mean the right to the same job)[4] hampers the shut-down of obsolete or inefficient plants. The resistance of workers to plant closures is also due to the fact that dismissal from a job often means moving to another location where housing may not be available.

1.3 SOCIAL SECURITY

1.3.1 Introduction

Social security is a comprehensive programme which takes care of a whole range of social problems. With some exaggeration it can be said that the programmes take care of people from the cradle to the grave. The social benefits resulting can be broken down in two ways: one according to the functions which they fulfil and which may overlap, and another according to the methods of providing benefits. The division according to functions includes, on the one hand, support of those members of society who cannot work because of illness, disability or old age, or because they have not yet reached working age. On the other hand, it means support for the reproduction of the work force. Assistance is provided by means of pensions, sickness benefits, maternity assistance, rehabilitation treatment, occupational training and retraining, etc. (Zacharov and Tsivilyov, 1978, p. 20).

Social benefits are provided in the form of services (medical care, rest homes) and transfer payments (pensions, sickness benefits, family allowances). Services are provided according to needs, while transfer payments are mostly linked to employment incomes and thus indirectly to performance in the workplace before retirement.

The scope of this chapter does not allow coverage of all the social programmes and therefore the discussion will be confined primarily to two which give quite a good insight into the social security system: old age pensions and health care.

1.3.2 Old Age Pensions

In the USSR, pensions were first introduced in 1928 in the textile industry where the labour supply was especially abundant. The introduction of pensions was aimed at creating jobs for young people but the system soon expanded to other sectors of the economy (Powell, 1987, p. 201).

Poland, Czechoslovakia and Hungary had pension systems before the Second World War, different, however, for blue-collar and white-collar workers. After the takeover of political power by the Communists, a uniform and comprehensive pension scheme – covering all employees – was slowly brought into being.

First, some principles underlying the policies on old age pensions (OAPs) will be discussed. All employed people of a certain age and with a certain number of service years are entitled to a full pension. Initially, collective farmers were not entitled to a pension from budgetary sources, and in some countries, even when they became entitled, they were still discriminated against. It was several years before they were put on the same footing as employees (Adam, 1983). Nowadays, the old age pension system is based on the principles of universality and transferability. Everyone, regardless of his or her economic activity (apart from household activity) is entitled to a pension, and service years wherever acquired are counted towards the number of service years required for eligibility.

With the exception of Poland, where the retirement age for men is 65 years, it is 60 in the USSR, Czechoslovakia and Hungary. Women have a lower retirement age. One can only speculate why the retirement age was set at such a low level in the USSR, Czechoslovakia and Hungary. Probably one of the motives was to ease the implementation of the full employment pledge. If this is the case, why has Poland chosen a higher retirement age? This question is all the more warranted because Poland has had a faster growth rate of population of a working age.

Due to the role which the working retirees play in the regulation of the labour supply, which will be discussed later, one could surmise that this was also one of the reasons for setting a low retirement age. This suggestion assumes that the planners' decisions were marked by great foresight, but this would give too much credit to an institution which has definitely not distinguished itself in this respect.

The number of service years needed for a full pension is not the same in all the countries. In the USSR, even in the 1930s it was 25 years, after the Second World War in Czechoslovakia it was 25 years, and in Hungary 10 years[5] (Powell, 1987, p. 201; Adam, 1983). People in some occupations need fewer service years in order to qualify for full pension.

All the countries have a minimum, and some also a maximum pension. In the USSR, a maximum was introduced with the pension reform of 1956 (Osborn, 1970, p. 70). In Czechoslovakia, unlike other countries, the maximum level of pensions is differentiated according to three distinct work categories based on working conditions and risks to life in economic activity carried out before retirement (for more see Adam, 1983).[6]

One would expect that when it comes to the level of pensions in a socialist system, all segments of the population would be treated equally within the adopted criteria. This is not the case. Usually, the repressive apparatus gets preferential treatment. What is even more important, the élite (high party and government functionaries) got and, in some countries, still get much higher pensions.

On the whole, OAPs for the ordinary retirees were set quite modestly, particularly in the beginning. In the USSR before 1956, when a new pension reform was introduced, the fifteen new rubles which most pensioners received monthly were hardly enough to make ends meet. Pensioners who did not save – and inflation devalued savings substantially – had to rely on the support of relatives (Osborn, 1970, p. 70) or had to work if they were still able.

In most countries under review the pension benefits were adjusted several times, but mostly only for new retirees. Since pensions are set as a percentage of employment income before retirement, and incomes mostly grow, the new retirees had an additional advantage. As a result, a gap has developed between the pension levels of old and new retirees. The authorities have promised more than once to solve the problem, but this has not yet been fully settled.[7]

The setting of pensions at a low level was motivated by budgetary considerations. Probably the idea of having a workforce in reserve also played a role. In all the countries under review, most pensioners are allowed to continue working for a limited period and collect their pensions. Alternatively, they may continue working full time without collecting their pensions. The deferment of pension collection is rewarded by a supplement in the form of a percentage of the pension.

Working retirees play an important role in regulating the labour supply. If there is a need for their work, they are encouraged to work by improved incentives. In addition, the authorities can direct them by incentives into sectors of the economy where their contribution is most needed. If there is a threat of unemployment, the conditions for their engagement can be restricted. Of course, all this manoeuvring is only possible with retirees who are still able to work.

The spousal survivors of retirees do not have an automatic title to their spouse's pension or a portion of it. In order to be eligible for a lifetime pension, widows must be disabled or of a certain age, or care for a certain number of children. Pensions are regarded as a privilege given by the authorities and not as a right which can be inherited.

Outlays for pensions, as well as for different types of derived pensions such as disability, widows', orphans', social pensions, are financed by the budget (from the collective consumption fund) and enterprises. (Hungary is the only country where, since 1968, employers are obliged to contribute to the pensions costs. Thus pensions are formally no longer a matter of social security, but of social insurance. Until recently, Hungary has not had an income tax.) Enterprises pay a social insurance contribution to the budget which is supposed to be a contribution to the financing of the whole social security package. The balance of the costs is paid from general revenue.

Needless to say, the financing of pensions from general revenue is reflected in higher taxes and lower wages. The state has to find the means from somewhere.

1.3.3 Health Care

In Russia, as early as 1919, the Second Programme of the Bolshevik Party called for 'generally accessible, free and qualified treatment and medication'. This call was gradually implemented in the post-NEP era; however, it took fifty years for rural workers to achieve formal equality[8] in accessibility to health services (Kaser, 1976, pp. 38–9).

Free health care for all citizens was embraced by all East European countries soon after 1945. Apart from some differences, the underlying principles applied in health care delivery were the same in all the countries under review. The care provided has been quite comprehensive. It has included medical treatment, hospitalisation, preventive care, dental care, medication (with some limitations), sanatoria, health spas, etc.

The idea of making health care accessible to all citizens is, no doubt, a progressive and noble idea. It has alleviated the concerns particularly of low income groups about major surgery or chronic disease, as well as the fears of more prosperous groups of financial ruin due to sickness. It has given people a feeling of security and certainty. Free health care also means an important contribution to narrowing the differences in the standard of living. In no other field perhaps was the difference between the haves and the have nots as large as in health care.

The principle of free health care was, of course, supposed to be combined with equal access to health care services. The quality and amount of health care services were not linked officially to any performance or merit in the work place. It was supposed to be distributed purely according to the principle of need and not work. From the beginning, though, it was violated by the establishment of separate health care facilities for the Party and government élite. It was also violated in another way. In all the socialist countries, politicians tried to deliver health services at the least possible cost, an aim which cannot be objected to as long as it is not made at the expense of the quality of services and the principle of free and equal access. However, because of the way in which the minimisation of costs was implemented, infringements on quality and the principle of free and equal access could not be avoided.

The costs of health care services were minimised at the expense of health care workers, mainly physicians. Before the takeover of power by the Communists, physicians were mostly self-employed professionals who set their own fees. The change in the regime turned them into salaried workers, a metamorphosis which was undoubtedly resented by many of them. On top of this, their salaries were set at a relatively low[9] level, bearing in mind that before the socialisation of health care doctors usually earned the most among self-employed professionals, and that distribution of income is supposed to be governed under socialism by quantity and quality of the labour expended. However, the policy-makers did not share such considerations; they believed in a wage policy marked on the one hand by an egalitarianism (or, more precisely, by narrow wage differentials) and on the other by preferential wage treatment of the material sphere, particularly heavy industry. In addition, whenever the economies were exposed to inflation or crisis, physicians' real salaries were usually hit the hardest. For example, the salaries of Soviet health service personnel made up 90.9 per cent of average wages in 1928, 77 per cent in 1940, and 75.7 per cent in 1950 (Kaser, 1976, p. 91; see also p. 12 of this chapter).

Needless to say, doctors viewed their low salaries as disrespect for their profession and deeply resented that policy. They manifested their dissatisfaction in various ways, particularly by hinting to their patients that they must contribute to their earnings if quality care was to be delivered.[10] These hints fell on fertile soil and quickly had a positive response as they coincided with the natural desire of a segment of the population for privileged health care, even at the cost of spending money for services which were, and are, supposed to be without charge. This is mainly true of the more prosperous people in society. Since health is the most precious good, most people sooner or later imitated the 'pioneers' in tipping. This does not mean that doctors are tipped for all services and that all doctors have the same chance of being tipped; in the main it applies to major services, such as operations, where tipping is generous. And so, in the course of time, health care ceased to be a free service, to a degree. Since different patients have different incomes and a different inclination towards tipping, access to health services was not and is not equal. Those who can afford to tip more (or have good connections) can receive treatment from doctors they trust or have access to the hospitals they prefer. Thus, the remuneration policy has eroded the very principle that the politicians promised to promote.

The corruption which penetrated the health service (after all, receiving tips was and is illegal in most countries) has undermined labour discipline. Doctors who take gratuities are not eager to enforce labour discipline at the work place since they are afraid that their subordinates may blow the whistle on them.

Another consequence of the policy of low salaries has been that many men who have not seen a calling in the medical profession have given priority to other professions. This is not to say that the countries are short of doctors. Women have taken up the slack and salary discrimination has thus accelerated the trend towards a prevailing share of women in the medical profession, formerly composed mostly of men.

Health care is financed primarily from general revenues and no premiums are paid by the public. This saves the authorities, on the one hand, from the dilemma of how to set premiums – equal for everyone or according to the size of income – and, on the other hand, from additional costs which the administration of such a programme would require. The financing of health care from general revenues enables the authorities to feel that whatever the amount spent on health care is enough. This hypothesis is borne out in practice. The sketchy figures which are available show that, from the beginning, the spending on health care has been modest in the USSR as well as in the East European countries. For example, expenditure on health protection and physical culture made up only 3.9 per cent of the Soviet Net Material Product in the Soviet Union in 1958, after quite an increase in expenditures on health care.[11] In the following years, Soviet expenditures on health care as a percentage of national income have more or less stagnated. In 1974, they made up 3.87 per cent (Ryan, 1978, p. 19)[12]. It is no wonder that the quality of Soviet health care, as recent revelations show, lags behind advanced countries.

1.4 LOW FOOD PRICES AND STABLE PRICES

In this section, I will discuss the system of retail prices for consumer goods and services. Prices (rents) for shelter will be examined in connection with housing policy.

The price system in the centralised system of management differs very much from that in a market economy. Prices in a centralised system are not the result of market forces; they are set by the authorities[13] and can be changed – with some exceptions – only by the authorities. They are not flexible; they do not react to changes in the relationship between the demand for and the supply of goods.

In setting producer prices, the authorities apply the formula cost plus profit; scarcity is hardly taken into consideration. In setting consumer prices, the authorities take market clearing possibilities into consideration, besides several other aspects which will be mentioned later. Retail prices are set by adding a trade margin to the wholesale prices plus turnover tax.[14] The latter is a differentiated amount which enables the authorities to pursue their objectives in pricing. This retail price system with its relativities was established in the USSR in the 1930s with some modifications in 1947, and in the smaller countries at the beginning of the 1950s (Chapman, 1963, p. 24; Adam, 1979, pp. 4–16). It is still – at the time of writing – almost intact in the USSR and to a lesser degree in Czechoslovakia. In Hungary, the process of its liquidation is in an advanced stage, while in Poland only traces of it have remained.

Concerning the distribution of the turnover tax in consumer prices, it is possible to observe several principles which have not always been consistently applied and which sometimes conflict.

The turnover tax differentiation has aimed at helping to:

(1) equate supply and demand;

(2) fulfil a social function, namely, mitigate social inequalities stemming from differentiated employment income and number of children. To this end, the turnover tax is differentiated according to the principle of how essential consumer goods are deemed to be. In practice, this means that the turnover tax on food staples (such as bread, milk and meat products) is set relatively low and in the course of time has turned into a subsidy, since the increases in agricultural procurement prices have not been (or have only partially been in some countries) passed on to the consumers. In addition, no tax is set on most services. Transportation and utilities rates, as well as prices of some personal services, are set below cost. The social function has not been applied consistently, of course, since other aspects have also been considered;

(3) implement taxation policy. The primary source of state revenues has been indirect taxes and the turnover tax has for a long time been the most important element of these. Therefore, as a matter of principle, goods which are deemed to be non-essential have been taxed heavily. This refers primarily to alcohol and tobacco, and also, though not to such an extent, to clothing, footwear and some other consumer goods. This is not to say that all goods are taxed evenly. On

the whole, staple products are taxed more leniently than luxury goods. Clothing and footwear for children have not been taxed at all or have even been subsidised.

The high turnover tax on clothing and footwear has also been motivated by the fact that light industry has been neglected because of the rapid development of heavy industry;

(4) bring about a proper (as the authorities viewed it) differentiation of real incomes between the agricultural and the non-agricultural population. The existing system of turnover tax distribution among prices disadvantages the agricultural population, which absorbs a great deal of food supplies from its own land and cannot take advantage of some of the low priced services (e.g. public transportation in the cities);

(5) contribute to the promotion of education and culture as well as to propaganda. To this end, prices of books, newspapers and entrance fees to theatres and cinemas are set low.

As a result of the existing distribution of the turnover tax, prices of consumer goods as a whole are set high in relation to prices of services. Within consumer goods, prices of food are set low in comparison to industrial consumer goods.

The use of retail prices for solving various social and income problems has introduced a great deal of distortion into pricing, which is damaging to the economy. Distorted consumer prices cause a distorted structure of private consumption, leading to a higher consumption of some food staples than there would be at rational prices, considering the level of income. The consumer, when faced with a choice of what to do with his savings, whether to buy expensive clothing and/or footwear or more cheap food, often gives preference to the latter. Consumption of meat in Poland is a good example. In the 1970s, the average annual amount was not far below 80 kg, some 20–30 per cent below the West German level, but compared to national income per capita the difference was huge.

The distorted prices contribute to food shortages and, in addition, are a source of inefficiency. Rational prices for consumer goods would increase the demand for clothing, footwear and consumer durables whose production can be expanded more easily, probably at higher productivity[15] and would reduce the demand for food, mainly meat, which cannot be produced in all the countries under review in sufficient amounts. But even if the countries were able to produce enough, high domestic consumption would damage exports, since meat and meat products are important export commodities. In addition, high consumption of meat affects the balance of payments unfavourably since large amounts of fodder must be imported from the West to sustain high meat production (see e.g. Poland).

Low prices for services create many inefficiencies and hamper the expansion of services which, in all the countries under review, are insufficiently developed. One of the main reasons for the reluctance of governments to expand services is that this means a greater claim for state subsidies.

Distorted retail prices have turned out to be what could be expected: one of the important obstacles to economic reforms. It is generally accepted that present reforms must lead in the direction of a market economy. And this requires, among other things, rational prices, that is prices whose relativities are not distorted by subsidies, which in the last two decades have increased to a high percentage of government outlay and, as a result, have become in some countries a factor of budget deficit. If the countries under review had booming economies, this would be no great problem. Since this is not the case, people resist elimination of subsidies even if compensation is promised.

1.5 HOUSING

After the 1917 revolution, Russia was faced with the problem of how to provide housing for the population living in overcrowded and unsanitary conditions, and also for newlyweds. In the beginning, Russia followed in substance Engel's advice expounded in his article, 'The Housing Question', which meant coping with the housing problem primarily by redistributing the existing housing space (Lenin, 1967, p. 310). To this end, soon after the October revolution, Russia nationalised or municipalised large residential buildings exceeding a certain value in towns of over 10 000 inhabitants. Two years later, a new decree specifically expropriated houses belonging to capitalists. The housing space used for residences was distributed on the basis of need and according to set norms for living space per person (Andrusz, 1985, pp. 13–15; Di Maio, 1974, pp. 8–9).

The NEP brought about several changes in housing policy. Small housing properties were returned to their owners and rents, which were abolished during the War Communism, were reintroduced.

However, the rents were not economic but were set at a level which could not even cover the cost of maintenance (Di Maio, 1974, p. 12). The Soviet government also changed its policy with regard to the financing of newly constructed dwellings – it encouraged individual and private financing. In order to promote the use of private capital, it promised investors in its January 1928 decree, 'On housing Policy', various concessions such as freedom to set rents and preferential tax treatment. All this had little effect; owners of capital had too little trust in the government to be willing to invest great amounts in housing, and the drastic change in attitude to the private sector which soon followed proved them right. In addition, the NEP encouraged cooperative housing construction (Di Maio, 1974, p. 13; Andrusz, 1985, p. 16).

In the 1930s, the Soviet authorities took almost full responsibility for housing construction. The underlying idea of the new system of management that planning must embrace all activities, and that investment must be under the strict control of the central authorities, was applied here too. It was argued that centralisation of resources for housing construction would allow a better use of available resources and would enable modern technology to be applied. In reality, this contributed to the housing crisis. In the national plans, housing – as part of the infrastructure – received low priority,[16] though industrialisation and urbanisation substantially increased demand for it. Shortages in construction capacity and materials were felt the most here. The low priority for house building resulted not only from greater stress on heavy and armament industries, but also from the reluctance of the authorities to increase expenditure on the construction and maintenance of houses. Every new dwelling unit meant an increase in the total cost of maintenance because of the low rents that were charged.

The housing crisis of the 1930s was aggravated dramatically by the Second World War, which brought about the destruction of a significant percentage of houses in the territories occupied by Nazi Germany. Not until 1957 did the Soviets exert great efforts to cope with the housing problem, when Khrushchev announced a programme for eliminating the housing shortage within ten to twelve years. His programme opened the door to the increased involvement of individuals in housing construction. Cooperative housing,[17] as a new form of housing tenure with similar privileges to those which individual builders received, was introduced in the USSR in 1962, later than in East European countries (Andrusz, 1985, p. 83).

After the Second World War, the housing situation in Poland was the worst of all; approximately 9 million inhabitants were deprived of living space (Rajkiewicz, 1974, p. 260). Czechoslovakia's residential areas, mainly in Bohemia, were little affected by the devastating effects of the war. The removal of approximately 3 million Germans from Bohemia and Moravia made a large number of dwellings available, primarily in the frontier areas. Nevertheless, Czechoslovakia did face a housing problem. During the war, new residential construction stagnated and the maintenance of existing stock was neglected. After the war, rapid industrialisation and collectivisation in agriculture brought about a great migration to the cities (Adam, 1974), a phenomenon which occurred to a greater degree in Poland and Hungary.

All three countries followed Soviet housing policy with some modifications. They nationalised (municipalised) apartment houses, and housing shortages were mitigated by a redistribution of living space. Strict norms were set, mainly for newly allocated apartments, and rents were kept low. With the start of medium term plans, housing became the responsibility of the government but was low on the list of priorities. In Hungary, for example, the first five-year plan envisaged only 13.5 per cent participation by individuals in housing construction (Pető and Szakács, 1985, p. 227).

In the middle of the 1950s, under political and economic pressure, all three countries committed themselves to paying more attention to housing. To this end, the financing of housing was modified and cooperative housing was given a great role.

Thus, in all the four countries at that time there were four forms of housing tenure, namely, state, cooperative,[18] enterprise,[19] and individual (private).[20] The main purpose of encouraging cooperative and private housing construction was, on the one hand, to expand the number of housing units built and, on the other, to reduce government financial involvement. This does not mean that people involved in cooperative and private housing construction were left to themselves. They received state loans at a very favourable interest rate and also, with the exception of the USSR, state subsidies.[21] Despite the new provisions, none of the countries managed to solve the problem; housing shortages still persist.[22]

The neglect of housing construction has been the result of the obsession with the industrialisation drive and national security. The handling of housing as a social service, which must be provided primarily from state funds and at low rents, has made the situation even worse, because housing has a low priority in government outlays. In addition, low rents have contributed to housing shortages because many families use larger dwelling units than they would if rents were economically realistic.

True, in the second half of the 1950s, Poland tried first, with no great success, to bring the level of rents closer to an economically justified level, and other countries followed, a process which even now has not yet been completed. Low rents have been perceived by the population as compensation for low wages, or, in other words, as an integral part of the social contract. Politicians have confirmed this perception by many of their pronouncements and thus any radical change in rents is resisted.

The expansion of different forms of ownership in housing construction has undoubtedly been a good move; it has contributed to an improvement in housing conditions. However, it has created a situation in which accommodation is available to different people under varied conditions. This differentiation is accidental to a great degree and has little to do with social justice. Housing at low rents in state-owned dwelling units is a privilege not only for low income families, but also for many with higher or high incomes. The advantage of low rents is enjoyed by everyone who had an apartment before cooperative housing was introduced. In addition, allocations from new state-owned housing are not limited to low income families; they are also given to people who, on account of their job or position, are entitled to a service dwelling or in a position to exact such an entitlement. And these are mostly well-paid people. The greater part of the population without apartments, including young people, must look for cooperative or owner-occupied housing. These two kinds of housing are considerably more expensive. Rents in cooperatives are much higher and a down-payment must be made which is not low, considering the earning conditions in the countries under review.

1.6 WAGE DIFFERENTIALS FOR SKILL

As is known, we distinguish different kinds of wage differentials. To mention some: within the same occupation, intra-enterprise, interenterprise, interbranch, for skills, etc. In my opinion, point four in the social contract refers primarily to differentials for skill – wage differentiation between unskilled, semi-skilled and skilled workers – and maybe even more so to wage differentiation between blue-collar and white-collar workers, particularly between workers and professionals. The most typical example is the wage differential between a skilled (or unskilled) worker and an engineer with a university education. Of course, wage differentials for skill have an effect on those others mentioned above.

In the USSR, wage differentials went through several changes. During War Communism, the differentials were quite narrow, the prevailing ideology at that time favoured wage levelling. According to Bergson (1954, p. 182), the ratio of the highest to the lowest wage rate for an industrial manual worker in 1919 was 1.75, which was not very low considering the rates set in 1975 (Chapman, 1988), which seem to be the lowest in the post-war period. By 1921, the difference in earnings between skilled and unskilled workers was already negligible (Lane, 1982, p. 21). During NEP, wage differentials widened substantially; market forces which had been restored had their impact here, too.

With the beginning of the first five-year plan, there seemed to be an opposite trend, but only for a short time. Stalin soon made it clear that there would not be a return to the wage differentials policy of War Communism. He attacked wage levelling as a petty bourgeois idea. In his talk with Emil Ludwig he said, 'Only people who are unacquainted with Marxism can have the primitive notion that the Russian Bolsheviks want to pool all wealth and then to share it out equally' (Stalin, 1955, pp. 120–1; quoted according to Lane, 1982, p. 22).

Stalin's policy was probably motivated by two considerations: (i) fast industrialisation required a large number of skilled workers and technicians, and narrow wage differentials hamper the acquisition of skills; (ii) the growing dictatorship needed a faithful managerial, administrative and repressive apparatus and an army of propagandists in order to protect the regime. Preferential wage treatment was one of the main tools used to obtain the loyalty and the obedience of these people.

After Stalin's death, Khrushchev began a process of narrowing wage differentials which has continued until recently. One could argue that the social contract in matters of wage differentials really started to work after Stalin's death, when it was possible to resume the tradition of War Communism to some extent.

In the smaller countries, the process of narrowing wage differentials started during the Second World War and was accelerated after the Communist takeover of power. This is true particularly of Czechoslovakia and Poland. In 1948–53, in Czechoslovakia, wage differentials between the material and non-material sphere narrowed dramatically, due largely to a reduction of wage differentials between blue- and white-collar workers. In 1948, average employment incomes in education and culture were 124.7, assuming 100 in the national economy, and in health and welfare they were 120.8, whereas in 1953 the figures were 88.9 and 88.6 respectively. A similar narrowing occurred in industry between engineering and technical personnel on the one hand, and manual workers on the other. In 1948, average incomes in the first group were 165, assuming 100 in the latter group; in 1953, the difference was only 32 (Hron, 1968, appendices X/1 and X/2).[23]

It would be wrong to assume that these dramatic changes were only the result of the authorities' desire for relative equality. There were other important reasons. One has to do with the way regulation of wages is applied. In profit-making enterprises, central control over wage increases is not watertight; even under a strict system of wage fund assignment, enterprises have had some devices for receiving additional funds. Manual workers are in a much better position than non-manual; the earnings of the former are dependent to a great extent on piece work and norms which can be manipulated, whereas those of the latter are fixed. In budget financed organisations, the wage bill is set from above and can be changed only by a decision from above. Whenever the economies of the countries faced some crisis, white-collar workers were affected more because of their political vulnerability.

Despite many promises in various periods to widen wage differentials, not much has happened until recently. Perhaps the best example of what wage levelling has achieved is that in some countries an average engineer (with a university education) in a non-managerial position earns more or the same as an average skilled worker. Needless to say, such average levelling is not an incentive to work hard or an encouragement to acquire skill and innovation.

1.7 CONCLUDING REMARKS

Leaders of the socialist countries have always argued that the profound social, political and economic changes which they carried out were intended for the well-being of the people, of course as they understood it. When Stalin formulated his basic law of socialism (1952), he wanted to make the same point. Judging from the history of these countries, those pronouncements, even if they were sincerely meant by some leaders, turned out to be largely of propaganda value. It would, however, be wrong not to see that in the first three decades of the post-war period the countries under review achieved positive results in certain areas of what we have called the welfare system. The present political, social and economic crisis which has engulfed more or less all the countries under review should not conceal these achievements. In the opinion of many people including the author, what should be most appreciated is the introduction of a comprehensive package of social programmes and the creation of full employment.[24] Though the achievements are not without their negative aspects, as I have already shown and intend to enlarge upon, they can nevertheless be valued positively on balance.

The social contract is now under attack on all sides. Some critics argue that social programmes, including consumer price subsidies, are too costly, that they exceed the possibilities of the economy and are at the expense of the level of wages, thus undermining incentives. In this context, it is also argued that the social contract is one of the reasons for recent huge budget deficits, mainly in the USSR. Some believe that people should bear greater responsibility for taking care of themselves and, in this way, they would learn to appreciate the laws of the economy.

Others believe that the social contract leads to the neglect of economic efficiency for the sake of social justice and equality. It is also criticised as an obstacle to economic reforms. It would exceed the scope of this paper to discuss all the criticisms. Therefore, only some comments, mainly about equality versus economic efficiency, will be made.

The cost argument has a certain validity. Since the second half of the 1970s, the economy has started to worsen, but, at the same time, the cost of social programmes has continued to increase as a result of the aging, and previous improvements in the programmes; thus a conflict arose between claims for funds for social programmes and the capability of the economy. On the other hand, inflation, mainly in Poland, and to a lesser degree in Hungary, has significantly reduced the purchasing power of pensions; but it has also reduced the real value of the loans extended to the population for housing. The social programmes are also such a heavy burden because of the high consumer price subsidies, especially in the USSR, which, as will be shown, do not fulfil their purpose.

Extreme adherents of the market have a tendency to favour economic efficiency without great regard to equality. A socialist system which puts equality at the centre of its goals cannot behave in such a way, but it cannot disregard economic efficiency entirely if it does not want the amount available for distribution to be significantly less than in a less equitable but more efficient system. Therefore, policy-makers in a socialist system must always have both principles in mind when making decisions. In balancing the two principles, the bottom line should be the rule that equality does not grossly hamper economic efficiency. To turn this principle into a practical tool is difficult in many cases because it is almost impossible to base it on accurate quantification. It seems that social security on the whole does not violate this principle. There is, however, one element which has the potential to do so and that is sickness benefits, if the authorities neglect to weigh all the factors properly when setting the levels of the benefits and rules for preventing abuses. Otherwise, more equality, particularly in health care, would not hurt efficiency.

It can surely be argued that the right to a job violates the principle of balancing equality and efficiency. It has already been mentioned that the negative effects of full employment can be greatly reduced by proper actions.

In my opinion, the retail price system is the one which clearly violates the principle of balancing equality and efficiency, for reasons already mentioned. In addition, it is not clear whether it contributes much to equality if taken as a whole. In 1956, computations were made in Czechoslovakia to find out how the distribution of the turnover tax into prices with the existing structure of consumption affects individual income groups. It turned out that it had little effect; though many prices favour low income groups, these advantages are offset by low prices which favour high income groups, because low income groups cannot afford to buy these goods in great amounts (e.g. meat). Low income groups could have been much better served if subsidised prices had been limited to a few staples, and pensioners and families with several children, who for the most part belong to low income groups, would have received higher pensions and family allowances, respectively.

There is no doubt that some elements of the social contract undermine incentives. Narrow wage differentials for skill definitely have a negative effect on the motivation of managerial and technical staff whose activities determine, to a great degree, the efficiency of the economy. Some believe that a reduction in social benefits in favour of wages may increase incentives. No doubt average wages compared to national income per capita are low in the countries under review, and their increase may, under certain conditions, increase incentives. However, an increase in wages at the expense of social benefits may not necessarily work as expected.

NOTES

1. Here I leave aside all the discussions about how to define full employment.
2. Poland and Hungary are going to omit this from the newly designed constitutions.
3. In some cases, the authorities assigned jobs, as in the case of university graduates. For more, see J. Adam, 1984.
4. In the USSR, this perception has been strengthened by bonuses for seniority.
5. In 1984, the number of service years in Hungary was increased to twenty-five.
6. The differences in pensions between the three work categories are quite big. In 1959, the maximum for the third category was Kcs 1600 monthly, second Kcs 1800 and first Kcs 2200.
7. This particularly affects pensioners of advanced age or with ill health.
8. Real equality has not been and cannot be achieved. Urban health care centres are equipped with better facilities and more qualified physicians.
9. In 1955–65, the monthly salaries of physicians in urban areas ranged between 74 and 110 rubles; at the same time, the average wage in national income was 71.8 rubles in 1955 and 96.5 in 1965. See V. Navaro, 1977, p. 73 and *Narodnoe Khoziaistvo SSSR za 60 let*, Moscow, 1977, p. 472.
10. This is not to say that all doctors behaved in the same way. In the beginning, there were many doctors who disliked the idea of being tipped, but gradually they were swayed by their colleagues.
11. In Canada (which also has a free health care system), in the 1970s, it was approximately 8 per cent of GNP, which is of a larger magnitude than net material product under the same level of performance of the economy. However, the higher percentage in Canada has, to a great degree, to do with the high salaries of health care employees, especially physicians. But it is also the result of medical facilities being equipped with the most modern equipment and technology.
12. Other statistical figures show that if we take the allocation for public health in 1940 for 100, in 1975 it was 1244; at the same time, national income increased to 1142. (Lisitsin and Batygin, 1978, p. 79; *Narodnoe Khoziaistvo SSSR za 60 let*, Moscow, 1977, p. 14.)

13. This was mostly done by the central authority, in some cases by regional or local authorities.
14. For a long time, the turnover tax was (in the USSR still is) a residual difference between retail (reduced by a trade margin) and wholesale prices. This method of tax construction means that wholesale and retail prices can have autonomous development.
15. In some countries, such changes would require new productive capacities.
16. In the period from 1929 to June 1941, the Soviet Union constructed only 206 000 housing units. The meaning of this figures becomes clear if it is mentioned that in the 1960s, when greater attention was devoted to housing, approximately 500 000 units were built during a quinquennium (Di Maio, 1974, p. 21).
17. Cooperatives were already possible earlier, and they got a boost in 1958 when they were recognised as a socialist form (ibid., p. 185).
18. Housing cooperatives, which initially were meant only for cities, were later also expanded in some countries to collective farms.
19. Enterprise housing aims at ensuring housing for skilled employees and thus at creating a stable nucleus of the enterprise workforce. Its share in housing construction is quite small.
20. Private housing was meant for the countryside.
21. In the 1960s, in Czechoslovakia, the state subsidies amounted to 59 per cent of total costs (*Hospodářské noviny*, no. 11, 1970).
22. Many families must still live in overcrowded conditions, many newlyweds must live with their parents and/or grandparents. The shortage of housing is an important cause of many broken marriages, family tragedies, and a strain on human relations. In brief, it adversely affects human life. All the countries under review deserve low marks for their handling of the housing problem; they have displayed great insensitivity to human hardship.
23. For more on wage differentials in the 1950s see Adam, 1984, pp. 192–208.
24. Talking about achievements, one should not forget the accomplishments in education and culture.

REFERENCES

ADAM, J. (1976) 'Housing Policy in European Socialist Countries: The Czechoslovak Experience', *Jahrbuch der Wirtschaft Osteuropas*, vol. 6.

ADAM, J. (1979, 1980) *Wage Control and Inflation in the Soviet Bloc Countries* (London: Macmillan; New York: Praeger).

ADAM, J. (1983) 'The Old Age Pension System in Eastern Europe: A Case Study of Czechoslovak and Hungarian Experience', *Osteuropa Wirtschaft*, no. 4.

ADAM, J. (1984) *Employment and Wage Policies in Poland, Czechoslovakia and Hungary since 1950* (London: Macmillan; New York: St Martin's Press).

ANDRUSZ, G. D. (1985) *Housing and Urban Development in the USSR* (New York: State University of New York Press).

BERGSON, A. (1954) *The Structure of Soviet Wages: A Study in Socialist Economics* (Cambridge: Third Printing).

CHAPMAN, J. (1963) *Real Wages in Soviet Russia since 1928* (Cambridge, Mass.: Harvard University Press).

CHAPMAN, J. (1988) 'Gorbachev's Wage Reform', *Soviet Economy*, no. 4.

DI MAIO, A. (1974) *Soviet Urban Housing: Problems and Policies* (New York: Praeger).

ELLMAN, M. (1979) 'Full Employment – Lessons from State Socialism', *De Economist*, no. 4.

GRANICK, D. (1987) *Job Rights in the Soviet Union: Their Consequences* (Cambridge: Cambridge University Press).

HAUSLOHNER, P. (1987) 'Gorbachev's Social Contract', *Soviet Economy*, no. 1.

HRON, J. (1968) *Změny v oblasti mezd v období 1945–1953* (Prague).

KALECKI, M. (1964) *Z zagadnien gospodarczo-społecznych Polski Ludowej* (Warsaw).

KASER, M. (1976) *Health Care in the Soviet Union and Eastern Europe* (London: Croom Helm).

KORNAI, J. (1980) *Economics of Shortage* (Amsterdam, volume A).

KORNAI, J. (1983) *Contradictions and Dilemmas, Studies on the Socialist Economy and Society* (Budapest: Akademia Budapest).

LANE, D. (1982) *The End of Social Inequality? Class, Status and Power under State Socialism* (London: Allen & Unwin).

LENIN, V.I. (1967) *The State and Revolution*, in *Selected Works*, Vol. 2, (Moscow: Progress Publishers).

LISITSIN, J. and BATYGIN, K. (1978) *Public Health and Social Security* (Moscow: Progress Publishers).

MATTHEWS, M. (1986) *Poverty in the Soviet Union* (Cambridge: Cambridge University Press).

NAVARO, V. (1977) *Social Security and the Medicine in the USSR* (Lexington, Mass.: D.C. Heath).

OSBORN, Robert J. (1970) *Soviet Social Policies: Welfare, Equality and Community* (Chicago: Dorsey Press).

PETŐ, I. and SZAKÁCS, S. (1985) *A hazai gazdaság négy évtizedének története 1945–1985*, Vol. 1 (Budapest: Közgazdasági és Jogi Könyvkiadó).

POWELL, D. E. (1987) 'Manpower Constraints and the Use of Pensioners in the Soviet Economy', in Adam, J. (ed.), *Employment Policies in the Soviet Union and Eastern Europe*, 2nd rev. ed. (London: Macmillan; New York: St Martin's Press).

RAJKIEWICZ, A. (1974) in Secomski, K. (ed.), *30 lat Gospodarki Polski Ludowej* (Warsaw).

RYAN, M. (1978) *The Organisation of Soviet Medical Care* (Oxford).

STALIN, J. (1955) 'Talk with Emil Ludwig', *Collected Works*, Vol. 13 (Moscow: Foreign Language Publishing House).

STILLER, P. (1981) *Systeme der sozialen Sicherung in der USSR, Polen, DDR und der CSSR* (Munich: Olzog).

ZAKHAROV, M. and TSIVILYOV, R. (1978) *Social Security in the USSR* (Moscow: Progress Publishers).

2 Drastic Changes in the Soviet Social Contract

Janet G. Chapman

2.1 INTRODUCTION

Gorbachev's reforms are breaking what for the past three decades or so has been the social contract between the Soviet leaders and the people, and he is attempting to develop and sell a new social contract more suitable to the current situation.

The old social contract, as Jan Adam's chapter points out, provided for job security, protection in old age and illness, free education and health services, a rather egalitarian distribution of income, low and stable prices of food and rent and an increasing, even if at times slowly, standard of living. In return, the people were to stay out of politics, show up for work, obey their superiors and maintain discipline. This worked well for years but more recently had obviously begun to unravel. Docility turned into apathy; drunkenness, absenteeism and other forms of indiscipline were increasing. The saying attributed to Soviet workers: 'As long as the bosses pretend they are paying us a decent wage, we will pretend that we are working'[1] sums up the situation and implies that the workers understood that there was – or at least had been – an underlying social contract.

The new contract takes away some of the old economic rights; so far, in particular, the guaranteed job and the egalitarian distribution of wages. It is argued, following Marx, that socialist justice requires that each contribute according to his ability and be paid according to his contribution. Paying slackers as much as effective workers is unjust.

A number of other questions of socialist justice are being raised. For instance, each ruble earned should have the same value so special privileges should be eliminated and price subsidies should go. The end of subsidised food and rent is in the offing but the leadership is treading hesitantly here.

While job security has been reduced, the safety net for those who cannot work or who lose their jobs will be improved.

With increased emphasis on payment according to contribution, some argue that justice requires greater equality of opportunity for people, especially children, to develop their abilities. Benefits provided by the state should be more equally distributed. Some propose that only the minimum benefits that society can afford to provide to all should be provided free. Additional benefits or services could be paid for by those whose income permits.

The new contract introduces some political rights and opportunities to participate in economic and political life. We hear talk of a 'civil state' and of the rule of law. Provision has been made for greater worker participation in enterprise decisions. This and some new forms of the organisation of labour, such as private and cooperative enterprise and leasing arrangements, are expected to give the workers a sense of proprietorship. Considerable power is shifting from the centre to enterprises and to republican and local governments. Elections now provide some choice of candidates. The new legislature – Congress of People's Deputies and its standing body, the Supreme Soviet – appears to have some real power.

By improving incentives, giving workers more political rights, and trying to inculcate a sense of proprietorship, Gorbachev hopes to 'activate the human factor'. He has acknowledged (for instance, in his speech to the Central Committee in early February, *The New York Times*, 9 February 1990) that neglect of human rights means the USSR has seriously lagged. He wants to turn people around, give them more incentive to put out, tap their creativity and give and demand more responsibility. In Marx's terms, Gorbachev wants to see work changed from a mere means of life to the prime necessity of life. This is considered crucial to improved efficiency and technological progress.

I will discuss the end of the guaranteed job, the new policy of increasing wage differentials, job-related rights, improvements in social security and the war on poverty and housing. Specifics on other aspects of the social contract are covered elsewhere in the volume. In the next to last section, some issues and trends are appraised and the last section examines prospects for the new social contract and the reforms.

2.2 THE END OF THE GUARANTEED JOB

The Soviet constitution guarantees everyone the right to an appropriate job and makes it a duty for everyone to hold a job. This has been interpreted to mean that a person is guaranteed not only a job but tenure for life in that job. And this interpretation reflects more than just tradition. Strict legal limits exist on the reasons workers may be fired and the trade union committee has to approve each case of firing.[2]

The main reasons a worker may be fired are violation of discipline, a finding that the person is no longer capable of performing adequately, and reduction of staff or closing down the enterprise. Further,it has long been – sometimes by law, sometimes by custom – the obligation of the employer who fires a worker to find him a suitable job either in the same enterprise or elsewhere.[3] This is a strong deterrent to firing. Economists have long been arguing that enterprise management should be freed of this obligation and that re-employment should be left to the placement service, which has been in existence since 1967.

Beyond this, a number of job-connected rights exist. General rules restrict the right to fire people and specific legislation protects the rights of various categories of workers – women, especially with young children; juveniles; and invalids.

The general rule about breaking the labour contract and releasing workers when an enterprise is reducing staff, is that the enterprise is entitled to keep those of superior skill and productivity and, where appropriate, to reallocate them to jobs from which others are released. The enterprise cannot make new hires while it is reducing staff. When skill and productivity are equal, preference in retaining workers is given the following:

(a) members of families with two or more dependants;
(b) a person who is the sole earner in the family;
(c) workers with a long stage of uninterrupted work in the enterprise;
(d) persons who have suffered work injuries or contracted an occupational illness at the enterprise;
(e) workers raising their qualifications at higher or specialised secondary education without a break from employment;
(f) war invalids and members of families of military servicemen or partisans killed or missing in action (Begichev and Zaikin, 1985, pp. 138–9; *Kodeks*, 1988, p. 18).

In addition, to fire persons absent for military service, sick leave, or annual vacation, while they are absent, unless the enterprise is being completely liquidated is prohibited.

Women are heavily protected. Pregnant women, nursing mothers and mothers of children under 18 months cannot be fired unless the enterprise is being completely liquidated, and even then, to find another job for them is obligatory (Kodeks, 1988, p. 65). This prohibition is designed to protect these women in view of the many privileges they have that would tend to make them less desirable employees.

Young people are also heavily protected. First, quotas are set for the percentage of the workforce in each enterprise that must be made up of people under age 18. They have special privileges. The main one is a shorter week (24 hours for those 14 to 16 and 36 hours for those 16–18, as compared with the standard 41 hour week) while paid the same weekly rate as adult workers (Livshitz and Nikitinsky, 1977, pp. 86–7).

The disabled and pensioners are to be fired only if there is no alternative (*Kodeks*, 1988, pp. 11–12, 17).

Policy towards job security has changed drastically. The economic reform emphasises more economical use of labour and contains provisions intended to squeeze out excess labour.

Also anticipated is a substantial structural shift in the demand for labour, from the material branches to services. The estimate is that 16–20 million fewer people will be needed in the material branches by the year 2000 (Kostakov, 1987); the service sector is to expand but it is not clear that it will be able to absorb all those released (Chapman, 1989b).

The wage reform in the material branches requires that wage rates be raised and the enterprise must finance these from its own funds. This is expected generally to impose economies of labour, including firing redundant workers. The new economic mechanism now in operation throughout the economy also emphasises self-financing and provides similar incentives to economise on labour.

The right to a job is no longer the right to a particular job but a guarantee (promise?) that an appropriate job will be forthcoming, with the expectation that a person will have to change jobs, occupation and place of residence during his life.

Economists are beginning to repeat the attitude taken in Hungary that 'full employment is the responsibility of the state' (Sziraczki, 1988, p. 399) while 'effective use of labour is the responsibility of the enterprise' (Kotliar, in 'Kak ne . . .'). Some, such as Kostakov (1987), believe too many people are working and that measures should be taken to relieve some of them of this necessity, such as longer leaves for mothers of young children and more generous student stipends and old age pensions. Some suggest that a little unemployment would keep workers on their toes. Others say that job creation must correspond to the need of the economically active population for labour. 'In socialist conditions, only employment which is at the same time both rational and full can be regarded as effective' (Kotliar, 1989).

In the transition from the old to the new view of employment, a number of issues are still to be faced. One set relates to the job rights, or rights not to be fired outlined above. These would seem to conflict with the economic interest of enterprises on full self-financing in their efforts to reduce the number but improve the quality of their work-force. In general, precisely the kinds of workers management would find least desirable – because of special privileges, restrictions on their activities, or because they are on leave and not on the job – are those most difficult to fire. Not clear is whether significant changes are to be made in these rights. So far, management has been given the right to let go persons who reach pension age and are entitled to a full pension (*Izvestia*, 19 February 1988); the implication is that those not entitled to a full pension should not be fired.

Not likely is that the privileges and protections for pregnant women and mothers of small children will be eliminated. But if not, women may find it harder to get jobs in the future. Rimashevskaia (1988) anticipates the development of a dual labour market, with women, youths, and elderly in the secondary jobs.

The other set of issues relates to the maintenance, retraining and placement of people who lose their jobs. The placement service, established in 1967, is being expanded and improved with additional duties of coordinating training programmes as well as finding jobs for the unemployed.[4] Not clear is how the training is to be financed. Those who lose their jobs are entitled to two to three months' pay at the level of their former earnings while job searching or retraining. So far, however, the former employer pays.

Financing of unemployment compensation has to be put on a sounder basis. First, the possibility of unemployment must be recognised. As P. S. Rudev (1989) of Goskomtrud puts it:

> Officially we have no unemployment. The status of the unemployed person has not been defined, nor are there statistics on this question. But this, of course, does not mean that everyone has a job. We will have to sign the international convention on promot-

> ing employment and protection from unemployment and change the Code of Labour Laws to define the status of the unemployed and measures to protect these persons. Today proposals have been prepared to create an All-Union Fund for Retraining and Redistributing Cadres (in effect a fund to support the unemployed).

He suggests the source for this fund could be either part of the payments enterprises make for labour or the social insurance tax on payrolls (ibid.).

Whether two to three months is long enough for persons to retrain and find a new job is yet to be faced. Apparently, it has not been long enough for some who have lost managerial jobs. Of them, Rudev says that if someone does not find a job within two months, his salary will be extended for another three months, and possibly even longer (ibid.).

Even proposed support for the unemployed would presumably cover only those who have been fired. It would be of no benefit to the many young, particularly in Central Asia, who have never had a job.[5]

2.3 INCREASING EARNINGS DIFFERENTIALS

The Soviet people appear to believe strongly in equality. This is rooted in historical and cultural traditions and in Marx's distribution principle for full communism: 'From each according to his abilities, to each according to his needs.'[6] Part of the post-war social contract was a policy that promoted substantial decreases in inequalities. Gorbachev is reversing this trend.

The beginning of the reduction in earnings differentials is 1956 when the first post-war wage reform was undertaken.[7] Although reducing inequalities in income was not initially stressed, it became an aim of the wage reform at the Twenty-first Party Congress in January 1959 and in the seven-year plan for 1959–65. The major features of this wage reform tending to reduce differentials was establishment of an effective minimum wage – at first 27–30 rubles a month, later 40 rubles (Chapman, 1970, p. 18) – and the setting of a ceiling on top pay rates, of around 230 rubles or more. In a study of this reform, I concluded that the primary function of the Soviet wage system, including these reforms, was still that of achieving the desired allocation of labour and stimulating better performance on the part of the workers, but that, in the case of the 1956–65 wage reform, efficiency criteria coincided generally with the goal of achieving a more equitable distribution of income (ibid., pp. viii, 101–7).

Notice that Khrushchev, who forecast the country would be on the verge of full communism by 1980, saw the transition to the distribution principle of full communism as being achieved through increasing the share in income of benefits in kind rather than through eliminating wage differentials (ibid., pp. 113–14).

The biggest step towards equality was Brezhnev's raising of the minimum wage by 50 per cent (from 40 to 60 rubles) for all on 1 January 1968. This was announced as implementing the party's policy of narrowing the gap between the incomes of low- and high-paid workers and creating the conditions for securing the material well-being of the families of all workers (Smirnov, 1967; Kunel'skii, 1968, p. 20; Chapman, 1970, pp. 126–8). Subsequent adjustments in wage rates above the minimum in the second wage reform, completed in 1975, somewhat increased differentials above the 1968 level but top wage and salary rates remained under a ceiling.

Another factor tending to keep earnings differentials narrow is the widespread management practice of paying relatively equal bonuses rather than making fine distinctions among the individual performances of workers in a group. Workers on incentive pay may sometimes pace their work so no member of the group comes out too far ahead or behind. And workers in a brigade with some discretion over the distribution of its bonus may often operate on the 'equal stomachs' principle.

The decile ratio[8] of the earnings of all full-time Soviet wage earners and salaried workers, which was 4.44 in 1955, just prior to the first post-war wage reform, fell to a low of 2.83 in 1968 after the 50 per cent increase in the minimum wage and has varied around 3 to 3.3 per cent between 1970 and 1985 (Chapman, 1989a, p. 16). The freeze on upper salaries meant an erosion of the relative pay of managerial and professional personnel. In industry, the earnings of engineering-technical personnel (ITR) exceeded those of wage earners by 66 per cent in 1955, but this advantage had fallen to 10 per cent in 1968. In construction, ITR earnings exceeded those of wage earners by 95 per cent in 1955 but in 1986 fell 2 per cent below earnings of wage earners (*Trud*, 1968, pp. 138–9, 145; *Narodnoe khoziaistvo*, 1987, p. 431).

Gorbachev's wage reform marks a clear change in policy. He found that the wage differentials had become so narrow as to stifle initiative, particularly among managers and highly qualified engineers on whom he must rely to further technological progress. This reform makes basic pay for similar jobs more equal but increases differentials in basic rates to reflect more closely differences in skill and responsibility. Professional salary rates are raised by 30–35 per cent against rises of 20–25 per cent for wage earners. Greater scope is provided in incentive and bonus rules for management to recognise and reward superior performance. (For further details, see Chapman, 1988). The decile ratio of earnings rose to 3.6 in 1986 as to 3.9 in 1989 (Chapman, 1990, p. 3).

Interestingly, the current wage reform makes no reference to a change in the minimum wage although it had originally been planned to raise it from 70 rubles to 80 rubles (Kunel'ski, 1987, p. 193).[9]

Marx's distribution prescription for socialism is: 'from each according to his abilities, to each according to his contribution.' While previous leaders subscribed to this principle, Gorbachev emphasises it more strongly and argues that justice requires that people who work more effectively be paid more than those who shirk. They are trying to sell this conception of justice to the population.

The drive against unearned income is part of this programme. Unearned income includes not only income from speculation on the black market, accepting bribes and the like, but also bonuses or other earnings from employment in state enterprises based on padded reports of output.

The policies permitting cooperatives and individual labour activity (small private business) and encouraging leasing arrangements provide new opportunities for earnings, which may be quite high. Much popular indignation is expressed over the high prices charged by cooperatives and the high earnings of coop members.

Concerns over cooperative incomes may be seen in the controversy about taxation of the incomes of their members. Some wanted to penalise the new 'millionaires' and proposed a marginal tax rate as high as 90 per cent (Tedstrom, 1989), but the majority in the Supreme Soviet believed these high taxes would stifle initiative and hinder development of the cooperative movement. The rational course, as proposed by some of the better economists, would be not to place any restrictions on the amount that can legally be earned but, to prevent an unacceptable degree of inequality, to establish a progressive income tax. This seems to be the course that will be taken.

A draft decree currently under consideration (published in *Pravda*, 16 April 1989) will apply equally to members of cooperatives and state employees and to all forms of income.[10] The new rates are more progressive than the old rates for state employees. Incomes up to 80 rubles a month are exempt, the tax on incomes of 81 to 100 rubles is reduced and incomes of 101 to 700 rubles are taxed at the current top marginal rate of 13 per cent. The marginal rate goes to 15 per cent for incomes of 701 to 900 rubles, to 40 per cent for incomes of 1301 to 1500 and to 50 per cent for earnings above 1500 rubles ('Taxes Based on Income', p. 16). This is a clever law in that the rates apply to all with earnings over 80 rubles but the progression only begins at 700 rubles a month. The 1988 average earnings of state employees were 217 rubles and only a little over one per cent of full-time wage earners and salaried workers earned more than 700 rubles (*Ekonomicheskaia gazeta*, no. 29 (May) 1989, p. 14).[11] Earnings of coop members in Moscow averaged 700 rubles in 1988 ('The Cooperatives: Surf and Foam', p. 83).

2.4 JOB-RELATED RIGHTS, FRINGE BENEFITS AND PERKS

In the Soviet Union, an extraordinary number of essential services are provided at the factory or office and are tied to a person's job. These may include housing, cafeterias, child care facilities, shops, vacation resorts, repair services, and so forth. This means, in the first place, that losing one's job may mean losing one's apartment and access to services. Secondly, the benefits are unequally distributed and questions are being raised about the justice of that.

The right to housing is probably the most important, given the extreme shortage of housing. Much belongs to enterprises[12] and a worker usually obtains his apartment through his employer. Once he has an apartment, it is true, he usually cannot be evicted even if he ceases working for the enterprise (Bogorad, 1988). A person who loses his job and finds another one in the same city has no problem. The problem arises for those who are on the waiting list for housing, especially those near the top of the list, for in a new job they would presumably fall to the bottom of the list. For some, losing one's place on the housing list is worse than having to take a new job at lower pay. In at least one case, an employee was allowed to take her high place on the housing list to her new job (Kurbatov, 1987, p. 83). But this creates problems for the new employer. 'They would rather not hire a person for work than allow him to "bump" one of "their own" from the waiting list' (Krasnopolskii, 1989, p. 83).

In redefining the social contract, some have raised questions about the justice of the widely varying benefits that are attached to the job. Some take the view that these benefits, financed from enterprise profits, represent an extension of the principle of payment according to contribution and are therefore just (Rimashevskaia, 1986). To the extent that the profits that pay for these benefits reflect efficient management and hard work, most would probably agree. Some point to the wide discrepancy in the amounts of such benefits, a discrepancy that may reflect circumstances not under control of the enterprise, such as favourable or unfavourable prices, modern or antiquated equipment (Rutkevich, 1986; Riazanov, 1984).

Wide variations in the provision of services do exist. A 1987 survey of 18 000 workers in five industries showed that one-fifth of the workers (one-third in ferrous metallurgy) were on the waiting list for improved housing and in the previous year, only 12 per cent of those on the waiting list had improved their housing. The same survey showed that 54 per cent of the enterprises had pre-school institutions (only 31 per cent in the food industry, where 53 per cent of the workers are women), 35 per cent had pioneer camps, 69 per cent had health care facilities, 86 per cent had cafeterias, 63 per cent had libraries, 52 per cent had houses of culture, and 56 per cent had sports facilities (*Vestnik statistiki*, 1988, no. 5, p. 59).

A similar survey of 46 000 workers showed that 71 per cent had cafeterias, 58 per cent medical services, 63 per cent had tourist and excursion services, 61 per cent had retail trade services, 62 per cent had transport services, 40 per cent had everyday services (such as repairs to clothing or household goods, repairs of apartments, dry cleaning) and 59 per cent had access to physical culture and sport facilities (*ibid.*, p. 53).

These services are so embedded in the system that it is not clear that they could be separated from the enterprises and opened to all.[13]

Of perhaps greater concern are the lavish perquisites of office of the élite, such as chauffeured cars, country dachas and access to closed shops. Some, led by Boris Yeltsin, are calling for the abolition of these perks. A committee of the Supreme Soviet is working on this question. So far, the number of official cars was to be reduced by 40 per cent by July 1988 (*The New York Times*, 4 February 1988), the special canteens for ministers were closed in 1988 (Ryshkov, 1989a) and the Moscow closed-shop food distribution system for the élite is to be ended (FBIS-SOV-90-031, p. 39). Some of the special hospitals for the élite are being transformed into child care hospitals or others open to the public.

2.5 SOCIAL SECURITY AND THE WAR AGAINST POVERTY

Although job security has decreased, all evidence suggests that the safety net for those unable to work will be raised. One might even say that a 'war on poverty' has begun. With *glasnost*, more information has become available on the distribution of income. This shows that 8.3 million people or 2.9 per cent have per capita incomes below 50 rubles a month, the poverty line established in the early 1960s. Another 11.8 million persons have income between 50 and 75 rubles, making a total of 36 million people or 12.6 per cent of the population with per capita monthly incomes below 75 rubles.[14] The new official poverty line is 78 rubles a month (*Ekonomicheskaia gazeta*, 1989, no. 25, p. 11). The publication of these data may well have been the inspiration for Gorbachev's expression of concern in his report to the Congress of People's Deputies on 30 May for the 'more than 40 million people with low incomes', for Boris Yeltsin's call in the Congress of Deputies the next day for an improvement in the living conditions of the poor and Ryzhkov's prompt response with a draft of a law, 'Emergency Measures for the Improvement of Pension Security and Social Maintenance of the Population' (Peterson, 1989, p. 8).

The major social security provisions relate to temporary disability, including pregnancy leave; old age pensions and pensions for the disabled, for veterans and those who have lost their breadwinner; various maternal and child benefits; and student stipends. Health care, not treated in this chapter, should be considered part of social security.

2.5.1 Temporary Disability and Pregnancy

For temporary disability resulting from an accident occurring at work or a work-related illness, the worker is paid his full former earnings for the entire period of the disability (unless it becomes permanent and he goes on a disability pension). This is also true of temporary disability benefits for invalids from the Second World War, for persons maintaining three or more children and for pregnant women. Otherwise, the benefits depend on the individual's earnings and on the length of uninterrupted employment. The benefit is 50 per cent of earnings for continuous employment under three years to 100 per cent of earnings for continuous employment of over eight years (Livshitz and Nikitinsky, 1977, pp. 137–9).

2.5.2 Old Age Pensions

Old age pensions are based in part on former wages with the percentage of former earnings declining as the level of earnings rises. The size of the pension is a mixture of incentive and need. Women are entitled to a full pension at age 55 if they have a total length of employment of at least twenty years and men at age 60 with a total length of employment of twenty-five years. Certain groups are entitled to an old age pension five to ten years younger and, in some cases, with a shorter work record. These groups include those working underground or in other heavy or hazardous conditions, war invalids, persons who have worked in the Far North for fifteen to twenty years, and mothers who have raised five or more children to age 8 (ibid., pp. 142–5).

The size of the old age pension ranges from 65 per cent of former earnings with earnings between 60 and 80 rubles, 55 per cent of former earnings for earnings of 80 to 100 and 50 per cent of earnings over 100 rubles (for those who worked on underground jobs, etc., the corresponding percentages are 70, 60 and 55 per cent) (ibid., pp. 145–7). A supplement may be paid for length of employment ten years longer than the minimum or for continuous employment in the same enterprise of fifteen years. Also, a supplement of 10 per cent for one dependant unable to work or 15 per cent for two or more dependents unable to work is paid.

The earnings that count may be either the average monthly earnings of the last year at work or the average of the highest earnings during a five-year period within the last ten years of work.

For wage earners and salaried workers, these rules were established in 1956, when pensions were greatly raised. At the time, a minimum pension was set at 50 rubles a month and the maximum at 120 rubles.[15] Old age pension rights were extended to members of collective farms in 1964 and their minimum pension was set at 40 rubles. This lower pension took into account that retired collective farmers are usually able to supplement their income from the private plot.

While these pensions were reasonably generous in relation to average earnings at the time they were set – 73.4 rubles in 1956

(*Trud*, 1968, p. 137) – they have become very low. In 1986, the average old age pension of wage earners and salaried workers was 89.4 rubles a month, compared to average earnings of working people of 195.6 rubles, and 8 per cent of the retired wage earners and salaried workers received the minimum of 50 rubles. For retired *kolkhozniki*, the average pension was 48.2 rubles, as compared with their average earnings from the socialised sector of 163.0 rubles, and 57 per cent of the retired *kolkhozniki* received only the minimum pension of 40 rubles (*Narodnoe khoziaistvo*, 1987, p. 439). These are low incomes indeed compared to the official poverty line of 78 rubles a month. Pensioners make up about one-fifth of the 36 million persons with per capita monthly income below 75 rubles in 1988 (*Ekonomicheskaia gazeta*, 1989, no. 25, p. 11). Some 40 per cent of all pensioners were receiving monthly pensions of less than 60 rubles in 1987 (Trehub, 1989).

Some improvements have been made and others are in the offing. The problem was particularly acute for long time pensioners who had retired when average earnings were much lower than they are today. In November 1985, the pensions of those whose pensions were under 60 rubles, and who had gone on pension ten or more years previously, were raised to levels approaching the pensions of current retirees of similar qualifications and in similar fields (Trehub, 1988, p. 27).

A complete reform of the pension system has been under consideration since 1986 but will apparently not be implemented before 1991.[16] In the meantime, emergency legislation was passed in August 1989 that will raise the minimum pension to 70 rubles in October 1989 (Peterson, 1989; Trehub, 1989). This brings pensions for both members of collective farms and state employees to the level of the current minimum wage.[17]

While little has been published about the proposed new pension law, some have suggested that it will include a subsistence wage for everyone, including those, such as housewives, who have no employment record and that there would be regular cost of living increases (Trehub, 1989). Both these provisions would mark a substantial improvement, especially as more mothers are being encouraged to stay at home with their young children and as inflation can be expected to be more significant in the future.

One issue that has apparently now been resolved is that of persons continuing to work while receiving a pension. Sarkisian (1983, p. 261), for instance, has argued that the pension is meant to support people who can no longer work and so should not be paid to those who are working. To encourage pensioners to continue working, various provisions had been made for them to receive both earnings and pension, but with a limit on the combined income. These limits have now been removed. In April 1987, it was announced that retired pensioners could engage in individual labour activity without affecting their pension payments (Gladkiy, 1987). The emergency legislation of summer 1989 includes lifting the ceiling on combined earnings plus pension (Trehub, 1989).

Alternatively, a person who continues to work past pension age without drawing on his pension will have the pension supplemented by a certain amount for each year he does not receive it.

Since January 1988, a wage earner or salaried worker may purchase additions to his pension. The extra pension can be from 10 to 50 rubles a month. Men aged 35 to 60 and women aged 30 to 55 may participate. Essentially, half the funding will come from the individual payments and half from the state budget. The size of the payment depends on the age at which a worker enters the plan and the amount of supplement (Moscow TASS International Service, 5 September 1987; FBIS-SOV-87-173, 8 September 1986, pp. 36–7).

2.5.3 Maternity, Child and Student Benefits

Large families made up almost half of the 36 million persons with a per capita income below 75 rubles in 1988 and most of these live in the Central Asian republics, Kazakhstan and Azerbaijan (*Ekonomicheskaia gazeta*, 1989, no. 25, p. 11).[18] Since 1947, a monthly child allowance has been paid to families with four or more children for each child from the fourth on until the child reaches age 5. In 1986, almost 2 million mothers were receiving such allowances (*Narodnoe khoziaistvo*, 1987, p. 437). A one-time payment is made at the birth of each child. This, now, is 50 rubles for the first child and 100 rubles for each subsequent child.

Since 1974, an allowance of 12 rubles a month has been paid for each child in families where the per capita income is below 50 rubles (75 rubles in the Far North, Siberia, and the Far East) until the child reaches age 8, the age by which the child would be in school. During 1989, the age was to be raised to 12 years ('Law on the 1989 Plan', p. 14).

Single mothers are paid an allowance for each child. Formerly, this was a maximum of 10 rubles a month for three or more children, until the child reached age 12. Recently, this has been raised to 20 rubles a month for each child and until the child is 16 (or 18, if at school without a state stipend) (Matthews, 1986, pp. 48, 122, 172). Since 1987, school age children of low income, single parent families (below 50 rubles or 75 rubles, depending on location) with three or more children under 16 are to receive free school lunches, school, athletic and young pioneer uniforms and free passes to pioneer camps and sanitoria ('Family assistance').

Many of these child benefits were probably initiated as pro-natal measures. More recently, they must be seen more as anti-poverty measures. There is surely no need – and no inclination on the part of the leadership – to encourage the women of Central Asia, Kazakhstan and Azerbaijan, where most of the large family benefits go, to have more children. Income supplements for large families may often relieve the mother from working and allow her to take care of her own children.

Some other child benefits are designed to make it easier for women to be mothers and workers. In addition to paid maternity leave (eight weeks before and eight weeks following the birth), a new mother is entitled to take twelve months of partially paid leave, plus an additional six months without pay, and is guaranteed she can return to her job. The monthly pay is 35 rubles generally, and 50 rubles in the Far North, Siberia and the Far East. The length of partially paid maternal leave will be extended to eighteen months. This will go into effect in the Far East, Siberia and the Far North on 1 December 1989; in the remaining areas of the RSFSR, and in the Ukraine, Belorussia, Moldavia and the Baltic republics on 1 July 1990; and in Kazakhstan, Central Asia and the Transcaucasus on 1 January 1991. Additional unpaid leave, with guaranteed return to her job, until the child reaches the age of 3 is granted to everyone effective 1 December 1989. Maternity leave is counted towards total and continuous time served in any job and also towards time served in one's speciality ('In the Interests of Mother and Child').

Child care facilities are crucial to the working mother, especially when there is no grandmother or the grandmother herself is still working. There has been a considerable extension of pre-school nurseries and kindergartens, especially during the 1970s. The proportion of the relevant age group, those to age 7, in permanent day care facilities was 13 per cent in 1960, 37 per cent in 1970 and 57 per cent in 1986. In 1986, 70 per cent of the urban pre-school children and 37 per cent of the rural pre-school children were in these institutions. The proportion of pre-school children in nurseries or kindergartens is quite low in those republics where large families prevail; only 15 per cent in Tadzhikistan and 20 per cent in Azerbaijan (*Narodnoe khoziaistvo*, 1987, pp. 540–1). Parents are charged for pre-school care, with the rates in inverse proportion to income. Payments by parents cover only about 20 per cent of the cost (Panchenko *et al.*, 1985, p. 190).

Stipends are paid to full-time day students at secondary specialised schools and universities, so long as they maintain adequate grades. Monthly rates established in September 1972 were 30–45 rubles for those in secondary specialised schools and 40–60 rubles for university students (McAuley, 1979, p. 281). The exact amount within those ranges was determined by class and performance. Stipends were raised in September 1987. One source says the increases are 25 per cent to 50 per cent, depending on grades (Yagodin, 1987). Another source says the increment is 50 per cent and that undergraduates who get good grades would get up to 130 rubles, and doctoral candidates may qualify for up to 180 rubles a month (*Izvestiia*, 1 September 1987). More generous stipends reduce the burden on parents of supporting students and reduce the opportunity cost of continuing education. Kostakov (1987) suggests that this will make it possible for more students to withdraw from the labour force to study full time instead of in the evening. In the 1986–7 school year, 64 per cent of the secondary specialised students were in the day programme and 53 per cent of the college students were also (*Narodnoe khoziaistvo*, 1987, p. 544). The quality of education is superior in the regular day programmes to that in the evening and correspondence courses.

The increase in pensions, the increase in length of maternity leave and in children's allowances, and the increase in student stipends should enable more individuals in these groups to leave the labour force, permanently or temporarily.

2.6 HOUSING

The constitution guarantees equal rights to housing for all citizens but the distribution of housing is quite unequal. In the first place, not all people have housing. In 1986, 22.7 million or 22.3 per cent of all families and single persons were on the waiting list for housing (ibid., p. 159). The length of the wait on the list can be long. Almost half (46 per cent) of newly married couples live with older relatives and are able to live on their own only after twenty years of married life (Rimashevskaia, 1988). And many complaints of arbitrariness and inequity in the assignment of housing are expressed.

Secondly, people living in state housing pay low subsidised rent that covers only one-quarter of the costs of maintaining the housing (*Narodnoe khoziaistvo*, 1987, p. 517). Others living in cooperative housing or owning their own houses or apartments have considerably higher costs. In a late 1970s study of Taganrog, said to be representative of the central industrial area of the RSFSR, costs for people in private or cooperative housing were found to be eight to nine times the costs in state apartments (Rimashevskaia, 1988).

In 1961, the party programme promised that every family would have an apartment of their own by 1981; now, this is the party's promise for 2000. Boris Yeltsin, at the time Minister of the Construction Ministry, indicated this will be difficult to achieve (Yeltsin, 1989). Currently, some 15 per cent of the urban population does not have separate quarters (*Narodnoe khoziaistvo*, 1987, p. 517) but live in communal apartments (with shared bath and kitchen), in dormitories or in rented rooms. In the Taganrog study, 47 per cent of the families had their own apartments (an increase from 19 per cent in 1968) but three-quarters of the one-room apartments were housing families of two or more people.

The amount of space and quality vary significantly. The Taganrog study found that 10 per cent of the families had less than 5 square metres of space per person while 17 per cent had over 15 square metres. Thirty per cent had as much space as to provide one room per person (Rimashevskia, 1988, p. 17). The USSR average living space in 1980 was 13.4 square metres and in 1986 14.9 square metres (*Narodnoe khoziaistvo*, 1987, p. 522). In Taganrog, one-quarter of the families had all utilities but almost half lacked running water or a sewage system or both (Rimashevskaia, 1988). In 1986, in urban state and cooperative housing, 92 per cent had running water, 72 per cent hot water, 90 per cent had sewage, 89 per cent central heating, 78 per cent gas and 84 per cent baths (*Narodnoe khoziaistvo*, 1987, p. 521). Rural housing is less well provided with utilities.[19] The quality of construction and the age of housing also differs significantly.

At the same time, rent for state housing is virtually the same per square metre for all housing, regardless of differences in location or quality.[20]

A number of economists see the necessity for a greater differentiation of rent to take into account all parameters of quality (Rimashevskaia, 1988). But they appear reluctant to raise rents to the level where they would cover maintenance of the housing stock (Rutgaiser and Sheviakhov, 1987). At the same time, it is believed that families with space above the standard norm should pay the full cost for the extra space (Sarkisian, 1983, p. 141; Rimashevskaia, 1988).

2.7 ISSUES AND TRENDS

One train of socialist thought is that the state should take care of children and other dependants, leaving the earners to enjoy their earnings. Timarenko (1986, p. 87) says that the fact that families bear expenses for children means a departure from the law of distribution according to labour in consumption. Others feel the desire to take good care of one's children is a powerful incentive that should not be removed (Chapman, 1989a).

Questions have been raised, mentioned above, about the justice of the widely varying benefits that are attached to the job.

Another trend is towards an increase in services for which the individual pays. Zaslavskaia says that a number of scientists (including herself) think that the free distribution of social consumption funds must secure an equal for all guaranteed minimum of such things as housing, education and medical services. Everything consumed on top of that should be paid for from a person's earnings or, in Rimashevskaia's view, his employer (Zaslavskaia, 1987; Rimashevskaia, 1986).

The right of individuals to purchase an increased pension was mentioned. Private and cooperative housing is being encouraged. Recreational facilities where people pay for accommodations, meals and services (as opposed to using a heavily subsidised travel voucher) are being expanded.[21] Free medical service continues to be available to all[22] but the number of state fee-charging clinics is being increased. It has long been possible to buy doctors' services in their off hours privately. Some 4500 cooperative medical clinics were organised by doctors but severe limitations on their activities were imposed in January 1989 (*The New York Times*, 6 January 1989). We do not know how many of the cooperative clinics have survived.

Providing more services for which the consumer pays should sop up some of the enormous 'ruble overhang' and make working harder to increase earnings worthwhile.

Social justice requires, besides payment for work according to results, an equitable distribution of benefits provided or subsidised by the state, such as education and health care, at least to the extent that the society can afford at a given moment to provide to all. Zaslavskaia (1986) stresses this, especially with regard to children; they should have as nearly equal 'starting conditions' as possible so they can fully develop their abilities. Free health care is available to all who need it; and free education is available to all and students in secondary specialised and higher education receive stipends. But wide variations in the quality of day care and health care,[23] and in the quality and choice of educational programmes are present. Some of the differences among children in access to education relate to the occupation of their parents. Access to and quality of education and health services seem to vary most with where the child lives, that is, between urban and rural areas, and among different geographic areas. To achieve anything approaching equality in the provision of these services would be a costly and lengthy process. But it would be a worthwhile investment in human capital.

The decentralisation process of the reforms includes devolving greater power and responsibility to republican and local governments for consumer and social needs of their localities. This is expected to provide an incentive for local authorities to concern themselves with improving the supplies of consumer goods and services.[24] Because of differing local budget resources, this is likely to increase rather than reduce local differences in the provision of housing and social services. If so, it will be even more difficult to achieve equal starting conditions for the children.

2.8 PROSPECTS

The new contract provides opportunities to earn as much as is justified by the results of one's work, the elimination of unearned income and special privileges, an improved safety net to compensate for decreased job security, a greater choice of types of employment (including self-employment), and increased rights to participate in economic decisions and the political process. Under discussion also is an increase in the equity of the distribution of social services.

By no means yet clear is whether Gorbachev can persuade the people to swallow the new contract. Complaints appear frequently in the Soviet press that five years of *perestroika* have done nothing for ordinary people. People tend to equate justice with equality. Wages are differentiated more than before. Some people have lost their jobs; others, probably not many, suffered some cut in pay with more careful attention to labour costs. Yet the winners in the reform, those whose pay or pensions have been raised, find less and less that the extra money can buy. The wage reform has led to an increase in wages that has exceeded the growth of productivity and the output of consumer goods.[25] The result is even emptier shelves in the shops. All kinds of efforts, some of them quite at odds with the logic of the economic reforms,[26] are being made to increase the supply of consumer goods and services at the expense of investment and defence ('Law on the 1989 Plan'; Romaniuk, 1989). But it will take time for increases in production to get to the shops. And it will take time, or drastic measures, to reduce the ruble overhang.

The leadership seems undecided whether to press on with radical systemic changes or to hold off until the consumer market is in better equilibrium. As announced by Ryzhkov (1989b) in December 1989, the plan for 1990 to 1992 emphasises heavily a change in structure of output, more consumer goods and services, less defence and investment, and provides for continued state price setting. This suggests an all-out effort to get more goods on the shelves in preparation for further market-type reform measures. Quotas are being restored for many major consumer goods, including cheap clothing for children and pensioners; and restrictions are being placed on exports of many consumer goods. Yet, once Gorbachev was elected President, it was reported that he would present a package of radical, market-like reforms to the Supreme Soviet (*The New York Times*, 20 March and 10 April 1990; *Wall Street Journal*, 13 April 1990). Initially intended to be enacted by 1 July 1990, Gorbachev wavered and finally presented his reform proposal on 16 October, 1990 (*The New York Times*, 17 October 1990). This provides for some radical measures such as privatisation and 'freedom of economic activity', sharp cuts in budget expenditures and a reform of the banking system but anticipates that prices of essential consumer goods will continue to be controlled even after 1992.

The impact of the drive to squeeze out excess labour and fire redundant workers has been rather modest for the USSR as a whole so far.[27] Nevertheless, release of workers has had significant, and probably often unanticipated, effects in particular areas of the country and on particular groups of the population. The policy seems to have contributed to the ethnic unrest in Central Asia and the Caucasus, where unemployment was already high, especially among young people. Reduction in employment, especially among managerial and professional personnel, has complicated the problem of finding jobs for the 100 000 officers to be released from the armed forces. The wage reform and the emphasis on self-financing has weakened the relative position in the labour market of segments of the population enjoying special job protection, such as women, youth and working pensioners (Chapman, 1989c).

Gorbachev's policies on increased political freedom and *glasnost* seem so far to have been more successful in activating the human factor than his economic policies. The movements for independence in the Baltics and elsewhere, the miners' strikes and the development of independent trade unions seem to indicate an increased desire on the part of many people to take more responsibility. The miners were not just demanding extra pay, sausage and soap but also greater autonomy from the coal ministry and implementation of the increased rights they were supposed to have been given in managing the mines (ibid., p. 4).

Yeltsin, often a critic that Gorbachev is not moving fast enough, expressed optimism about the changes that have been taking place among the people:

> the people are changing – the people who were in a state of apathy, who took no interest in politics, whose personal dignity was crushed, and the people who are now – in the midst of the democratization of society – acquiring or regaining their own dignity, becoming politically minded and have a civic position. (Film Panorama programme Russian Television Service, 4 August 1989; FBIS-SOV-89-150, 7 August 1989, p. 85)

Getting the people to accept the new social contract and activating them is crucial to the success of the economic reforms. As Aganbegyan (1989, p. 58) said recently:

> This is perhaps the central problem of the new economic system: how to make people care about the results of their work, how to inculcate, as part of the economic reform, feelings of personal responsibility. Since human beings are the most important of the productive factors, much depends on their attitude to work.

Considerable scepticism abounds in both the USSR and the West about the likelihood of success. Implementation of *perestroika* and changed definition of the social contract create hardships for various groups and the increase in *glasnost* and in freedoms leads to expression of ethnic conflicts and social unrest that may threaten the unravelling of the union or a reaction that could lead to the ousting of Gorbachev. The people and leaders are anxious. Painful though it may be, the future of the USSR depends on a changed attitude to work and revision of the social contract.

NOTES

1. Cited first, to my knowledge, by H. Smith, 1976, p. 215.
2. In the case of juveniles, approval must also be obtained from the local Commission on Juvenile Affairs.
3. In April 1984, the Supreme Court ruled that the employer's obligation was limited to giving a dismissed employee a job in the same enterprise, if one was vacant (Hauslohner, 1987, p. 67). However, the 1986 Wage Reform Law and the 1987 Law on the State Enterprise state that the enterprise and ministry will secure the placement of released workers 'first of all' by reallocating them within the enterprise or elsewhere within the ministry ('Vremennoe polozhenie o poriadke trudoustroistva . . .').
4. One might anticipate that managers would finally be relieved of the obligation to place people they fire. Of those released as a result of the reforms by July 1988, almost half of those who did not retire were rehired in the same enterprise (Chapman, 1989b, table 2, p. 6).
5. For estimates of the extent of unemployment, see Adirim, 1989.
6. Anecdotal evidence suggests that this belief is a bit perverse and unambitious. G. Arbatov, Director of the USA-Canada Institute has said the thinking of many people runs this way: 'Okay, maybe I'll have to go hungry, but just don't let my neighbor prosper' (*The Washington Post*, 8 January 1989).
7. Some reduction in earnings differentials had already been effected in September 1946 when a 'bread allowance' was introduced to compensate lower paid workers for the increase in retail prices to accompany derationing (Chapman, 1970, pp. 9–10).
8. This is the ratio of earnings of those at the ninth decile from the bottom to earnings of those at the first decile, or the spread in earnings among the middle paid 80 per cent of earners.
9. The 80-ruble minimum had been predicated on the assumption that manual labour would have been largely eliminated (Kostakov, personal interview, Moscow, 15 May 1987). Manual labour is still widespread.
10. At the same time, however, taxes on the revenues of the cooperatives appear to have been increased over the initial proposal.
11. The data relate to earnings from their jobs in state enterprises. Outside earnings, e.g. from publications or moonlighting in cooperatives, are not

included. Such earnings are to be included in taxable income under the draft law.

12. In the 1980s, about 73 per cent of all housing built was state housing, including housing constructed by governments and enterprises (*Narodnoe khoziaistvo*, 1988 p. 455). Enterprises may be assigned housing space in municipal built buildings.
13. However, the 20 December 1989 resolution of the Congress of People's Deputies on the thirteenth five-year plan calls for 'a gradual shift to the principle that labour collectives and individuals earn their housing through their own labour (while retaining state distribution of housing for the needier segments of the population)' CDSP-XLII-2, p. 26.
14. The surveys of family incomes and expenditures have been severely criticised by both Soviet and Western writers. See Rabkina and Rimashevskaia (1972); McAuley (1979).
15. Special pensions higher than this may be awarded to selected individuals.
16. This delay may reflect differences of opinion or a concern for the inflationary impact of raising pensions for almost 60 million pensioners. Possibly, also it was hoped to delay increases in pensions until the reform of retail prices so that the pension increases could be presented as compensation for the increase in the cost of living.
17. A number of improvements were made also in pensions for invalids and veterans.
18. While the percentage of the population with a per capita monthly income below 75 rubles averaged 12.6 for the USSR, the proportions in those republics were: Uzbekistan, 44.7; Kazakhstan, 15.9; Azerbaijan, 33.3; Kirghizia, 37.1, Tadzhikistan 58.6; Turkmenia 43.6 (*Ekonomicheskaia gazeta*, 1989, no. 25 (June), p. 11).
19. Elizabeth Clayton's chapter deals with rural housing.
20. The original rent law of 1926 (as modified in 1928) that is still in effect provides for differentiation of rent on the basis of location and quality and also for rent increases with the wage of the renter; the maximum rent of 13.2 kopeks per square metre was reached at a wage of 41 to 53 rubles. Even the minimum wage is well above these levels now (Chapman, 1963, pp. 303–4; Bergson, 1946, pp. 43–6, 132–4).
21. The USSR adopted a resolution 'On Measures to Radically Restructure the Sphere of Paid Services to the Population' (*Pravda*, 24 August 1988, pp. 1–2; FBIS-SOV-88-174, 8 September 1988, pp. 80–5).
22. There are constant complaints of having to bribe nurses and doctors for even the most routine services.
23. See Urban, 1988; Shmelev and Popov, 1989, pp. 188–90 and M. Feshbach's chapter in this volume.
24. It will also take some of the heat off the centre.
25. During 1989, the average wage increased by 9.5 per cent while social labour productivity increased by 2.3 per cent (CDSP-XLII, 9 (1990), pp. 17, 18).
26. The requirement that all enterprises, no matter what their main line of production, should increase their output of consumer goods and services is one such.
27. By 1 July 1988, of the 72 million workers in the material branches who

were scheduled to transfer to the new pay conditions, 2 million had been released. Of these, 40.7 per cent were rehired in the same enterprise, 17.8 per cent retired and 41.5 per cent had to find jobs elsewhere (Chapman, 1989b, pp. 5–6). By the end of October 1989, over 3 million persons had lost their jobs as a result of economic reforms (*Pravda*, 31 October 1989, p. 2).

REFERENCES

ADIRIM, I. (1989) 'A Note on the Current Level, Pattern and Trends of Unemployment in the USSR', *Soviet Studies*, XLI-3.

AGANBEGYAN, A. (1989) *Inside Perestroika: The Future of the Soviet Economy* (New York: Harper & Row).

BEGICHEV, B. K. and A. D. ZAIKIN (1985) (eds) *Sovetskoe trudovoe pravo*, 2nd ed (Moscow: Iuridicheskaia literatura).

BERGSON, A. (1946) *The Structure of Soviet Wages* (Cambridge, Mass: Harvard University Press).

BOGORAD, V. A. (1988) 'Candidate of Jurisprudence Answers Readers' Questions', *Izvestiia*, 17 March; JPRS-UEA-88-018, 18 May.

CDSP, *Current Digest of the Soviet Press*.

CHAPMAN, J. G. (1963) *Real Wages in Soviet Russia Since 1928* (Cambridge, Mass: Harvard University Press).

CHAPMAN, J. G. (1970) *Wage Variation in Soviet Industry: The Impact of the 1956–1960 Wage Reform*, Memorandum RM=6076-PR (Santa Monica: The RAND Corporation).

CHAPMAN, J. G. (1988) 'Gorbachev's Wage Reform', *Soviet Economy*, vol. 4, no. 4.

CHAPMAN, J. G. (1989a) 'Income Distribution and Social Justice in the Soviet Union', *Comparative Economic Studies*, vol. XXXI, no. 1.

CHAPMAN, J. G. (1989b) 'Lay-offs, Employment Shifts, and the Ability of Soviet Institutions to Management This', University of Pittsburgh, Department of Economics, Working Paper No. 250.

CHAPMAN, J. G. (1989c) 'Ramifications of Lay-offs Resulting from Soviet Economic Reform', University of Pittsburgh, Department of Economics, Working Paper No. 249.

CHAPMAN, J. G. (1990) 'Recent and Prospective Trends in Soviet Wage Distribution', University of Pittsburgh Department of Economics, Working Paper no. 262.

'The Cooperatives: Surf and Foam', *Pravda*, 18 February 1989; FBIS-SOV-89-039, 1 March 1989.

'Family Assistance', *Trud*, 16 January 1987; JPRS-UEA-87-027, 3 September 1987.

'The Fate of the New Cause in Danger: Two Million Cooperators Are Sounding the Alarm', *Literaturnaia gazeta*, 28 June 1989; FBIS-SOV-89-139, 13 July 1989.

FBIS-SOV, Foreign Broadcasting Information Service, *Daily Report*, *Soviet Union*.

GLADKIY, I. I. (1987) 'Prestige of the Honest Ruble', *Trud*, 28 April; JPRS-UEA-87-020, 30 July 1987.
GOLOVACHEV, V., Interview with A. P. Dementov, *Trud* 29 June 1989; FBIS-SOV-89-133, 13 July 1989.
HAUSLOHNER, P. (1987) 'Gorbachev's Social Contract', *Soviet Economy*, vol. 3, no. 1.
'In the Interests of Mother and Child', *Pravda*, 23 August 1989 and *Izvestiia*, 23 August 1989; CDSP, XL-34 (89).
JPRS-UEA, Joint Publications Research Service Report, *Soviet Union, Economic Affairs*.
'Kak ne dopustit' bezrabotitsky' ('za kruglym stolem' zhurnala *Voprosy ekonomiki*), *Voprosy ekonomiki*, 1989, no. 2.
Kodeks zakonov o trude RSFSR, Moscow: Iuridicheskaia literatura, 1988.
KOSTAKOV, V. (1987) *Kommunist*, no. 2.
KOTLIAR, A. (1989) 'Is Full Employment Necessary?' *Pravda*, 14 November 1989; FBIS-SOV-89-226.
KRASNOPOLSKII, Iu. (1989) 'Man and Work: Finding One Another', *Trud*, 7 February; FBIS-SOV-89-027, 10 February 1989.
KUNEL'SKII, L. (1968) *Sotsialisticheskii trud*, no. 12.
KUNEL'SKII, L. E. (1987) *Povyshenie effektivnosti truda v promyshlennosti* (Moscow: Ekonomika).
KURBATOV, A. (1987) 'Reportage from the Commission for Job Placement of Workers Made Redundant by the Merger of Two Ministries', 'Your Job Is Being Abolished', *Sotsialistickeskaia industriia*, 10 November; FBIS-SOV-87-218, 12 November 1987.
'Law on the 1989 Plan', *Pravda* and *Izvestiia*, 29 October 1988; CDSP XL-46(88).
LIVSHITZ, R. and NIKITINSKY, V. (1977) *An Outline of Soviet Labour Law* (Moscow: Progress Publishers).
MATTHEWS, M. (1986) *Poverty in the Soviet Union* (Cambridge/New York/Melbourne/Sydney: Cambridge University Press).
McAuley, A. (1979) *Economic Welfare in the Soviet Union* (Madison, Wis.: University of Wisconsin Press).
Narodnoe khoziaistvo SSSR za 70 let (1987) (Moscow: Finansy i statistiki).
Narodnoe khoziaistvo SSSR v 1987 g. (1988) (Moscow: Finansy i statistiki).
PANCHENKO, N. F., PIVNEV, V. A. and NOSOVSKII, E. E. (1985) *Proizvodstvo i lichnoe potreblenie* (Kiev: Vishcha shkola).
PETERSON, D. J. (1989) 'Supreme Soviet Adopts Emergency Pension Measures', Radio Liberty, *Report on the USSR*, vol. 1, no. 33, 18 August.
RABINA, N. E. and RIMASHEVSKAIA, N. M. (1972) *Osnovy differentsiatsii zarabotnoi platy i dokhdov naseleniia* (Moscow: Ekonomika).
RIAZANOV, V. T. (1984) *Raspredelenie po trudu; ekonomicheskii i sotsial 'nyi aspekty* (Leningrad: izd. Leningradskogo Universiteta).
RIMASHEVSKAIA, N. (1986) *Ekonomicheskaia gazeta*, no. 40 (October).
RIMASHEVSKAIA, N. (1988) *Ekonomika i organizatsia promyshlennogo proizvodstva*, no. 7.
ROMANIUK, V. (1989) 'A Programme of Urgent Measures', *Izvestiia*; FBIS-SOV-89-175, 12 September.
RUDEV, P. S. (1989) 'Interview With', *Izvestiia*, 7 August; FBIS-SOV-89-164, 25 August.

RUTGAISER, V. M. and SHEVIAKOV, Iu. E. (1987) 'Distribution According to Labour', *Ekonomika i organizatsiia promyshlennogo proizvodstva*, no. 3, JPRS–UEA–87–001.

RUTKEVICH, M. N. (1986) 'Equality and Justice Are the Goals of the CPSU's Social Policy', *Voprosy istorii*, no. 1, pp. 37–52; CDSP XXXVIII-5.

RYZHKOV, N. I. (1989a) 'Interview With', *Argumenty i fakty*, no. 33, FBIS-SOV-89-164, 25 August.

RYZHKOV, N. I. (1989b) Report to Second Congress of USSR People's deputies, *Pravda* and *Izvestiia*, 14 December; CDSP XL1–51.

SARKISIAN, G. S. (1983) *Narodnoe blagosostoianie v SSSR* (Moscow: Ekonomiki).

SHMELEV, N. and POPOV, V. (1989) *The Turning Point: Revitalizing The Soviet Economy* (New York: Doubleday).

SMIRNOV, A. (1967) 'The Party's Chief Concern', *Komsomol'skaia pravda*, 30 September; CDSP, XIX-39.

SMITH, H. (1976) *The Russians* (New York: Quadrangle, The New York Times Book Company).

SZIRACZKI, G. (1988) 'Redundancy and Unemployment in a North Hungarian Steel Valley', *Labour and Society*, vol. 13, no. 4, October.

'Taxes Based on Income', *Pravda*, 17 April 1989; CDSP XLI-19 (1989).

TEDSTROM, J. (1989) 'New Draft Law on Income Taxes', Radio Liberty, *Report on The USSR*, vol. 1, no. 24.

TIMARENKO, A. P. (1986), in T. V. Riabushkin (ed.), *Demograficheskaia politika sotsialisticheskogo obshchestva* (Moscow: Nauka), pp. 85–91.

TREHUB, A. (1988) 'Social and Economic Rights in the Soviet Union', in George R. Urban (ed.) *Social and Economic Rights in the Soviet Bloc* (New Brunswick, NJ: Transaction Books).

TREHUB, A. (1989) 'The Congress of People's Deputies on Poverty', Radio Liberty, *Report on the USSR*, vol. 1, no. 24.

Trud v SSSR (1968) (Moscow: Statistika).

URBAN, G. R. (1988) (ed.) *Social and Economic Rights in the Soviet Bloc* (New Brunswick: Transaction Books).

'USSR Economy: Half-Year Results', *Sovetskaia Rossiia*, 28 July 1989; FBIS-SOV-89-145, 31 July 1989.

'Vremennoe polozhenie o poriadke trudoustroistva i perepodgotovki rabotnikov vysvobozhdaemykh iz ob' edinenii i s predpriiatii i organizatsii', *Ekonomicheskaia gazeta*, no. 49 (October) 1986.

YAGODIN, V. A. (1987) 'VUZ Takes an Examination', *Sovetskaia Rossiia*, 15 March; JPRS-UEA-87-015.

YELTSIN, B. N. (1989) 'Interview With', *Komsomol'skaia pravda*, 31 December 1988; FBIS-SOV-89-001, 3 January.

ZASLAVSKAIA, T. I. (1986) 'The Creative Activeness of the Masses: Social Reserves of Growth', *Ekonomika i organizatsia promyshlennogo proizvodstva*, no. 3; JPRS-UEA-86-024, 16 July.

ZASLAVSKAIA, T. I. (1987) 'The Reconstruction Is for Us', *Moscow News*, 1 March; FBIS-SOV-87-052.

3 The Social Contract: Soviet Price and Housing Policy

Elizabeth Clayton

Property ownership and management, always a concern of Marxists, have quietly undergone significant discussion in the recent Soviet reforms. New powers have been proposed for enterprises, farms, and local government; new obligations have been added to their existing burdens. The goal, of course, is to enhance productivity; but these changes also revise the social contract that made nationalisation, central planning, and redistribution of income attractive to society, and they have proved more difficult to write than to implement.

The widespread attempt to reorganise property rights of ownership and management reshapes a bundle of powers and obligations that are defined and enforced by law, attached to a productive asset, and assigned to a legal entity. The bundle answers such economic questions as who can sell, rent, or give away land; who can change the price of a product; whether workers can withhold labour in a strike. The land, the product, and the labour – each a saleable asset in some sense – are governed by the legal property rights which delimit their possession, use, and distribution.

The bundle of rights and obligations that govern property can be unbundled and reassembled with a new configuration, and this has been a major tool of Soviet reformers. For example, the land once possessed and controlled by a Russian tsar or noble only recently was owned by the national government and loaned out, with zero rent and 'in perpetuity', to a collective farm. Now a collective or state farm may subrent (lease) land to individual farmers for rents defined in only the most rudimentary fashion.[1]

The Soviet reforms, however, while vigorously reorganising powers and claims, also require a close attention to the social contract. If citizens are to accept a new configuration of property rights, they must be persuaded that they can reap some benefits; otherwise, they may ignore the proffered reform and continue in old ways. (Such has been the fate of several Soviet reforms.) In the terms of Vinogradoff (1928, chapter 20), three elements are required for new property rights to succeed: the rights must prove valuable; they must be enforceable; and they must be recognised by society. All three requirements integrate the bundle of property rights and the social contract. Society, in its differentiated legal parts, must agree that the rights apply to something valuable (e.g. the asset is economically desirable and scarce), that the state can enforce ownership rights (e.g. non-owners can be excluded), and that non-owners can acknowledge the social benefits of the rights.

This chapter will be based on two powerful forces that motivate a society to agree to a set of property rights and to accept a social contract regarding property. The first is the belief that the bundle of rights will tie together labour and its product. Marx himself, especially in his early work, was much taken with the labour theory of value that flows from this view. It is earlier associated with the work of John Locke, who linked labour productivity with personal (private) ownership. Today, using this Lockean principle, the Soviet Union would allot land to farm labour to encourage the farmers to produce and market food. The principle is probably more popular with the reformers than with the workers.

A second force for the social acceptance of a set of property rights is the desire for security and reduced risk. Under this philosophy, associated with the work of Hegel, people want a stable and predictable environment and will defend the property rights that promise it. It is the promise of security that has sustained the conventional Soviet social contract for property ownership and management. It is probably more popular with workers than with reformers. One way of analysing the reforms is that the Hegelian insecurity that accompanies Lockean property rights strains the social contract and threatens the reforms themselves. A corollary is that insecurity, from both change and relative redistribution, improves labour productivity. In either case, the Lockean and Hegelian principles conflict with one another.

Using housing and price policies as examples, and emphasising rural–agricultural change, this chapter examines some changes in property rights: how they might create or destroy economic welfare, and might redistribute gains and risks among members of society. It examines new rights, powers, and obligations, and who would lose and win, and where the consequence is still in doubt. Property right reforms can in theory improve labour incentives, promise a new economic era, and shift around risk and insecurity, but the social contract must define them as valuable if they are to be recognised and enforceable by the population at large.

3.1 RECENT CHANGES IN THE SOVIET ECONOMIC WELFARE SYSTEM

3.1.1 Price Policy

There is widespread agreement, even in the Soviet Union, that the price system is cumbersome and antiquated, but any price reform is hotly contested. An important issue to decide is who has the power to set price. A property right recently discussed, occasionally offered gingerly, and seldom accepted with alacrity is that seller-owner has the right to set a price, and the buyer has the right to refuse it. Stable prices, however, have been a significant underpinning to the social contract because they provide security. Although fixed prices have an implicit cost – as Kornai (1986) has shown, the insecurity of fluctuating prices is replaced by the insecurity of fluctuating supplies, and queues – fluctuating prices require painful adaptations. Buyers must live with scarcity prices, sellers must learn about services, and both must live with insecurity.

The pricing of food has been particularly troublesome. To give away the power to set food prices arouses a primal fear. The known Soviet state food distribution system, with fixed-price, subsidised products, reassures consumers, who highly prefer it to a quasi-market distribution system, with floating-price, unsubsidised products. The fluctuating food prices and loss of subsidy are a powerful challenge to the social contract, and the complaints from consumers have been correspondingly loud. When Soviet coal-miners struck in summer 1989, they demanded more food, especially meat, but also that 'private entrepreneurs' (that is, private farmers and their higher, floating prices) be forbidden the city.

The miners rejected the Lockean view, that higher prices would elicit more food, and reflected a rejection that is heavily entrenched in the Soviet population. In a survey of former Soviet citizens (Millar, 1987), the dominant view held that higher prices, which would compensate farmers' labour, would not elicit more food. Living in an economy dominated by a culture of central planning, the consumers' view is rational, but the power of the higher price to improve food supplies remains leashed.

The supplier's power to set price is confounded by the consumer's right to receive a subsidy. The floating food prices that stress the social contract point out a Hobson's choice for the state: it must continue to absorb mounting food subsidies or shift costs to the population and risk their wrath, because the social contract is breached. In 1989, *Izvestiia* (27 September) reported that food subsidies equalled 87.8 billion rubles (b.r.), or far more than the total annual investment in agriculture. In 1990, they will reach 95.7 b.r. Meat that sells for 1 ruble per kilo in the state retail store costs more than 4 rubles to produce and more rubles to market; milk and its products are similarly subsidised. Food distribution through state stores closed to the general public but open to a favoured few, whose supply uncertainty is reduced at the expense of a compounded distress for the ordinary population.

How much do Soviet farmers value the power to set price? Probably not much. A Soviet farmer-entrepreneur (FBIS 6 April 1989, p. 54) has said: 'I take my produce to the city market. I have to tip the train conductor or he'll claim that by bags clutter up the aisles and won't let them on the train. I have to pay a taxi driver, there's a "surcharge" for a night in a hotel, too. That's why my little tomatoes aren't cheap.'

The infrastructure for private farmers to take products to market is poorly developed, erratic, and expensive; the customers are vociferous critics accustomed to highly subsidised food. Despite the new powers, small-scale, private farming is exceedingly unattractive in the north, where labour has good alternatives, and its growth is occurring only in the south, where labour has few industrial opportunities, and in enterprise subsidiaries, where it is an expensive but necessary burden on industrial activity.

To empower farmers with the right to set price, a powerful property right because it shifts economic power to the seller-owner from the state, raises the spectre of price inflation and its insecurity, a critical breach in the social contract. Prices in farm markets have indeed risen steadily, as shown in Table 3.1. But this food is not subsidised, so the price increase is confounded with the loss of subsidy.

Price empowerment, furthermore, arouses the traditional cultural antipathy to speculation and middlemen and an attack on cooperatives. Although worker and consumer cooperatives are highly promoted as ideologically desirable institutions intermediate between state and private enterprise, they are frequently censured for corrupt

Table 3.1 Food prices in urban collective farm markets (rubles per kilo)

	1985	*1986*	*1987*
Potatoes	0.56	0.65	0.73
Vegetables:			
Cabbage, fresh	0.74	0.79	0.76
Cabbage, chopped	1.38	1.46	1.50
Carrots	0.77	0.83	0.80
Fruits:			
Apples	1.80	1.95	2.30
Pears	2.21	2.38	2.83
Berry (kliukva)	4.94	5.29	5.50
Beef	4.85	4.90	5.08
Pork	4.36	4.48	4.69
Milk	0.75	0.75	0.77
Eggs (in tens)	1.20	1.16	1.13

Source: *APK* (1989) p. 24.

behaviour that in Western markets would be perfectly legal, that is, for 'speculation'. Although sometimes the cooperatives have sold goods that were stolen or embezzled from state enterprises, which is clearly corrupt behaviour, more often they have simply sold for more than they paid, which is a Western tenet of ordinary marketing but still a Soviet shibboleth.

There are elements of truth to the fear of corruption, and the term 'unearned income' is defined widely. Il'iasov and Mukhammetberdiev (1988), reporting on public attitudes in Turkmenistan towards unearned income, place bribes, bride prices, and speculation highest on their list. Shelley and Kislinskaia (KIARS, 14 November 1989), reporting on organised crime, which engages in bribery, blackmail and prostitution, say that it has strengthened as the economy has deteriorated. The cooperative movement as a whole, however, seems more a victim of cultural opposition and of social contract failure than of purely legal restrictions.

The twin beliefs that farmers have become wealthy because of price empowerment and that that is a deplorable state of affairs is a remnant of an old social contract, which held that farmers were obligated to provide low cost food for industrial and intellectual workers. It no longer accommodates the new reality that in some areas agricultural labour, and food, is in short supply. Public or private labour, either or both, must be compensated to produce and to stay in agriculture. The Lockean bargain that offers the right to set price with the expectation of more food has little or no advantage for farm workers, and it antagonises those who have a wistful and romantic gaze towards an improbably secure past, and who yearn for a subsidy without limit.

The criticism of giving Soviet farmers the right to set price is founded on the belief that the consequent income is 'unearned'. A miner (FBIS, 6 April 1989, p. 54) has said: 'It is time to recognise this [i.e. the "unearned excess income stemming from the market situation"] and deprive private traders of the opportunity to make a fortune.'

At the time of writing, the miners seem to have routed the farmers, who have been given no subsidy to sustain them and their buyers. It has been widely reported that the miners 'won' their demands; it might also be observed that the farmers 'not won' theirs, probably by default. In a paradox, the miners have strongly advocated that coal prices be tied to world price, which fluctuates around a level higher than the domestic Soviet price, which presumably, if enacted, would replicate their own outcry among the coal buyers.

In a further complication, a decentralised power to set price contravenes a principle of regional equality that has permeated Soviet policy and the social contract. For example, a radio report (FBIS, 6 April 1989, p. 54) cites a price of potatoes (one kilo) as:

10 k State store
73 k Moscow market
1.00 r Tbilisi market
1.21 r Baku market
1.50 r Ashkhabad market

and asks: 'Why is the cooperative system not doing something?' The price differentials, which are roughly proportional to collective farm production costs in each republic, violate a social contract principle of equality towards buyers and fail to distinguish between equality towards buyers (which implies regional uniformity) and equity (which could allow regional variety and food diversity).

The same search for regional uniformity, abolishing the differences in consumption, can be found even at the oblast level. One well-known example is the policy to stock capital city stores, but not smaller city stores. Cherniak (*Pravda*, 1 September 1988), comparing meat consumption within the Saratov oblast, cites consumption in the capital city of Saratov (36 kg per capita, or two-thirds of the oblast supply), in the nearby cities of Engels (26 kg), Balashov and Vol'sk (12 kg), and Marx and Atkarsk (7–8 kg). Consumption, and presumably supply, grows thinner with distance from the oblast centre. While there may be rational explanations for the difference (for example, private marketers may supply the smaller towns but be restricted in opportunities for arbitrage), there is clearly an expectation of equality and uniformity within the oblast.

Farmers, in addition to the power to set price, have been offered some Lockean rights to link labour, land use, and income. They have been offered long-term land contracts, at rents in money or in kind. By and large, the farmers have rejected the bargain as ungenerous. It is unsupported by labour-saving capital equipment, which would release them from the worst of back-breaking, dead-end, low-caste work.[2] It shifts the natural risks of farming (climate, weather, insecure supplies, and sheer incompetence) from the farm to the farmer, but denies him (or her) the power to add a risk premium to food prices or to receive a guarantee or subsidy. While there are today more 'brigades' and other results-oriented work units, there is by no means a spurt of individual entrepreneurship. The new social contract has little to offer individual farmers, except perhaps those who strongly desire its lifestyle.

Incentives to farmers apart from price have occupied much of political discussion. One policy, which was adopted enthusiastically in mid-1989 but faded within months, bought from farmers with hard currency the above-plan product that would otherwise have been left unsold but purchased abroad (for the same hard currency) by the state. It was an imaginative programme, but foundered on burdensome demands for enforcement and administration: how to define 'above-plan', how to establish a trade based on the demand of individual farmers, not a ministry, etc. Meanwhile, yet another agricultural price revision, with central control, is contemplated even as its defects are acknowledged. One reform, however, envisages controlled prices for meat and other staples, with prices for fruits and vegetables left to fluctuate within bounds.

Reading the price reform discussions, in food policy and elsewhere, brings a sense that economists are reasonably familiar with the rudiments of price effects but that policy-makers have little experience or vision about how to change or experiment. One domain poorly explored in Soviet literature lies in the difference between a policy that affects the general price level in the macro economy and one that changes only a specific relative price level in a micro economy. There is little attempt to separate discussion of the two, and legislators focus on their microeconomic needs, such as a subsidy on the price of fuel or feed, with little thought for the overall impact on, say, inflation. Another example of inexperience is the discussion about where and where not to introduce decentralised prices. There is apparently little experimentation, for example, in renting land for a price.

A common thread running through the problem of establishing a price reform is the inability to picture an economy that uses face-to-face decision-making between buyer and seller instead of a hierarchy. In a study of centrally planned change, Mayer *et al.* (1974, chapter 4) differentiate between a system that relies on negotiation and bargaining to work out a social consensus among participants, and a system that relies on rationalism, technical means, and a systemic approach, which has better described the centralised Soviet economy. The first system better coordinates the pluralism, trade-offs, and inconsistencies that are typical accommodations to conflicted social goals. In it, for example, the social contract would accept some regional inequalities as a trade-off for different regional preferences. It also requires a new mind-set, where no one answer is 'best' for everyone, no one side is a 'winner', and diversity is a virtue. A new social contract, where Soviet citizens are to shift their mind-set to floating prices and bargaining, introduces the idea implicit in a private contract of a 'win-win' negotiation; it also requires a recognition of modern life's ambiguity, diversity, and uncertainty.

Only a few visionaries are willing to consider full devolution of the power to price, rather than a tinkering with centralised price-setting power. As argued above, the opposition emphasises the confused babble of insecurity, inexperience, envy, and the dislocation of regional equality. While this chapter focuses on food supply, because it is both more competitive (potentially) and more publicised, similar observations can be made in the industrial and transport sectors whose problems are equally intractable. In these sectors the pessimists of reform who expect massive bankruptcy and unemployment from unplanned losses are joined by those who fear monopoly pricing; together they defend centralised pricing and resist the pricing reform in the name of upholding the social contract for security. (The monopoly problem is both real and endemic; there is, for example, only one pulp and paper mill in all the Soviet Union that produces ice cream wrappers.) The reformers persist and win where they can; they, for example, have broken the iron exchange rate for the ruble. They would go much further.

3.1.2 Housing Policy

Housing, another asset that is part of the Soviet social contract, can be similarly viewed as a bundle of property rights, but in this area the power to set price is not an important part of the reforms. In contrast to the property rights that affect food, the private ownership of urban housing is not a high priority and it remains solidly in the public sector.[3] This reflects sensible politics: in a survey of Soviet urban emigrants (Millar and Clayton 1987), public housing was a major source of satisfaction with Soviet life, and private housing held no particular attraction.

To the contrary, expanding public housing to rural areas has been a major labour incentive to keep labour from migrating to cities. It has brought a major change to the northern countryside, where agricultural labour shortages are acute. Socialised housing, moreover, is associated with more amenities such as water, sewage disposal and gas. According to Soviet statistics (*Sel'skoe khoziaistvo*, 1988, p. 492), socialised housing in 1980 comprised 23 per cent of Soviet rural housing; and rose by 1987 to 30 per cent. The republics, however, differed: in Georgia and Azerbaidzhan, less than 5 per cent of rural housing was socialised; but in Estonia, Latvia, and Kazakhstan, more than 50 per cent was socially owned (ibid.). Still, on average, private housing dominates the rural scene, and private housing investment grew between 1986 and 1987 by a whopping 17 per cent.

In housing, the property rights of significance are obligations and duties: who, if not a private sector, shall provide housing? In the past, housing provision has been the explicit domain of the enterprise, the *kolkhoz*, and local government, all of whom in their ways have failed to satisfy demand at low prices. As with food, there is a subsidy burden, not only of construction costs but of operating and repair expenses. As other reforms have pressed on enterprise profits, they have squeezed out the ability to provide for housing. Local governments, equally ill-prepared to take on the burdens of providing housing, have evaded the new responsibility. As documented by Bahry (1987), their tax base is small; their claims on construction materials are weak, because they cannot compete against the powerful ministries; and their obligations are numerous.

The result is a housing shortage that strains the social contract. The state's implicit contractual obligation is to guarantee low priced housing, with urban amenities, in a location of the citizen's choice. In housing, rising expectations have beat against the authorities' reluctance to spend more money on housing. Migration to cities, higher income, and more sophisticated tastes have augmented demand, overwhelmed investment plans and induced crowding. Seemingly unrelated social change has taxed the housing bureaucracy and its patrons. A miner, for example, demonstrating his ideas of what the social contract on housing should offer him in the way of occupational and sexual status, complains: 'She was allotted an apartment rather than me, a miner. After all, it is I, the man, who is responsible for the welfare of the family' (FBIS, 11 April 1989, p. 67).

Similarly, the housing shortage is offered as the reason why people leave Siberia, the non-chernozem zone, and other high priority regions, where local government is so weak as to be unable to assume the burden. It has also been a focus of interethnic conflict.

As the basic housing fund, however, has inexorably but slowly inched upwards, amenities such as schools, hospitals, and retail facilities that have been the system's stepchild, have assumed a new and equally strident importance. Local government has a titular obligation to provide the amenities, similar to that in housing, but few resources and claims to carry it out. In one report on the shortage of consumer retail trade outlets (FBIS, 15 May 1989, p. 105), *kolkhozes* of Kaluga, Novgorod, and Ryazan oblasts essentially constructed no trade facilities and were taken to task for their omission. This, in the favoured non-chernozem zone, left some rural inhabitants with no stores at all, let alone goods to stock the stores. When rayon consumer societies were encouraged to meet the deficiency with thirty mobile stores, they parked their mobile trade vehicles in rayon centres and ignored the small villages that they were intended to serve.

Under these circumstances, one critic asks: 'Where is the local authority here?' assuming that this problem is to be resolved not by entrepreneurship, negotiation and trade, but by turning to an authority, local, which has been imbued with a rationalism and a power that approaches the mythical. Central authority in only the recent past answered the very question posed above by declaring that small villages would become 'futureless': that is, they were by fiat to be bypassed by modern amenities. While this policy reflects an outcome common to economic modernisation in most developed countries, it was here imposed by the fiat of technocrats.

The absence of facilities brings no insecurity of change, but fails to match expectations from the social contract, again because of budgetary and resource limits. While the explicit programme of futureless villages has apparently died a quiet death, the result – the drain of population from small villages – continues. The responsibility for housing investment appears to be shifting from industry and central government to local government, whose resources are strapped. It cannot keep up with rising expectations. In retail provisioning, a degree of economic rationality means that the trading agencies, which face shortages of petrol and spare parts, limit the use of mobile stores and restrict the trade in tiny villages that is so unprofitable. Villagers, on the other hand, lack the roads and transportation to take them to the ration centres, and so on. To grant new property rights will not alone promise relief.

Another amenity of some importance to citizens is the perception of personal safety in urban areas. In a comparative study in 1989 (Trehub, 1989, p. 19), the citizens of Moscow were more fearful of being alone on a neighbourhood street at night than were the citizens of Detroit or San Francisco, and ethnic uprisings can only have exacerbated this fear. Nurturing human, political rights probably competes directly with meeting the acknowledged need, and there are few institutions for melding conflicting obligations. Furthermore, the police system, relatively inexperienced in new police methods, suffers from lack of resources, too.

One republic, Latvia, has tackled head on the problem of evaded responsibilities in housing and other infrastructure (FBIS, 10 March 1989). It would charge an enterprise 25 000 rubles per person to employ someone not now living in its vicinity. This would be the fee in Riga; an enterprise in a small city would pay 15 000 rubles. The fee would apply to an immigrant both from Latvia and from another republic. It would be used for housing and 'the food programme'. Registration of citizens without housing would be forbidden. In effect, this plan would explicitly shift the burden of housing and infrastructure from the enterprise, which would now pay a tax on incremental labour, to the municipality and perhaps the republic. The Latvians have proposed a similar tax of the public and private sectors in consumer cooperative trade.

Rural consumers have similar problems about who has the legal responsibility to provide amenities. In the pricing discussions, it has been noted that collective farms must provide schools, housing, and roads that industrial enterprises increasingly receive, however imperfectly, from local government; but, they complain, the farm prices are calculated in the same way as other prices, without allowance for these social obligations. If collective farms must compete and offer lower prices, it would deplete the funds for housing and other municipal functions now handed over to the collective farm. The Latvian proposal above makes no mention of the needs for municipal services in agricultural enterprises such as the collective and state farms, who in 1987 employed 264 000 persons.

Other amenities, the subject of intense discussion, can be provided only with ever more expensive measures. The Soviet Union's farms and enterprises, like those of other modern nations, have claimed well-entrenched 'rights' to pollute and destroy the natural environment in exchange, under the social contract, for industrial progress. The effects have spilled over on to bystanders who now complain vociferously. A miner has eloquently said (FBIS 19 July 1989, p. 63): 'The Kuzbass was constantly told: Give us metal and coal and we will feed you. In exchange the Kuzbass got smoke, dirt, polluted water, lifeless landscapes, disease and more of the same . . . [Now] we are told: we have perestroika, feed yourselves . . . but we have no land – it has all been eaten up by slag heaps and quarries – and the peasants have fled in all directions.'

Like most nations, cleaning up has become a part of the government's obligations, but the taxes to pay for it, the incentive to pollute no further, and the shift of burdens between regions will continue to bedevil the problem solvers.

3.2 THE SEARCH FOR A NEW SOCIAL CONTRACT

This chapter has defined the Soviet reforms in terms of a trade-off between productivity and security, and implied that more insecurity and change is necessary for gains in productivity. In realigning the institutional power over productive property, from Hegelian rights to Lockean, old goals have been abandoned but the new ones are not acceptably in place. Over the years, the population has responded to the new rights such as migration, which has a new appeal today. In the articles used to prepare this text, migration – out of the Kuzbass, into Latvia, on to the farms – is often noted. But such decisions, not lightly undertaken, may proclaim either a certain faith in change and a pull to new opportunities; or it may be a backlash against change and a push out of desperate circumstances. There is some evidence for the latter. The rise of ethnic nationalism; the passionate support of local language and literature; a strong sentiment against farmers: these do not, for the most part, enhance economic productivity, but instead ask for security from the social contract.

Soviet reform seems from outside to be monolithic, but it has many components, each with its own agenda. One way to break down these elements of the reform is to separate them by a simplified hierarchy of needs, where people satisfy first their physical needs of basic food and shelter, then their social needs of friends and family, and finally their personal needs for identity and expression. The first level is represented by the miners cited earlier who wished to have more food and soap – basic needs by all standards. The second level seems to have entered the reform discussion primarily in the demand for travel and family reunification.

At the third level, the need for individuality and personal expression, there are numerous, open conflicts. The pluralism, ethnocentrism, and expanded powers and rights of the new economic and political reforms emphasise this need. The third level can, in the Hegelian view, be satisfied by new property rights and obligations, which have the power to define personality and identity. At its worst, this is the Western materialism that the Soviets and others have traditionally deplored. At best, it can open up new support for the social contract. The right to proclaim one's ethnic identity, to publish one's poetry and hear the music of one's ancestors or cousins abroad, to vote as one wishes: these are personal expressions of identity that assume particular importance after material and social needs are satisfied.

Third-level needs can be called the demand for diversity, but may manifest itself in exclusion. Three examples will illustrate. The first is the rise of Russophilia, or Russian nationalism, and the ethnic and personal identification with a historical people. This satisfies a deep third level need, but has an intolerant side. Andrei Sinyavsky (KIARS, 9 January 1990), citing an article by Russophile Alexander Solzhenitsyn, argues that Russophilia opposes pluralism and that there is still a notion that a 'Russophobic Satan is preventing things from getting better'. (The anti-Semitism of some Russophiles can also be mentioned in this context.) The point is that ethnic movements such as this will satisfy their own third-level needs but oppose the diversity and tolerance that would give satisfaction to others. It seeks security by exclusion, by extending the domain of its own ethnocentrism.

In a second example, a survey by 'Rukh', a popular movement in Ukraine whose leadership is dominated by highly educated members, differed from a broader republic-wide survey made by the Central Ukrainian branch of the All-Union Centre for the Study of Public Opinion (Marples, 1990). The 'Rukh' respondents, who had the higher income and education typical of those seeking to satisfy third-level needs, emphasised the goals of democratisation, political sovereignty, and Ukrainian culture. In the wider sample, respondents, although they generally supported 'Rukh', named an uppermost need on the first level: a satisfactory standard of living. This split demonstrates the fact that nascent political movements will need to blend their policies carefully to bring in votes and overcome the centrifugal force of third-level needs.

Finally, Fyodor Burlatsky (KIARS, 5 December 1989), a member of a Supreme Soviet Committee who spoke of Soviet legislators' support for diversity as well as their legislative inexperience, notes that there are established political interest groups that are both regional and ethnic (the Interregional group; the Baltic, Russian, and Ukrainian groups) and professional (the economists, the scientists, and the agriculturalists). The political groups based on professional identity are a counterpoise to those based on ethnicity, and a more productive force whose growth will contribute to needs at all levels. Echoing Sinyavsky's concern about the Russophiles, Burlatsky notes that they are conservative, suspicious of progressive people and Western ideas, and isolationist.

The focus of this study, price and housing policy and the change in the institutions of property, has merely touched on the forces that provoke and shape a reform as profound as that going on in the Soviet Union. Bardhan (1989, Chapter 1) observes that a new social contract, between citizens and leaders, may define a new and productive set of socio-economic institutions, but that opposing forces may resolve their differences by ideology and that dysfunctional institutions may persist for a long time. It is possible that the current reform movement will blow up into armed conflict or fizzle out. The same observations that were made of Great Russians might be made of other ethnic groups, e.g. Marples reports a similar feeling among Ukrainians, the Lithuanians have engaged in anti-Polish activity, and the conflict between the Azerbaijanis and Armenians has brought bloodshed. In analysing the burgeoning ethnic developments in Communist nations, Brzezinski (1990, p. 10) has proposed five stages of ethnic national development, from preserving the language to full independent sovereignty. The Soviet social contract deliberations will determine the final course.

NOTES

I would like to thank my coauthors for their helpful reviews of an earlier version of this chapter and, especially, Janet Chapman, Professor of Economics at the University of Pittsburgh, for her considerable help in providing source materials.

1. Stuart (1972, pp. 199–228) shows the statutory development of collective farm authorisations, including the obligations to provide consumer goods and services. *Polozhenie* . . . (1989) shows the latest legal environment for land relationships.
2. According to Swafford (1987), farmers are ranked particularly low in any social status study. This, plus the low capitalisation, particularly on small-scale units, discourages farmers from staying in agriculture.
3. According to Soviet statistics (Narodnoe Khoziaistvo 1987, pp. 470–3), urban housing increased 23 per cent and rural housing 16 per cent between 1980 and 1987. In each sector, growth in privately owned housing was slower than that in publicly owned housing, including cooperatives.

REFERENCES

APK: Ekonomika, upravlenie (1989), no. 6

BAHRY, D. (1987) *Outside Moscow* (New York: Columbia University Press).

BARDHAN, P. (1989) *The Economic Theory of Agrarian Institutions* (Oxford: Oxford University Press).

BORNSTEIN, M. (1987) 'Soviet Price Policies', *Soviet Economy*, no. 3, pp. 96–134.

BRZEZINSKI, Z. (1990) 'Post-Communist Nationalism', *Foreign Affairs*, winter.

CHERNIAK, A. (1988) *Pravda*, 1 September.

FBIS (Foreign Broadcast Information Service): 6 April 1989; 11 April 1989, p. 67; 15 May 1989, p. 106; 10 March 1989, pp. 59–61; 19 July 1989, p. 63.

FEDOTOV, A. (1989) *Pravda*, 19 July.

IL'IASOV, F. and MUKHAMMETBERDIEV, O. (1988) *Sotsiologicheskie Issledovanie*, no. 5, pp. 52–7.

KIARS (Kennan Institute for Advanced Russian Studies) *Meeting Report*: 5 December 1989 (Burlatsky); 14 November 1989 (Shelley; Kislinskaia); 9 January 1990 (Sinyavsky).

KORNAI, J. (1986) *Contradictions and Dilemmas: Studies on the Socialist Economy and Society* (Cambridge, Mass.: MIT Press).
MARPLES, D. (1990) *Report on the USSR*, no. 2.
MAYER, R. *et al.* (1974) *Centrally Planned Change: A Re-examination of Theory and Experience* (Urbana: University of Illinois Press).
MILLAR, J. (ed.) (1987) *Politics, Work, and Daily Life in the USSR: A Survey of Former Soviet Citizens* (Cambridge: Cambridge University Press).
MILLAR, J. and CLAYTON, E. (1987) 'Quality of Life' in Millar (ed.) pp. 31–57.
Narodnoe Khoziaistvo SSSR v 1987 g. (1988) (Moscow: Finansy i statistika).
Polozhenie: Ob ekonomicheskikh i organizatsionnykh osnovakh arendnykh otnoshenii v SSSR, (1989) SSSR: Council of Ministers, 7 April, no. 294.
Sel'skoe khoziaistvo SSSR (1988) (Moscow: Finansy i statistiki).
STUART, R. (1972) *The Collective Farm in Soviet Agriculture* (Lexington: Lexington Books).
SWAFFORD, M. (1987) 'Perceptions of Social Status in the USSR', in Millar (ed.), pp. 284–6.
TREHUB, A. (1989) *Report on the USSR*, no. 23.
VINOGRADOFF, P. (1928) *Collected Papers* (Oxford: Clarendon Press).
WORTLEY, B. A. (1967) *Jurisprudence* (New York: Manchester University Press).

4 Health Care in the USSR

Murray Feshbach and Ann Rubin

This chapter describes the state of Soviet health care and the efforts to improve it which are currently under way. Since there is a no more telling indication of the quality of health care in the USSR than the country's morbidity and mortality record, we begin with a summary of the current health situation. It is, after all, the at last publicised 'outputs' of the Soviet welfare state that have compelled the leadership towards a re-evaluation of its viability.[1]

Health care problems in the Soviet Union have taken on a particular urgency in the Gorbachev era. *Glasnost* has publicly unveiled health and environmental degradation of such depth and magnitude that leadership inattention to these social issues is no longer morally or politically feasible. This is particularly so under conditions of *demokratizatsiya* which has dramatically intensified the nexus between politics and health. In contrast to the past, constituent demands are heeded by now 'elected' Soviet officials. Environmentalism has been a key campaign issue in recent political contests, often facilitating the emergence of more dissident contenders, while support for the Soviet Union's Popular Fronts has largely derived from these organisations' commitment to improvements in the health and environmental sphere. That in some republics nationalities conflicts have been fuelled by ecological and related health concerns has further raised the political risks involved in continued neglect of these most profound social problems.

Nor can the economic and military implications of poor health be ignored any longer. The economic losses from diminished productivity, disability benefits and payment for treatment of the sick are alarming to Soviet authorities, reported at 90 billion rubles in 1987, or 11 per cent of the Soviet official GNP measure.[2] Of this amount, the burden from environment-related losses has been estimated at 30 to 50 billion rubles per year.[3] At the same time, demographic trends have placed constraints on the Soviet labour force and military which greatly enhance the importance of the health factor. Prompted by diminished manpower and fiscal resources, Gorbachev has initiated an intensive economic growth policy. But the prospects for intensive growth rest on the ability of the Soviet Union to challenge problems of chronic disability, underproductivity of an unhealthy workforce and premature invalidism and death.

4.1 THE CURRENT HEALTH SITUATION IN THE SOVIET UNION

The troubling reality of the Soviet Union's health situation is discernible, to begin with, in morbidity rates for the country's children. In 1989, 53 per cent of all school children in the USSR were allegedly seriously ill.[4] In the same year, 15 per cent of 6 year olds were reportedly functionally and physically unprepared to begin school.[5] A 1989 report by the Collegium of the Ministry of Health, in which it was revealed that more than half of general secondary school graduates in the Soviet Union are limited in their choice of profession because of deviations or defects in their health status, suggests that sickness does not diminish even in the upper grades.[6]

Infectious disease rates for the Soviet population provide further indication of the seriousness of the country's health situation. In 1988, the Soviets, with a population only 15 per cent larger than that of the US, registered 716 436 cases of hepatitis compared to just over 56 000 reported cases of hepatitis (all types) in the United States in 1987. There are several hundred cases of typhoid per year in the United States versus a Soviet figure of 11 000 to 19 000 cases annually for the past decade, down to 'only' 8096 cases in 1988. Incidence of diphtheria has decreased in the Soviet Union from 53 200 cases in 1960 to 870 cases in 1988. But this rate is still astonishingly high in comparison to the current US level of 0 to 3 cases per year for the last ten years.

Yet the all-union figures do not fully depict the severity of the Soviet Union's morbidity problem. In areas surrounding the highly polluted Aral Sea, two-thirds of the population reportedly have typhoid, hepatitis or cancer of the digestive system. While the all-union incidence rate for typhoid was 2.8 per 100 000 population in 1988, the comparable figure for Tadzhikistan, was 40.6; in the same year, infectious disease illnesses occurred at almost twice the national rate in this republic. In the case of viral hepatitis, the overall figure was 251 cases per 100 000 population in 1988 compared to 942 in Uzbekistan, 816 in Kirgizia, 529 in Tadzhikistan and 474 in Turkmenistan.

The regional disparities in illness rates are particularly worrisome in the face of current demographic trends. During the 1979 to 1989 intercensal period, Tadzhiks grew by 45 per cent and Uzbeks by 34 per cent, compared to the Russian population which experienced a slightly less than 6 per cent increase, the Ukrainians who grew by just over 4 per cent and the Belorussians who increased by barely over 6 per cent. The figures confirm projections that the Soviet labour and draft pool will be increasingly drawn from the southern tier of the country. Between 1979 and 1989, 70 per cent, or 5 million of the 7 million person growth in the population of able-bodied ages (16–59 years of age for males and 16–54 years of age for females, inclusive) was among residents of the four Central Asian republics and Kazakhstan. In 1988, already 37 per cent of Soviet draftees came from the seven southern republics of Central Asia (Kirgizia, Tadzhikistan, Turkmenistan and Uzbekistan) and the Transcaucasus (Armenia, Azerbaydzhan and Georgia), up from 28 per cent in 1980.

The continuing shift in the conscriptee pool to the southern periphery of the Soviet Union concerns not least of all the military leadership, already dismayed over deterioration in the health of recruits. As early as 1984, hints of the health problem in the Soviet military surfaced in the Ministry of Defence newspaper, *Krasnaya Zvezda*, which announced the formation of an Extraordinary Anti-epidemic Commission in every military unit.[7] Under *glasnost*, innuendo has given way to frank reports in the Soviet press that an increasing number of 18-year-old males are being rejected for military service for medical reasons, including liver and kidney disease, ulcers and nervous disorders. Since 1986, narcotic and psychological specialists have been assigned to each medical commission of conscription boards throughout the country to contend with increasing drug and mental health problems. (This, of course, may also reflect, in part, an effort to control false claims to ineligibility.) It is reported that in the Soviet Union's Karaganda oblast, the number of potential draftees rejected for military service increased by 40 per cent between 1985 and 1987.[8] Only one in fourteen young males passed the (admittedly more demanding) physical examinations to serve as aircrews when reporting for active duty in 1987.[9]

The challenge before the Soviet health care system in detecting and alleviating morbidity has now been further complicated by the Chernobyl tragedy. Medical evaluations only now detailed in the Soviet press are conflicting and thus the full scale of Chernobyl's impact is difficult to ascertain. Doctors who have studied patients in the zone report dramatic increases in anaemia, heart attacks, enlarged thyroid glands, skins and other cancers, miscarriages, genetic mutations, birth defects, gynaecological problems and general lowering of the immune system.[10] Until quite recently, the medical establishment had claimed that these higher morbidity findings were due to more comprehensive medical observation. Available transcripts of interviews with residents of the affected areas, as well as reports from local Belorussian and Ukrainian physicians and commentators, however, suggest that the recorded increases in illness rates are real and are related to the nuclear fallout. In any case, the burden on an already strained Soviet health care system has been one of Chernobyl's incontestable consequences. Many additional resources are now being devoted to contend with the medical and other consequences of the incident. The Belorussian state budget will double in the next five to six years to incorporate an incremental 70 billion rubles, from 10 to approximately 20 billion rubles per year. The Ukraine will require an additional 16 billion rubles.

The consequences of high morbidity are nowhere more evident than in the Soviet Union's mortality rates. While overall improvements in crude death rates (with the exception of 1988 and 1989), age-specific death rates and infant mortality rates (especially affecting life expectancy at birth) have been recorded since 1985, the Soviet levels are still dramatically inferior to those of the rest of the developed world. Life expectancy in the Soviet Union is currently worse than in Turkey and comparable to that in Paraguay. The death rate for Soviet men of able-bodied ages (16–59) from all causes is 1.82 times that of men in the West. (The death ratio between Soviet able-bodied women and those of Western countries is 1.43.)[11] Indeed, in the Soviet Union, the problem of male mortality is as profound as that for American black males.

Although the infant mortality rate in the Soviet Union has seemed to improve over time, relative to other developed nations it is still very high: the officially reported figure of 22 per 1000 live births contrasts with 8 in France, 9 in the former FRG, 11 in Italy, 6 in Sweden and 10 in the United States.[12] Meanwhile, there is abundant commentary in the Soviet press that in regions of Central Asia, the infant mortality rate is in fact increasing, or in any case not improving, as official Soviet reports would suggest. Chief obstetrician-gynaecologist, Martynov, of the Tashauz oblast in the Turkmenistan has written that often newborn babies and infants are not registered for a year or longer and that in many cases physicians misrepresent the facts. A child who is in fact deceased may be reported as gaining weight, a live birth may be misclassified as a stillbirth, or an infant death may be reported many months after the fact, too late for inclusion in 'infant' mortality counts. According to Martynov, the responsible physicians have been misinforming higher authorities and the public with their claim to a 25 to 50 per cent reduction in infant mortality; in fact no positive changes in approach or results in the area of infant mortality have occurred in this region of the USSR.[13]

However, as in the case with reported morbidity statistics, all-union rates sadly do not reveal the gravity of the country's infant mortality problem. Thus, again, in Karakalpakia (Uzbekistan), for example, a region devastated by the dessication of the Aral Sea and excessive pesticide use, an infant mortality rate as high as 111 deaths per 1000 live births has been reported.

4.2 PROVISION OF HEALTH CARE IN THE SOVIET UNION: THE CURRENT SITUATION

The myth of good universal health care under the Soviet welfare state has been irrevocably damaged by *glasnost*. The Soviet Union's abysmal morbidity and mortality record has become public knowledge, as have the basic systemic roots of the health crisis. However impressive the quantitative picture, *glasnost* has undermined all claims to the qualitative successes of the Soviet centralised health care system. Moreover, the now acknowledged failures of the Soviet health care system have contributed to disillusionment with socialism itself; for it has become increasingly clear that the general malaise of the Soviet centralised economy is responsible for the profound shortages in the medical area, from aspirin to heart medications to foetal monitoring devices.

The fallacy of Soviet health care became strikingly apparent in the early stages of medical *glasnost* when former Minister of Health, Yevgeniy Chazov announced that 40 per cent of new medical school graduates cannot even read an electrocardiogram. Chazov's revelation provided some perspective on a favourable doctors per capita figure in the USSR *vis-à-vis* the West. Likewise, the truly impressive number of medical facilities in the Soviet Union turned out to be quite meaningless in light of newly acknowledged major quality and sanitation problems. Chazov has stipulated that only half of all Soviet medical institutions have hot water or sewage.[14] Almost 45 per cent of all hospitals in the Soviet Union were built in 1960 or earlier, and only 37 per cent meet Soviet standard requirements; capital and current repairs are needed by 66 per cent, and almost 10 per cent are in full disrepair.[15] Even more startling is information now published about health care facilities in rural areas of the Soviet Union. Thus, even today 65 per cent of all rural district hospitals lack hot water, 27 per cent were built without sewage pipes and 17 per cent have no water at all.[16]

New data also suggest that the abundance of hospital beds, like the plethora of doctors, may be equally a detriment as an advantage to Soviet health care. The norms for bed space in the Soviet Union is 7 square metres but Chazov has noted that the actual average alloted space in hospitals is only 4.2 to 4.3 square metres.[17] Due to overcrowding, as well as lack of control of visitors, and poor sanitation, there is probably a high incidence of nosocomial, i.e. in-hospital acquired, infections.

The Soviet health care system also suffers from both shortages and quality problems in the area of medical equipment and medicines. Overall, the demand for medical equipment in the Soviet Union is satisfied by only 60 per cent, and only 30 per cent of the equipment coming off the line meets 'modern levels'.[18] However, it is often the case that domestically produced equipment is not only of an insufficiently 'modern' level but rather does not function at all. This was the situation in 1989, for example, when of 850 spectrophotometers produced only 100 were in working condition.[19] Whereas the United States has 4800 CAT scans for a population of 250 million, and Japan 4000 for its 120 million citizens, the Soviet Union has just 62 for a population of 290 million. But only 25 of these, all imported, are capable of reading the whole body. Soviet foetal monitoring devices are good for, on average, only 500 uses, compared to 30 000 for US devices.

Based on information collected by the USSR People's Control Committee, the demand for medicines in the Soviet Union in 1989, even accounting for imports, is satisfied by only 75 to 80 per cent. The total volume of production per capita is about 14 rubles per year, or eight to ten times less than in the developed capitalist countries. (Domestic production accounts for only 57 per cent of total available medications.) Furthermore, the committee noted that domestic medications do not meet international requirements, with significantly lower shelf lives than their foreign analogues; also that 'the condition of equipment and production capacity of the overwhelming majority of enterprises do not meet sanitary-technical norms and cannot guarantee the purity of their output'.[20]

And yet the Control Committee's report paints a more favourable picture than that of the Soviet medical establishment itself. Both former Minister of Health, Chazov, and Head of the Pharmaceutical Administration of the USSR Ministry of Health, A.D. Apazov, have claimed that only 70 per cent of the country's needed medicines are available, a rate of demand satisfaction approximately the same as sixty years ago. Chazov has on numerous occasions also condemned the poor quality of those medications which are accessible. Nor is the medicine supply problem apparently getting any better. In 1989, overall shortfalls of medications were reported to have increased by more than six times since Gorbachev's accession to power.[21]

4.3 EFFORTS TO RECTIFY THE HEALTH SITUATION

While the challenge before the Soviet Union in the area of health care is enormous there are some grounds for optimism. The current leadership has initiated fundamental organisational changes accompanied by dramatic increases in budgetary appropriations to the health sphere for the next five-year plan. Whether the approved resources will in fact be allocated and/or appropriately dispersed remains to be seen, as does the impact of *perestroika* in the health sector. Even under the best of circumstances, the question must be asked whether the scale of need can be effectively addressed with the designated level of funding.

The shake-up in the health care system began in January 1987 with massive personnel turnover. Within two months of Gorbachev's replacement of USSR Minister of Health Burenkov with Yevgeniy Chazov, two deputy ministers, the head of the maternity and child health care administration of the ministry, the president of the Academy of Sciences, the head of the military medical services for the Southern Group of Forces, and several others were fired; many others were reprimanded. In addition, 350 000 of the more than 1 million physicians in the Soviet Union were recertified (on a, reportedly, relatively lenient basis), some 1000 were fired immediately and an additional 10 per cent were given only temporary certificates to continue their practice of medicine.[22]

Leadership acknowledgement of the low level of physician preparedness in the Soviet Union has also set in motion comprehensive change in the medical education system. In September 1988, after public (and, perhaps, even greater internal) denunciation of the insufficient cardiology-related capability of new graduates, the entire medical school curriculum was revised. Not only were new medical students required to have clinical hands-on time in their last three years of training (for the first time) and more years of study, with tests at benchmark dates, but additional training for older physicians was also planned. While in the past independent medical practice was permitted after only one year of internship, reforms call for two to three years of mandatory supervised work at this stage. Moreover, licensing exams are to be introduced in an effort to bring Soviet medical training practices closer to international standards. Plans also provide for new textbooks and equipment and revised methods of teaching. The appointment of a former rector of a medical institute, Igor Denisov, as the new Minister of Health, perhaps reflects Soviet recognition of the need for medical training expertise at the highest level.

Perhaps most impressive are the proposed budgetary increases. Chazov demonstrated his political skill in obtaining agreement from the leadership for a doubling of state budgetary allocation to the health sector in the thirteenth five-year plan, and a tripling for the last quinqennial period of the century. For the current five-year plan period, Chazov had managed to secure some 5.4 to 5.6 billion additional rubles for the health sector from the 'peace dividend', i.e. from the reduction in defence sector expenditures. Whether, given all the competing demands for resources, this will hold under the new minister remains to be seen.

In general, in the future the health sector's relative allocation from the state budget is to be attuned to the gross national product (GNP) rather than to national income, and to the relative size of the population. The new methodology will permit adjustments on the basis of regional distinctions, although just how such differentials will be factored into the calculus is at this point unclear. Indeed, the proposed system of allocation raises questions concerning the accuracy of Soviet statistics, particularly GNP estimates. Will individual republic figures be used to determine respective shares and how will policy-makers resolve republic claims to greater relative contributions to GNP? In the future, the Soviet republics will be given greater freedom in utilising funds distributed to them. To what extent any national system of standards can endure once republics and their local soviets are permitted more authority to distribute funds between institutions on their territory is another open question.

Apart from increases in budgetary allocations and changes in the criteria for their distribution, also envisaged is a comprehensive shift to cost-accountability (i.e. self-financing). Under the terms of the new *khozraschet*, medical institutions will be permitted greater leeway in expenditure of allocated funds and use of any profits. As in the case with the republics, medical institutions will receive money on a per capita basis (medical help and services rendered), but also in accordance with performance indicators. Medical institutions will now ultimately be responsible for their patient's well-being, while the direct relationship between funding and success of treatment will presumably guarantee the appropriate and effective use of resources. It remains to be seen if a system of payments to cost-accounting polyclinics based on reported performance indicators, which are known to be of questionable accuracy, will be effective.

Budgetary financing of health care institutions will be supplemented by contract agreements with enterprises, organisations and institutions on a cost-accounting basis, along with development of services to the population for which fees will be charged. Non-budgetary sources will also include allocations from the local soviets and sums levied by the sanitary-epidemiological service on enterprises, organisations and citizens for damages to the health of working people in connection with violations of sanitary and anti-epidemic norms and regulations. In addition, funds will be generated from reimbursements of expenditures for treatment of persons who have experienced on-the-job injuries and poisonings, road transport accidents for which transport organisations and private individuals are to blame, as well as voluntary payments from enterprises, institutions, and organisations, charity funds, cooperatives and individual citizens.

In areas where there are several medical institutions, cost-accounting medical establishments are to be organised into territorial medical associations with a leading role assigned to the polyclinic. The polyclinic will distribute its normative budgetary allotments and additional sources of funding among teams of sectional physicians, including midwives, paediatricians, and combination-type midwife–paediatrician therapists. Once funds are dispersed, these teams are in charge of the funds designated for medical help to the patients attached to these teams. The remaining associated hospitals, diagnostic and consultative centres and dispensaries, first aid, and specialised medical services are to 'earn' funds for their activities, obtaining them from the teams as payment for the services rendered. In the interest of profit, the polyclinics will, when possible, treat patients itself rather than pay its associated organisations. Patients are to be allowed a free choice of physician, as well as of institution within the association, an arrangement intended to foster 'healthy' competition.

While an immediate decision has been made to reorient the Soviet health care system along the lines described above, discussions of alternative models continue in the Soviet press and participants urge that experimentation in the area not be considered finished. Insurance medicine, based also on self-financing of medical institutions and patient choice, is a second option now being seriously debated in the Soviet press. Denisov has confirmed that investigation into the best public health concept is still under way, including team forms of organisation of labour, collective contracts, leasing and cooperatives.[23]

Advocates of insurance-based medicine oppose state-financed health care on principle: first, they write, the budget is funded primarily through levies on enterprise business activity, which under *khozraschet* comes directly from the workers' pockets. To compel these same workers to then pay (if only partially) self-financing clinics, cooperatives or private practitioners is denounced as 'highway robbery' and a 'violation of social justice'. Moreover, say the proponents of insurance-based care, any system financed directly from the state is susceptible to accountability problems since 'funds disbursed by the Treasury belong to no one'. The suggested alternative is that money allocated from the state budget for medical care be returned to the enterprises. Enterprise funds will be created for treating all members of the collective, but every individual will retain essential control over his or her share. Employees will not as a rule be permitted to receive their allotted amount in cash but are free to transfer it to the medical institution of their choice for use when necessary. Funds to treat retirees are to be transferred to social security offices and those to treat children to public education institutions.[24]

In Latvia, restructuring of the health care system is already occurring along similar lines. In this Soviet republic, financing is being converted to a system of hospital insurance. Patients will be free to select their own doctor and the republic's 'insurance society' will pay doctor's fees through the hospital insurance fund, comprised of state funds, wages and fees from individual citizens. Denisov has stated that the future of all Soviet health care lies with insurance-based medicine, though no specific time frame has been announced.[25]

While the current innovations in health funding policy reflect a concession to the failures of 'administrative methods', they do represent an attitudinal shift concerning the merits of the welfare state. The principle of free and universally available health care continues to be upheld as inviolable and pay services are cautiously advocated only as impetus for competition. In any case, fee services are to play only a minor role in the new health care system. The total volume of fee-based services in 1986 amounted to 274.6 million rubles, or approximately 1.31 rubles per capita. By the end of 1987, the volume of these services reached 378.3 million rubles. During his tenure Chazov had proposed a quintupling of the 1987 level by the year 2000, a still relatively insubstantial contribution to overall health care services.[26]

Related to this, the fate of medical cooperatives in the Soviet Union's evolving health care system will be interesting to observe. Over the past several years, medical cooperatives have played an important role in filling the health services gap, although they have been systematically restricted since their initial introduction. Indeed, public and official resistance to cooperative medical establishments reflects the distance to go in the Soviet Union towards acceptance of market forces, particularly in the sacrosanct area of social services. None the less, between January and July 1989, the number of cooperatives providing medical services increased from 1900 to 2800, employment increased from 32 000 to 47 000, and the value of services from 68 million for all of 1988 to almost double that amount (119 million rubles) for the first half of 1989.

Whether it is envisioned that insurance funds be available for use at cooperatives is unclear from the literature. How medical cooperatives will fare under the new organisational system will most likely depend upon the successes of the self-financing and territorial model. It seems doubtful that the quality of medical care will be sufficiently improved and overcrowding enough reduced under the proposed measures to render the medical cooperative movement obsolete in the short term.

4.4 PROSPECTS

It is still too early to evaluate the impact of the transition to economic management methods in Soviet health care. Whatever the ameliorating effects of organisational change, however, the basic issue of funding remains. And the evidence suggests that the resources proposed for the future are grossly insufficient to meet the overwhelming needs in the health sector.

The discrepancy between projected expenditure and official Soviet designated need for hospitals and equipment provides a useful example. Chazov statements comparing Soviet expenditures on building and equipment per hospital bed (18 000 rubles) with 'needed' rates of expenditure, comparable to those for the GDR (40 000 rubles) or Czechloslovakia (80 000 rubles), indicate that for the Soviet Union to attain even its minimum goal for modern new construction and remodernisation of existing facilities, allocations are far short of need. Cumulative expenditures for new and upgraded hospitals and equipment over the next fifteen years is estimated at 82 billion rubles, or 40 per cent short of the necessary 142 billion to meet a 52 000 rubles per bed level Soviet stated goal. However, this calculation is based on the current Soviet artificial prices for equipment; thus the shortfall will in fact be even greater as world prices are introduced and costs are adjusted commensurately. Moreover, the approximately 60 billion ruble shortfall is based on needs for hospital construction alone while the 82 billion rubles reflects the cumulative amount available for all curative–preventive institutions, including polyclinics, diagnostic centres, dispensaries, etc. While alternative sources of funding such as enterprise and charity funds, loans, etc. will mitigate the shortfall, these will be far from sufficient to compensate for a 60 billion ruble gap for hospitals alone.

Given such a major shortfall for just hospitals, the Soviets will be hard pressed to obtain funds to meet officially proclaimed needs for 150 diagnostic centres scheduled for operation by 1995; for 30 laser ophthalmology centres to open by 1990; for 70 consultative–diagnostic polyclinics by 1991; for 14 000 medical labs attached to rural pharmacies, and many more. Likewise in the case of resources necessary to satisfy equipment demands for existing polyclinics, the cornerstone of the proposed self-financing associations. In 1989, Goskomstat revealed the enormous deficiencies in this area:

> The scale of production of medical equipment is inadequate as demonstrated by the level of supply of medical institutions. Thus, from the sample survey data (of October 1988), approximately one-half of [all] polyclinics and hospitals are short of x-ray therapeutic and lab equipment, as well as fluorographic equipment, more than one-third are short of x-ray diagnostic, physical therapy and dental surgery equipment, as well as electrocardiographic

devices. Only 2 per cent of polyclinics can satisfy public requirements for ultrasound diagnostics, 5 per cent for endoscopy, and somewhat more than half, for laboratory analysis.[27]

However, the provision of medical establishments with the necessary equipment is more than simply an issue of adequate funding. Medical institutions, no matter how effectively organised, are still dependent upon the vast network of ministries for supplies. And despite efforts under Gorbachev to push ministries towards greater accountability, profound problems with plan fulfilment persist. Recent Soviet experience with production of single-use syringes is a case in point, particularly relevant in light of a now potential AIDS epidemic.

In accordance with a directive issued in December 1986, the Ministry of Precision Instrument-making (Minpribor SSSR) and the Ministry of the Medical and Microbiological Industry (Minmedbioprom SSSR) were to produce 30 million and 77 million single-use syringes, respectively, in 1987 and 1988. Only 7 million were in fact produced and these by Minmedbioprom itself. A single machine, purchased fifteen years earlier and with an original capacity of only 2 to 3 million units per year, was the only piece of equipment at Minmedbioprom's disposal for the syringe production – hence its non-fulfilment of the plan.[28] (About 57 000 single-use syringes were imported by the Ministry of Health in 1988, approximately half of which were virtually useless since they were supplied with no disposable needles.)[29]

Current plans for syringe production call for 1 billion disposable syringes for 1989, 2 billion in 1990 and 3.5 billion in 1991. To prepare for this expanded production run, four rotary assembly lines capable of yielding 400 million syringes per year were to have been installed in 1988. However, by 1989 not a single one had been placed on line. Thus, as one commentator on the situation observed in *Sovetskaya Rossiya*, 'the entire programme planned to commission capacities this year to produce 2.2 billion syringes has failed', in part because, 'there is no Soviet equipment to produce syringes and needles'.[30]

Why is syringe-producing equipment so scarce? The list of culpable ministries goes on and on and reflects the basic failings of the Soviet economic system. The machine-tool industry frustrated work in the design stage, the Ministry of Chemical and Petroleum Building failed to deliver 'automatic lines for the sterilization of polymer syringes', the Ministry of the Electrical Equipment Industry failed to produce equipment necessary for needle production, the Ministry of Chemical Industry failed to provide polythylene, polypropylene, special glues and other required materials to make appropriate parts, and the Ministry of Timber Industry failed to produce the necessary paper for packaging the syringes.[31] The system survives for better or worse.

4.5 THE HEALTH AND ENVIRONMENT LINK

As if the news were not bad enough, the Soviet Union's health care system is also beleaguered by a serious environmental problem and its deleterious health implications. It is telling that in the Soviet Union deaths among able-bodied males due to respiratory illnesses occur at a rate of 2.8 times that of the West.[32] Last year the Soviets reported that 70 million Soviet citizens lived in cities where maximum permissible levels of pollutants had been exceeded by five or more times, 50 million in cities where such norms were exceeded by ten or more times, and 43 million in cities where norms were violated by fifteen or more times.[33]

A Vremya broadcast in March of this year added new information to already startling evidence about the health consequences of the dessication of the Aral Sea.[34] Not long ago the fourth (now the sixth) largest area of inland water in the world, the Aral has shrunk by 40 per cent in the three decades since 1960, and one prediction is that it will disappear by the year 2010. Pollution of the Aral Sea has rendered water in the lower reaches of the Syrdar'ya and Amudar'ya rivers unsuitable for consumption. According to the broadcast, average life expectancy in the Kara-Kalpak Autonomous Soviet Socialist Republic, where potable water is drawn from the Amudar'ya, is five years less than in other areas of the country, and maternal mortality is probably the highest in the USSR. Infant mortality is several times higher in this region than for Uzbekistan as a whole.

Between 1972 and 1986, there were thirty-six outbreaks of infectious diseases in the regions adjacent to the Aral Sea. Typhoid cases increased twenty-nine-fold between 1972 and 1984, jaundice, seven-fold between 1971 and 1987, and kidney disease, four-fold between 1976 and 1986. In the last five years, incidence of typhoid fever among children under age 15 increased from 34.5 per cent to 43.9 per cent, and infectious digestive diseases among the same age group from 73 to 82 per cent.[35]

There is, however, hope in the fact that the environment, like health, has been addressed with unprecedented seriousness and commitment in the Gorbachev era. Capital investments assigned to this sector will quadruple over the next fifteen years, an All-union Committee for Nature Protection (Goskompriroda) has been established to replace an unwieldy network of environmental control agencies, and a law on nature protection is in progress.

As in the case with health, the solution to ecological degradation is more complex than just political will. Aside from equipment shortages and bureaucratic obstacles, in implementing environmental enhancement measures the Soviets confront a host of other dilemmas that complicate the clean-up process. The classic predicament of economy versus ecology has a particular saliency under *perestroika*. For while improvements in the environmental situation seem crucial to economic recovery, sufficient funds for ecology programmes will not be forthcoming if the economic situation does not markedly improve. And environmental interests collide with output goals nowhere more forcefully than in a country with virtually no air and water purifying technology or equipment; that is, in a country where the only realistic environmental enhancement strategy is simply to shut down offending enterprises.

This dilemma has its direct consequences for the improvement not just of health conditions in general but also health services *per se*. For the fact is that pharmaceutical enterprises are among the worst offenders of clean air. In one city of the USSR, bronchitis and asthma were recorded to have increased thirty-seven times in just one year after the opening of a biochemical plant for production of protein-vitamin concentrate. In the city of Volgograd, bronchial asthma rose by only five times, but pneumonia increased seven times, and deaths increased within the year after a similar plant, but without purification equipment, began producing gaprin.[36] But the closing of pharmaceutical production sites threatens the supply of desperately needed medicines. And which is the more detrimental to the future health status and productivity of Soviet citizens? Moscow expresses frustration that local authorities simultaneously protest the shortage of medicines and the construction of pharmaceutical plants on their territories. The complaint reflects not just the myriad problems the Soviets confront in resolving their health crisis, but the changing dynamic between social concerns and politics in the age of *demokratizatsiya*.

There are no short-term solutions to the Soviet Union's health care problems and indeed the evidence suggests that the situation will significantly deteriorate before it improves. The economic, military and political implications of poor and worsening health in the USSR are serious. The damages to the economy are especially unaffordable in a period of profound economic strain, while the consequences for the military are exacerbated by current demographic trends. Politically, the recognised failure of the Soviet welfare state to provide one of the most basic guarantees of the 'social contract' has accelerated and widened the demand for radical political change, a demand which has increasing force under the now prevailing conditions of relative freedom.

REFERENCES

1. Much of the material in this chapter is derived from Murray Feshbach (with Alfred Friendly Jr), *Breakdown: The Neglect of Soviet Health and Nature* (New York: Basic Books, 1991) (forthcoming).
2. Ye. Chazov, 'Zdravookhraneniye: pul's perestroyki', *Meditsinskaya gazeta*, 30 October 1987, p. 1.
3. 'Environmental Damage Causes Losses of Billions Every Year', *Handelsblatt*, 4 November 1988, p. 15.
4. Dr Aleksey Dobrovskiy, Radio Moscow, cited in Radio Liberty Report, 'USSR Today', Soviet Media Features Digest, 16 November 1988.
5. 'Tyazhelaya rasplata, tsifry i fakty', *Agitator*, no. 17, September 1989, p. 32.
6. *Meditsinskaya gazeta*, 25 January 1989, p. 2.
7. 'V interesakh zdorov'ya voinov', *Krasnaya zvezda*, 7 January 1984, p. 1.
8. S. Brish, 'Sound the Alarm', *Voyennyye znaniya*, no. 2, February 1989, pp. 9–10.
9. Aleksey Dobrovskiy, Radio Moscow, April 1989.
10. Elizabeth Shogren, '4 Years Later, Chernobyl's Ills Widen', *Washington Post*, 27 April 1990, p. A1.
11. West defined as USA, former West Germany, France, Great Britain and Japan. Base data for the Soviet Union are from Goskomstat SSSR, *Press-vypusk*, no. 191, 5 May 1989, p. 2.
12. Newly available information regarding the falsification of Soviet official infant mortality statistics suggests that the actual infant mortality figure is closer to 33, or 50 per cent greater. As a consequence, life expectancy at birth is half a year lower than the already low figure officially reported in Soviet statistical sources. The information, recently published in *Argumenty i fakty*, suggests that lower than actual infant mortality rates have been reported in an attempt to demonstrate the success of recent efforts to reduce mortality rates.
13. Ye. Myatiyeva, 'Secret Figures', *Turkmenskaya iskra*, 5 March 1989, translated in JPRS, *USSR Political Affairs*, JPRS-UPA-89-039, 12 June 1989, p. 37.

14. *Komsomol'skaya pravda*, 18 June 1989.
15. *Meditsinskaya gazeta*, 7 July, 1989, p. 1
16. Interview with Chazov, 'Sotni voiteley stoit odin vrachevatel' iskusnyy', in *Ogonyek*, no. 42, 1988, pp. 1–3.
17. *Komsomol'skaya pravda*, 18 June 1989.
18. A. V. Tokar, 'This Concerns Us All', *Kommunist Ukrainy*, no. 12, December 1988, pp. 34–50, translated in JPRS, *USSR Political Affairs*, JPRS-UPA-89-004, 10 July 1989, pp. 53–66.
19. *Moscow News*, no. 8, 19 February 1989, p. 13.
20. B. Zyuganov and I. Kireyev, 'Gde kupit' aspirin?' *Pravda*, 12 April 1989, p. 3.
21. 'Rubezhi perestroyki narodnogo zdravookhraneniya (tsifry i fakty)', *Voyenno-meditsinskiy zhurnal*, no. 5, May 1989, p. 11.
22. In the spring of 1990, Chazov was himself replaced by his first deputy minister I. N. Denisov.
23. TASS in English, 22 September 1989.
24. See, for example, M. Krylov, 'A Proposal: More Profitable to Provide Better Medical Care', *Trud*, 11 January 1990, p. 4, translated in JPRS, *USSR, Economic Affairs*, JPRS-UEA-90-005, pp. 77–8.
25. *Izvestiya*, 24 April 1990, p. 2, translated in FBIS, *Soviet Union. Daily Report*, FBIS-SOV-90-081, 26 April 1990, p. 2.
26. V. P. Korchagin, M. P. Roytman, *et al.*, 'Platnye meditsinskiye uslugi naseleniyu SSSR', *Sovetskoye zdravookhraneniye*, no. 10, October 1989, p. 18.
27. Goskomstat SSSR, *Press-vypusk*, no. 251, 14 June 1989, p. 3.
28. From letters signed by the Ministers of Minpribor, Minmedbioprom, and Minstankoprom USSR, M. Skarbardin, V. Bykov, and N. Panichev, respectively, to General Secretary M. S. Gorbachev, 'O proizvodstve shpritsev i igl odnokratnogo primeneniya', dated 6 May 1989, in *Izvestiya TsK KPSS*, no. 6, June 1989, pp. 124–5.
29. Nelyudov, in *Meditsinskaya gazeta*, 17 February 1989, p. 3.
30. S. Blagodarov, 'Multiple Injections', *Sovestkaya Rossiya*, 6 May 1989, p. 2, translated in FBIS, *Daily Report. Soviet Union*, FBIS-SOV-89-098, 23 May 1989, p. 76, and *Argumenty i fakty*, no. 20, 20–26 May 1989, p. 8.
31. Ibid.
32. Goskomstat SSSR, *Press-vypusk*, no. 191, 5 May 1989, p. 2.
33. From S. Turanov, 'It Is Still Not Too Late', *Sotsialisticheskaya industriya*, 5 July 1989, p. 3, translated in JPRS, *USSR. Political Affairs*, JPRS-UPA-89-051, 16 August 1989, p. 1.
34. Vremya broadcast, 12 March 1990, translated in FBIS, *Soviet Union. Daily Report*, FBIS-SOV-90-051, 15 March 1990, p. 94.
35. Rusi Nasar, 'How the Soviets Murdered a Sea', *Washington Post*, 4 June 1989, p. B3.
36. A. Lebedinskiy, 'Pervaya pobeda "zelyenykh"', *Meditsinskaya gazeta*, 9 July 1989, p. 2. Gaprin, a new product, is a protein-vitamin concentrate.

5 Social Policies in the 1980s in Poland: A Discussion of New Approaches

Henryk Flakierski

In this chapter I will concentrate the discussion on three aspects of social policies: (i) new approaches to the welfare system; (ii) changes in the incomes policies in the 1980s; and (iii) price policies in connection with redistribution of real incomes. The largest part of the chapter, however, is devoted to the discussion of new approaches to the welfare system. Other aspects of social policies in Poland, especially the social welfare system narrowly defined, will be discussed by Z. Fallenbuchl in Chapter 6. Such a division of the subject matter is not accidental. We have divided beforehand the field of inquiry between us.

5.1 THE WELFARE SYSTEM

Changes in the welfare system cannot be discussed separately from the broad changes in the socio-economic system, that is, from the reforms in Poland. The view expressed in what direction the welfare system should go is a subordinated part of the discussion about the future of the socio-economic system in Poland. However, the debate around changes in the welfare system has its separate aspects and the battle lines are not identical to the battle lines in the socio-political sphere.

We can distinguish a broad spectrum of views from extreme egalitarianism to pure neo-liberalism, the latter rejecting any role of the state in the welfare system.

5.1.1 An Overview of Different Approaches

The major proponents of the paternalistic-egalitarian point of view (Winiewski, 1988; Rosner, 1989; Goralska and Wiktorow, 1988; Czajka, 1989; Rajkiewicz, 1979) historically are the children of the broadly understood traditional left.[1] They perceive a highly developed social benefit system as part of the egalitarian ethos of socialism.

Repeating Marx's ideas from the Gotha Programme and other socialists' ideas, they emphasise that public consumption (education, culture, pensions, child care, sport and recreation) should increase faster than the national output and the individual consumption fund. For the Marxists this is a social imperative for the gradual building of a new Communist society, for the gradual achievement of the goal to provide for everyone in accordance with their needs.

Living socialism of today does not in any meaningful way conform to Marx's vision of a socialist society. Nevertheless, certain elements of Marx's arguments have some validity for the countries of 'real socialism'. Namely, the smaller income differentials in East European countries than in most capitalist ones are mainly a result of elimination of earnings from property. The increase in the share of public consumption in the national output and in the total consumption fund has continued for a long time in East European countries. This tendency, given the relative dispersion of incomes from employment, is an equalising factor of income distribution, although the role of public consumption in this matter is not without its pitfalls and contradictions, especially as far as common access to goods and services of public consumption is concerned. However, we should not overlook the fact that an increase in the share of public consumption in the national output is not typical solely of East European countries. We can observe the same trend in any welfare state for at least a few decades. True, this tendency is narrower in scope (only for some countries) and of shorter duration than in the socialist countries (Pryor, 1973).

But the supporters of the welfare state in Poland are far from united, in how far the protective umbrella of the state should spread.

Between supporters of the welfare state both in the East and West there were always differences in the strategic objective of such a state. Should the welfare system: (a) decrease relative inequalities created by the wage system, or (b) alleviate poverty, or both. An expert in social welfare policies, M. Ksiezopolski (1988, p. 351), has formulated this very succinctly:

Is the objective to have a society where the individual behaviour will be subordinated to the laws of the market, or a society where the entitlement of the citizens would be increased in expense of weakening the market mechanism. Or differently, will the main criteria of redistribution be based with one's place in the division of labour in the workplace or would another not less essential criteria of distribution be the scale of unfulfilled needs of the individual or family.

Different answers are given to this question. Two general points of view can be distinguished briefly:

1. Social benefits (health care, education, family allowances, child care, care of disabled and elderly, subsidies of housing and transport fares, etc.) should not be used as a tool for reducing income disparities. To take away with one hand what the state provides with the other is inconsistent with the principle of distribution according to work and is a hindrance to improving labour productivity. If the state wants to reduce inequalities, it should use wage differentials or the tax mechanism. The major function of social benefits is not so much egalitarianism as to provide as much as possible for everyone to ensure equal opportunity. Those who contributed more to society in terms of work and hence have higher earnings should receive more in social benefits as well. The most desirable situation from a social point of view is that benefits in total have a neutral impact on absolute income disparities. In other words, disparities in social benefits should be in total more or less the same as disparities in earnings (Pohorille, 1975).
2. Social benefits should be used as a tool to redistribute income in favour of lower income groups. Equal opportunity is an empty slogan if we do not reduce not only relative but also absolute differences in per capita income (Tymowski, 1979).

In the pre-Solidarity period the prevailing point of view, shared also by the Gierek government, was the neutral approach to social benefits. However, since the downfall of Gierek, the authorities in Poland, under pressure from Solidarity, have moved to implement a more equal distribution of social benefits. But many concessions in the social welfare system made by the Communist government in the Gdansk Accord, in 1981, were gradually eroded by inflation.

Considering the very difficult economic situation in Poland, the increase of inequalities, and the sharpening of social conflict, the followers of the paternalistic state are opting now at least for a constant share of social benefits in the national income, and connected with it a constant ratio of social benefits to work-related incomes.[2] What is more, the followers of the paternalistic state both in Solidarity and in the Communist élite agree that to help the poor should not be the only objective of the social benefits system. Social policies must be designed to ensure social security for all members of society, but certain elements of those funds must be distributed in accordance with the egalitarian principle, namely, funds for education, health, culture etc.[3]

The underlying ideological assumption of the traditional left, both in the East and the West, was, for many decades, that there is no contradiction between the ethical principles of socialism like equality, solidarity, security, etc. and the requirement of economic efficiency.

Furthermore, the followers of this stream emphasise that to treat social benefits only as a cost out of the production possibilities of society is unjustified. The dependence between social benefit and the level of production is not one sided. It is true that the level of social benefits depends on the size of income created, but what is overlooked is that social benefits positively influence production. Education, health care, proper nutrition, etc. are investments in human capacities; all are conducive to full utilisation of human resources (Dahl and Lindblom, 1953; Czajka, 1989). Social benefits, broadly speaking, are an active part in production, they cannot be treated as something unproductive, burdening the national income.

However, the belief that there is no contradiction between equality and efficiency is nowadays very much questioned, not only by the liberals but also by some economists of the socialist tradition. The best expressed view in this respect are the ideas of J. Kornai (1980), linking the difficulties of hardening the budget constraint in socialism with certain specific characteristics of that system. He writes: 'Profit incentives clash with the ethical principle which prescribes that everybody should have his share in material goods according to his work and that there should be equal pay for equal work' (ibid., p. 150).[4]

This contradiction prevents a far-reaching hardening of the budget. As a result, a compromise between efficiency and ethical requirements emerges. Kornai believes that such a compromise is workable and desirable. Socialism must admit its limitations in terms of efficiency and look for its strength somewhere else. A claim that one social system must be better than another from every point of view is utopian. It is reminiscent of perfect models that combine all the best features from all systems. In every system, Kornai claims, we must take the good aspects with the bad ones. Although socialism will always be to a certain degree an 'economy of shortages', this fact does not mean that those societies cannot function and develop if the right compromise can be struck between the contradictory elements of the system.

Needless to say, the difficulty in reaching such a 'successful' compromise is enormous. Kornai quietly assumes that the contradiction between efficiency and the socialist value system does not prevent a certain continuous equilibrium between these two elements. More specifically, this means that efficiency can continue to improve, although not as fast as it would be without the socialist ethical requirements. Hence Kornai assumes that there will be sufficient material means to support socialist values. We cannot, however, exclude the possibility that this equilibrium of countervailing forces, as Brus and Kowalik (1983) call it, will not hold and a deterioration of efficiency will not only prevent the growth objectives of society from being achieved, but will also make it impossible materially to support the realisation of the ethical and egalitarian values of socialism. Recent developments in the countries of 'real socialism' support this view (Brus and Kowalik, 1983).

The followers of the paternalistic state, apart from the dogmatic followers of the old regime, agree that the highly centralistic system of the welfare state is very bureaucratised, lacks flexibility, limits choice, offers services of poor quality that do not always reach those most in need, and creates preferential treatment of certain groups, especially the power structure. What is more, the existing system has deprived society of any control over the welfare system. The majority of adherents to the paternalistic state also agree that the absolute monopoly of the state in the field of social services is undesirable both from a socio-political point of view and from the view of efficient operation of the system. Although the state should continue to play an important part in the welfare system, its role should undergo serious changes. Its monopolistic position and autocratic ways in decision-making and resource allocation, which make the receivers of social benefits passive objects, must be replaced with a more democratic model.

A variety of socialisation concepts is proposed. The main objective of these is to transfer control over the welfare system from state to non-state organisations. The variant of socialisation, supported by the broadly understood left, is a wide interaction between state institutions and organised citizens. However, it should be emphasised that socialisation for the followers of the left means not so much the direct provision of services, but rather social control over the state-run welfare system, over municipalities and other agencies operating in this sphere. Followers of the paternalistic–egalitarian approach oppose limiting the state's role solely to the function of financing the system or reducing the welfare system to charity. Needless to say, the traditional left opposes commercialisation of the basic sphere of social policy (education, health care, culture, etc.). Socialisation should be, according to them, an antidote to commercialisation – not its breeding ground. Non-state institutions like the Red Cross, Associations of Children's Friends, social organisations of the Church, some genuine cooperatives, associations of consumers, women's organisations, etc. should have a say not only in how social benefits are distributed, but should also augment some state services and thus create a more diversified system of benefits. An increase in social activities in this field would allow the state to provide better services and create an alternative to state welfare institutions in some areas.

Although the state should still maintain full responsibility for social policies, for their direction in general, this does not mean it must administer their every aspect (Morecka, 1989, pp. 280–8). Socialisation of social benefits need not eliminate the state. Rather, what is necessary is a clear division of prerogatives between central authorities, local communities and social organisations. The centre should determine the directions of development of the welfare system, formulate alternatives, and take care that those policies are consistent; but non-state social organisations, which have an interest in social policies and certain expertise, should take an active part in formulating such policies. Indeed, the implementation of those policies should be to some degree given over (together with finances) to the local level, to non-state organisations, and so on.

The broadly understood left rejected also the concept of reducing the role of the state welfare system merely to helping the poor and the handicapped (Sztanderska, 1989, pp. 270–9), leaving all other services to be provided by the commercialised and non-state socialised sector.[5] It is worthwhile mentioning that some of the representatives of the left treated the socialisation of the welfare system very instrumentally, as a sort of emergency in time of crisis, to help the state to manage in a difficult situation (Tymowski, Rajkiewicz, 1988). But in the future, when the crisis is overcome and normal times return, many of the non-state socialised institutions, according to them, will not be needed.

We can also detect in the broad discussion about the welfare system different socialisation concepts more in tune with the neo-liberal agenda, namely, to limit the function of the state to providing financial resources to the socialised welfare sector.[6] This approach is perceived by paternalistic followers as a Trojan horse to eliminate the state entirely from the welfare system. The discussion about socialisation has raised a few questions not yet fully answered: (i) is this an alternative to commercialisation of social benefit services, or is this institution preparing the ground for commercialisation; (b) should the independent non-state institutions be self-financed or not, and if the answer is in the affirmative, should it affect the way services are distributed? The discussion of these and other problems related to the interaction between the state agencies and the non-state institutions will surely continue in Poland for some time, especially since the welfare system, as with all other elements of the socio-political scene, continues to evolve.

The Polish neo-liberals' opposition to the welfare state is theoretically inspired by neo-conservatives in the West, specifically by their chief theoretician F. Hayek. Their ideas have a strong influence on the social policies of the Solidarity led government. The main objective and role of economic policy in general and social policy in particular should be, according to the neo-liberals, conducive to the broadest possible autonomy of the market and should prevent any attempts to introduce non-market solutions. In a certain sense, the best economic policy of the state is to abstain from any policy.

According to the neo-liberals, the distribution pattern produced by the market cannot and should not be subject to moral judgment: the demand to make the distribution process 'just' is, according to Hayek (1988, p. 73), 'a result of naive anthropomorphism'. The market is the final judge about who gets what; any arbitrary attempt to intervene in the process of distribution of income will distort the whole economic process and endanger prosperity. Those who do not succeed in the market game and find themselves without means, 'poor' in an absolute sense, should get help from those who were successful in the market. The best form of such help would be voluntary organised charities. On the other hand, those who do succeed should not discard the possibilities of defeat in the market place in the future; hence, they should take out private insurance against illness, death, old age, and so on.

In the pure neo-liberal approach, the responsibility to solve social welfare problems belongs to the individual, who, alone, is the subject and object of independent implemented policies. Individuals should rely for help in solving their social welfare problems foremost on private insurance based on commercial principles, and secondly, on the family. Only when these two institutions are not available should charity organisations, different foundations, or associations provide help. The state is distrusted as a subject of social welfare policy; its even more narrowly defined functions are perceived as 'necessary evils'.

For the specific Polish environment, according to the neo-liberals, an excessive social benefit system limits the work effort of individuals, reduces the amount of resources for commercial capital, and leads to a bureaucratisation and waste of resources which could be better used by private individuals. It is, especially in time of economic crisis, a hindrance to economic reform, to marketisation of the economy. Neo-liberals criticise the exclusive responsibility of the state for social security and welfare on a moral ground: exclusive responsibility by the state erodes the individual responsibility for his and her family's well-being, weakens the family ties and other forms of social solidarity (Kisielewski, 1988; Walicki, 1988; Toczynski, 1989).

What are the positive suggestions of this anti-egalitarian stream as far as social policies are concerned? They propose a reprivatisation of social services. The market will produce these services much cheaper and will provide a larger choice. Another proposition of the neo-liberals is to revitalise the so-called non-formal sector: different forms of self-help, community based philanthropy and family help.[7] The idea of privatisation of social services is not going unchallenged in Poland. The neo-liberals present family care of the old and disabled as a past, lost paradise. Apart from painting the picture of the past in rosy colours, what is overlooked is the fact that nowadays a much bigger percentage of women are in the workforce than in the past. Hence the amount of women who traditionally have taken care of the elderly has drastically declined in relation to people who need to be nurtured. It is unlikely that there will be a return to the traditional family where women will be sent back to unpaid work at home (Ksiezopolski, 1989).

In Poland, however, not only problems of state or non-state forms of the social welfare system are debated. The old organisation of the social benefit system is put into question. There is a general consensus between the reformers in the Communist Party and Solidarity that the system should be decentralised. Municipalities, towns, countries, etc. should take over many functions both organisational and in terms of financing as far as social benefits are concerned. The justification for this approach is not only linked with the general philosophy of the reformers that communities should have a much bigger say in all aspects of their life including education, health care, help for the elderly and the poor, but also with the fact that organised services from the centre are inefficient. The centre lacks detailed specific knowledge about the need of individuals. This is especially visible in solving the problem of poverty, the disabled, and social pathology.[8] Only in the framework of smaller communities can the problem be properly addressed. But radical organisational change in this field will not take place before the election of regional councils in the spring of 1990. Only after, when genuine self-governing regional councils emerge, will it be possible to transfer many prerogatives, including those in the field of social benefit from the central government to the regional powers.

The economic reforms in Poland have also put in question the role of the enterprise in the welfare system. Enterprises in socialist countries up to now have played an important role in providing social benefits both in cash and in kind. It is enough to say that in 1986 social benefits provided by enterprises constituted 3.3 per cent of the national income and 5.4 per cent of the total income of the population (Mech, 1989).[9] Enterprises are providing the employees with housing, hostels, canteens, health care, schools for specific trade training, holidays for adults and for children, sport facilities, small agriculture plots, and cultural events. To provide these services obviously requires a sizeable personnel and a lot of time spent by management on these functions.

This broad engagement of the enterprise in social welfare met with a wide range of criticism both by the followers of paternalism and their opponents. Social welfare benefits provided by the enterprise in the form in which it now exists is not an equalising factor in the standard of life. More prosperous enterprises are able to provide many more social services out of their profits than the less prosperous. There is a positive correlation between the size of average wages and the size of social services per employee (Wisniewska, 1985). What is more, the relative dispersion of social welfare services between enterprises is larger by a big margin than the relative dispersion of wages. As a result social welfare services, instead of equalising the standard of living between employees of different enterprises, are actually adding a new dimension to inequality. Such large differences in social services between enterprises defeat the purpose of this kind of welfare system.

The egalitarian character of social benefits is also negated by the fact that the better educated, the high earners, and the professional élite receive much more than the low earning groups. Employees with low wages very often do not use any social services, especially when it is linked with minimal payment (Kwasniewski, 1989). In view of this shortcoming, followers of the paternalistic welfare state propose to guarantee to every employee equal eligibility to social services in the enterprise, irrespective of the place of work or connections in the enterprise.

In contradistinction of this point of view, followers of market-oriented solutions are demanding an end to the enterprise role in providing the majority of social services, including housing. Funds allocated previously to finance these services should be earmarked for wage increases. Those services, which for economic reasons the enterprise will still decide to provide (like canteens), should be managed by specialised organisations.

The proposal to abolish most of the social services and transfer those funds into wages will inevitably create a lot of opposition from the majority of the workers. A broad survey conducted between March and July 1987, in some regions of the country, indicated that there is no unanimity between workers about the structure of social services or its way of funding, but 95 per cent of the employees firmly believe that the enterprise is obliged to be engaged in social welfare activities (Piatek, 1988). It will be a tall order to overcome this nurtured egalitarian sentiment between Polish workers.

Changes in the welfare system in the direction of socialisation and commercialisation are facing very serious economic and socio-political barriers in Poland. Three in particular need to be mentioned.

First, Poland is in the process of changing into a market economy. This will require bigger pay differentials. Assuming there will be no growth or a slow growth of the wage fund (in real terms) in the near future, any substantial increase in relative dispersion of wages will only be possible at the expense of a relative decline of social benefits.[10] But at the same time there will be strong pressure on the state to create a cushion against the negative consequences of marketisation such as bankruptcies, unemployment, and linked with it the need to reallocate workers and to retrain them for new jobs. Needless to say, this will require large increases in social benefit funds. Polish economic reforms will therefore face a serious contradiction: to implement a market economy will require a reduction of social benefits, using these extra funds for increasing wage differentials; but cushioning the negative consequence of marketisation will require more social funds. Only time will show how this contradiction can be solved.

Second, the current Polish situation is very paradoxical. On the one hand, the fiasco of the state monopoly in the field of social policies (expressed by the low quality of social services and difficult access to services) creates a tendency to de-etatisation of this sphere; but on the other hand, the numbers of those who are in poverty and need urgent help (approximately 30 per cent of the population) are much larger than those who could finance non-state social welfare organisations. Even if society would accept a substantial reduction of state involvement in social welfare policies and a broadening of the different non-state social welfare agencies (charities, foundations, private–commercial institutions), the resources of society are too meagre to become an alternative to the state (Filar, 1989).

Not without importance also is the fact that during the forty years of state monopoly in the social welfare system all non-state institutions were thoroughly eradicated. It would now be very difficult rapidly to create the right atmosphere to find enough people in order to restore those institutions to life. Considering these and other obstacles, the chances of implementing the liberal concept of social policies in Poland are very slim. The major obstacle is not in the social perception or in the will of the state to prevent this kind of change, but in the objective limitations for change. The reduction of the state role in the social welfare sphere would close access to social benefits to numerous social groups, because for the time being society is able to create non-state structures only on a limited scale. Hence the most likely variant to be implemented in the near future is, as D. Filar (1989) calls it, the 'imperfect social-democratic variant'. The state will continue to provide a broad variety of services of rather low quality.[11] At the same time, a gradual expansion of non-state service institutions will take place, which will not only augment and enrich state activities in this field in the future, but also provide for urgent need where the state fails to do so in a satisfactory manner.

Thirdly, we cannot expect a substantial part of the trade union movement (both in Solidarity and in the Communist-led unions) to be sympathetic to neo-liberal ideas about the welfare system. After all, the Solidarity trade union movement, at its inception in the 1980

Gdansk Accord, has asked for a more developed welfare system than the Communist regime has provided. The incomes policy package formulated by Solidarity in 1980 is one of the most egalitarian programmes ever defined in a socialist country and this is not accidental. The majority of the constituents of Solidarity – employees of the socialised sector – are rather hostile to reprivatisation of social benefits. But the future shape of the social benefit system will not be determined by the ideology either of Solidarity or the Communists but by the hard realities of a lack of means, especially for the social infrastructure, irrespective of who will govern Poland.

5.2 WAGE AND INCOME POLICIES

With the ascendancy of the Communist regime in Poland after the Second World War, wage differentials have been dramatically reduced in comparison with the pre-war period, a tendency discernible in other socialist countries too (Flakierski, 1989, p. 89; Adam, 1984, p. 193). These dramatic changes are exemplified by narrowing the differences between real incomes of manual and non-manual employees. Kalecki's estimation (1964, pp. 91–101) of manual and non-manual workers real incomes for the years 1937 and 1960 shows a substantial narrowing of incomes between those stratas; manual workers have increased their real income by 75 per cent, whereas for non-manual employees those incomes have declined by 20 per cent. As a result, the discrepancy of incomes between these two stratas, very high before the war, have been reduced in 1960 nearly to parity; in 1937 the income ratio of non-manual employees to manual ones was 2.63, but in 1960 this ratio was only 1.18. This tendency to equalise earnings between the major urban stratas has continued in the 1960s (Flakierski, 1986, p. 73), although at a slower pace than before.

The Gierek regime at the beginning of the 1970s, in connection with the impeding economic reform, promised to widen skill differentials. In the first years of Gierek's reign (1972–4) skill differentials increase as promised. Gierek, however, after the deflationary policies of Gomulka, immediately granted substantial increases in wages, in 1971, unprecedented in scale in previous decades. These increases embraced all categories of employees, but different groups did not gain in the same degree. The more skilled manual workers and top management gained the most – hence increasing skill differentials [12]

This increase in the material sphere was achieved by widening pay scale tariffs and reducing progressive taxes, especially unfavourable for highly skilled labourers. At the end of the decade there was also a substantial widening between the minimum and maximum wage.[13]

This process has changed abruptly with the ascendance of the Solidarity movement, whose demands for a more egalitarian income distribution were partially implemented between 1980 and 1981.

In a nutshell, on the basis of the Gdansk Interfactory Strike Committee twenty-one points (16 August 1980), the Gdansk Accord (31 August 1980) and various Solidarity[14] documents, the following demands were put forward by the new social force as far as incomes policies are concerned:

1. To increase wages for all employees evenly by 2000 zl. per month as recompensation for inflation. This sum was substantially scaled down by more than half in the process of negotiation with the government. Additionally, the Interfactory Strike Committee has also given up the idea of a lump sum paid equally to all employees. In the Gdansk Accord, both sides have agreed to move all employees upwards by one grade in the branch tariff scale. Negotiations about the wage increases were delegated to the branch and enterprise level. This decentralised form of implementing the Gdansk Accord in this matter has led to a wave of uncontrolled strikes for wage increases. In some enterprises, striking committees have demanded an equal lump sum for all workers as originally requested by the Interfactory Strike Committee in Gdansk. In other enterprises, a differentiated increase in wages in favour of the lower wage group was demanded. By and large, the process of wage increases as recompense for price increases has reduced relative wage disparities, because additional wages were less unequally distributed than the old wages. However, the increases in wages were too small to affect the overall relative dispersion of wages substantially.
2. The Gdansk Accord stipulates that a social minimum indicator be established, on the basis of which a formula for compensating cost of living increases should be worked out. Here again the original demand was not fully implemented. Social minimum indicators were systematically worked out and publicised, but such a minimum was not guaranteed in practice and neither was this indicator used as a basis for real recompense for cost of living increases.
3. A ceiling on the highest wages; the highest wages should not be

more than 7 times the minimum wage and 3.5 times the average wage. Once again, this principle did not become properly operational and after a while was forgotten.

4. For the same job, function, and skills, payment should be equalised throughout the country, sectors, and branches. A minimum national wage should be implemented which should be half the average wage, but not smaller than the social minimum. This demand has become an empty slogan; it was never implemented.
5. Piecework payments should be abolished wherever possible.
6. There should be a substantial increase in welfare funds, especially family allowances, pensions, and annuities, etc. These funds must be protected from inflationary erosion by indexing. Under pressure from Solidarity the government agreed to increase all family allowances, but the increases had to be preferential for families with lower income per capita. Solidarity representatives demanded that family allowances also be differentiated according to the age of the child. The union adhered to a general policy that compensation for price increases must protect the real earnings of the least prosperous workers and their families. In 1982, Solidarity called for the implementation of a social minimum as a guideline for an income policy. The union believed that an increase in social benefits would be the best tool to protect the poor and overcome poverty.
7. Annual pensions should increase systematically and be linked to changes in the lowest wages. The government should raise pensions to the level of the social minimum and gradually equalise the old portfolio of pensions with the new one. In establishing the level of pensions, increase in the cost of living should be taken into consideration. However, indexing of pensions and the liquidation of the old portfolio of pensions was never fully implemented. In spite of several increases in pensions, the ratio of average pensions to the average wage has continued to decline and the gap between the newly granted pensions and pensions granted in the past (the so called old portfolio of pensions) has widened constantly in the period of 1978–82 (Goralska and Wiktorow, 1985).
8. The state should grant maternity leave for three years. For the first year after birth pay should be 100 per cent of normal earnings. In the second year it should be 50 per cent of earnings, but not less than 2000 zl. per month. The demand for a three-year maternity leave was to be met gradually in the first half of 1981.

This postulate was fully implemented in accordance with the Solidarity demand, as were the increases in family allowances.

As we can see from the demands analysed above, some were not implemented at all, others partially and only a few were implemented fully. The impact of the implemented measures on the general disparities in income distribution is difficult to judge. The official statistical data for this period of turmoil are particularly unreliable due to the chaos of open and hidden inflation, as well as wild speculation caused by shortages. Actual income disparities probably did not conform with the official statistics on income inequalities. Thus, scepticism concerning the spectacular reduction of income inequalities that is claimed in the official statistics is well founded. In addition, some economic steps the government agreed to were not egalitarian in intent; namely, rationing of many goods. This measure resulted from a catastrophic decline in production. Although it is true that rationing is a great leveller, there is no reason to make a virtue out of necessity.

However, this honeymoon of egalitarianism did not last very long. Already in 1982 pay differentials started to climb again, evidenced by a deliberate policy of faster increase of wages of the non-manual over manual employees in the period 1983–5 – especially those in the upper echelons of this category. What is more, between manual and non-manual workers the faster increase in wages is observed for highly paid employees with the slowest increase for low paid workers. Whereas in the short period of egalitarianism of 1980–2 we observed the opposite. Another indicator of wage differentiation is the ratio of the highest 1 per cent of earnings to the minimum wage. During the period 1983–5 this ratio for the entire socialised sector increased by nearly 50 per cent; from seven times in 1983 to ten times in 1985. In industry, in 1982, this ratio was 13.1 times for manual workers (and 14.2 times for non-manual workers), whereas in 1985 it climbed to 15.6 times for manual workers (and 16.5 times for non-manual workers), in spite of the fact that the minimum wage increased substantially in this period. The above figures show that this ratio grew faster for manual workers than for non-manual ones in the period 1982–5. However it must be stressed that for the majority of workers (80 per cent of employees) the dispersion of wages measured by the decile ratio increased rather insignificantly in the period 1980–5 (Krencik, 1987, 1990).

From the second half of the 1980s onwards, only minimal data are available. Based upon fragmentary observation, a chaotic increase in wages has taken place to catch up with inflation. This has occurred not in those industries and branches which for one reason or another were more deserving (like higher labour productivity or systematic underpayment), but rather in those enterprises which the state feared might create unrest and organise strikes.

How this chaotic increase in wages has affected differentials is difficult to judge. One thing is certain, though, it has made the wage structure even more anti-motivational, removing further the link between wages and productivity. It can be expected that privatisation and marketisation under the non-Communist regime will bring an increase in wage differentials. But the general feeling that this will be the case is quite uncertain. Only the events in the 1990s in Poland will give an answer to this problem.

5.3 PRICE POLICY

One of the social policies of the Polish Communist regime from its inception was to subsidise some consumer goods, especially items such as food, rent, heating, transport, etc. The rationale of this policy was that cheap food and shelter protect the weak group in society and reduce inequalities between different income groups. An additional reason for introducing subsidies immediately after the war was the exhaustion and poor health of the Polish nation. Cheap food was considered the tool to rectify this situation. But once such a policy was established and identified as an 'important feature of socialism', it was very difficult to escape from it. The state was stuck with a policy of low wages and low subsidy prices for most consumer goods.

To make the situation even worse after the price increases in 1953, the state pledged not only that there would be no more price increases of consumer goods, but that prices would be gradually reduced. Needless to say, such a promise could not in the long run be fulfilled. But the perception of stable prices as a part of the socialist system was taken for granted and this has had serious consequences for the attempt to reduce subsidies in the 1980s.

The view that cheap food and other basic consumer goods are favourable for less affluent groups in society, because those items represent a larger part of their total consumption expenditure than for the more affluent, was for many decades commonly shared.

However, with time, the negative aspects of subsidies have become more apparent.

This problem has been well described in the economic literature of Poland and other East European countries (Lipinski, 1977; Kolodko, 1987; Jendrychowski, 1986; KRG, 1982, 1989; Round table, 1982, 1989; Sztyber, 1978; Krasinski, 1981; Makowiecki, 1989). A few of the negative aspects of widespread subsidies will now be mentioned:

(1) The price of administering subsidies is very high because of the wasteful way the bureaucracy handles the process of buying and distributing agricultural products. Generally, consumers as a whole do not gain or lose from subsidies because they are financed from different kinds of taxes; the public gets back in subsidies a sum exactly equal to the amount of taxes they have paid to finance those subsidies. But in reality, as a result of the high cost of the bureaucracy and the low quality of those services administering subsidies, the consumer is losing out on this type of redistribution: he puts into it more than he gets out of it (Lipowski, 1989; Krasinski, Mruk and Szulce, 1985).

(2) Subsidies – especially on food prices, which attract the largest proportion of financial aid – encourage consumption of goods usually requiring a high cost of production. It therefore prevents a transition from a consumer pattern characteristic of poor societies with a high proportion of food in consumption expenditure, to a more developed model where expenditure on basic food items is relatively low.

(3) Persistent subsidising of consumer goods has a tendency to increase very fast. This is so because if prices do not change with the increase in consumption of subsidised goods, the increased volume of sales of those goods will automatically increase the absolute size of subsidies. A need therefore arises to allocate more means to subsidies which would reduce the available resources for wages and social benefits in cash. Hence, it is justifiable to say that the larger the subsidies on consumer goods, the smaller is the incentive role of wages.

(4) The fast increase of consumption of subsidised consumer goods not only increases the absolute size of the subsidies, but has a tendency also to increase its relative size; subsidies are becoming a larger fraction of total budget expenditures and of the total sales value of all consumer goods.

(5) The fact that non-profitable enterprises producing consumer goods receive subsidies to cover their losses does not induce them to save on inputs. These enterprises are quite convinced that each cost incurred will one way or another be covered by a subsidy. This kind of wasteful behaviour increases the social cost of producing consumer goods and reduces the size of their output. Output is not determined by market needs but by the planned targets of subsidies, which do not stimulate production above a certain limit.

(6) Large subsidies distort the informational function of prices, so neither the producers nor the consumers can behave rationally and make the right decision.

(7) Waste takes place on a big scale in the household use of consumer goods which are highly subsidised. Many subsidised consumer goods are used as raw materials for further processing and for fodder for the animals (e.g. bread, milk, etc.).

(8) The social achievement of subsidies as an instrument of redistributing income in favour of the less fortunate is questioned by some economists (Podkaminer, 1988; Juhasz, 1979). The price mechanism as a tool for redistributing income works very often as a blind force: the gainers and the losers are accidental and very often the subsidies do not reach those who need them most. It is a fact that the more affluent income groups use more subsidised consumer goods than the less affluent (meat, some dairy products, fuel). Hence the affluent are the major beneficiaries of subsidies, what cannot be considered very fair.

Recent studies indicate that the more affluent groups gain more from subsidies than the less affluent; that white-collar employees fare much better than manual ones. Other studies claim that subsidies are in the aggregate distributed equally to different strata, hence prices in this respect have a neutral effect on income distribution. Be this as it may, non-equilibrium prices do not play an important role in equalising real incomes. Considering their negative impact on market equilibrium, efficient production and use of subsidised items, market-oriented reformers suggest that subsidies be abolished and equilibrium prices be established. It would be much more just and less wasteful if retail prices of subsidised goods were raised to their real cost level and the subsidies transformed into income increases for all consumers evenly, or selectively for the less affluent families.

There is no necessity to equalise real incomes by using the price mechanism. A proper wage and incomes policy, tax policy and social benefits policies can better serve to achieve a more desirable income distribution pattern.

Irrespective of the nature of the critique of subsidised consumer prices, a consensus emerged in the 1980s that the economy cannot be successfully reformed if subsidies are maintained on a substantial scale. But to abolish subsidies was easier said than done.

All attempts in the 1980s to reduce subsidies substantially by increasing prices have failed. In February 1982, as part of the first phase of economic reform, the government increased retail prices of consumer goods, especially food items. Subsidies in relation to the price paid to the agricultural producers declined, but a year later (1983), as a result of increases in prices paid to agricultural producers, the share of subsidies in the full price of food again increased. In 1982, the share of food subsidies within the total amount of all subsidies financed by the budget declined from 22 per cent (in 1981) to 17 per cent. By 1983 this ratio had jumped back to 21.7 per cent (Krasinski, Mruk and Szulce, 1985, p. 62).[15] What is more, in 1982 prices for consumer goods increased on average by 102 per cent, whereas wages increased only by 51 per cent; in the next year – 1983, wage increases outstripped prices of consumer goods. In subsequent years up to 1987 nominal wages continued to grow slightly faster than prices (Krencik, 1989). As a result, inflationary pressures on the consumer market were not eased and market equilibrium did not improve substantially. The inflationary overhang continued to increase and with it the unfulfilled demand for consumer goods.

In 1988, as part of the second phase of economic reform, the Communist government decided again to reduce subsidies on consumer goods including rent, heating and basic food items (Sadowski, 1988). The scale of price increases in consumer goods was originally planned to be on 40 per cent average. But in a referendum (held in December 1987) the more ambitious variant of price increases was defeated and a lower average price increase (27 per cent) was implemented by the authorities in February of 1988.

The income–price policy of the second phase of the reform offered recompense for price increases. The architects of this second phase claimed that increases in prices achieved by reducing subsidies are not meant to drain purchasing power from the population but reduce the burden of the state budget *vis-à-vis* subsidies. To prove that their intention is not to reduce the purchasing power of the population, they offered wage recompensation for price increases. But the population has not seen it in this way, especially since basic food items, heating and rent increased more than the overall average price increases of consumer goods. This income–price policy was perceived by the population as an attack on their standard of living, and a wave of strikes hit Poland in the spring of 1988. The government did not properly assess the mood in the country, or other socio-political realities, falsely assuming that it would be able to neutralise pressures on wage demands by granting everyone an equal recompense of 600 zl. per month. But they were wrong. Workers in the factories and the populace at large were not prepared to accept belt tightening from a government which was completely discredited and illegitimate in their eyes. As a result of strikes and pressures on wages, the growth of nominal money incomes substantially outstripped price increases within the first three months of 1988 alone. Such an income–price policy not only brought a deterioration in equilibrium on the consumer market, but also discredited the so-called second phase of the economic reform in general.

It has become clear from the experience of price increases in the 1980s, that as long as the population is not prepared to accept restrictions on wage demands, any attempts to increase consumer prices by abolishing subsidies will not work; it will merely unleash a spiral of wage and price increases chasing each other.

In August 1989, the last Communist government with Rakowski as its Prime Minister introduced marketisation of food prices. Nearly all subsidies were abolished on food items. The only fixed administrative prices for food were maintained for low fat milk, cheese and cheap bread. But the ill-prepared reform of food prices created chaos in the market, the supply of agricultural products, especially meat, actually declined in spite of price increases much above the expected rate.[16] The Rakowski government failed to: (i) provide a sufficient amount of goods whose prices are still fixed administratively and mainly consumed by low income groups; (ii) stimulate an increase in agricultural production in spite of the fact that peasants were selling their product at market prices; (iii) intervene both in excessive price increases and ensure more food on the market, especially in big towns; this lack of ability to intervene was due to the fact that it did not prepare proper commodity reserves; (iv) break the monopolistic position of such giant organisations like the state meat industry, dairy cooperatives and the grain and flower industries – organisations which dictate prices both to farmers and consumers.

As a result of these failures wild price increases began destroying what little credibility the Communist regime still possessed.

The fall of the Rakowski Communist government and the ascendance of the Solidarity-led Mazowiecki government has not reversed the abrupt increases in food prices. Solidarity has criticised the way fixed administrative prices for food were abolished and with it all subsidies, but commercialisation of food prices was also a part of Mazowiecki's programme to free the majority of consumer prices and of means of production.

The Stabilisation Programme of the Mazowiecki government[17] has further reduced many other subsidies as of January 1990. Administrative prices fixed by the state for coal and other inputs for producing energy have increased five-fold, and those for fertilizers, pesticides, drugs, rent and heating have increased sharply. As a result, subsidies for all these items were greatly reduced, but not abolished entirely. In view of the fact that coal and other sources of energy are inputs for nearly all goods produced, production costs have risen abruptly, together with all prices both of consumer goods and means of production. Another important factor which has abruptly increased the cost of production in the enterprises was a sharp rise in the interest paid for circulating capital (inventories, work in progress, etc.). Suddenly, for some enterprises, the servicing of their bank credit comprised 30–50 per cent of their cost of production. At the same time, the Solidarity-led government was able to hold money wages in check, limiting its increases to only 30 per cent of the price increases. This drastic reduction in real wages has successfully diminished effective demand by the population. The balance between supply and demand on the consumer market has improved not because of a larger volume of goods available, but because these goods are too expensive for a substantial number of households.

It is too premature to judge the success or failure of the Mazowiecki Stabilisation Programme. However, we can already say that the drastic reduction in real wages and incomes accepted by the population, and harsh credit conditions combined with high taxes on enterprises, has allowed the Solidarity government to create an effective demand barrier for consumer goods. For the first time in many years the supply of numerous consumer goods is larger than its demand. But this improvement in market equilibrium has taken its toll; many enterprises, due to lack of effective demand, are reducing production and laying off workers. The decline of output was much higher than expected for January and February of 1990. There is a danger that a further decline in output can trigger a second wave of inflation in spite of the initial success at reducing price increases in the first three months of the stabilisation programme. We must bear in mind that sooner or later the draconian measures to limit wage increases introduced by the government will be relaxed, and effective demand will again outstrip the shrinking supply. As a result further adjustment in prices will become necessary.

It is difficult to say for how long a consensus will exist for belt-tightening, for growing unemployment, or for how long will people agree to take this strong medicine. It will depend on how successful the Mazowiecki government is at curbing inflation. For the time being, the strong support of the Polish nation for the Solidarity-led government, has given them some space for manoeuvre, some chance of succeeding in stabilising the Polish economy.

NOTES

1. I include in the broadly understood left, the following groups: Communists, Social Democrats, leftist Catholics. In this chapter I very often interchange the terms paternalism, egalitarianism, and leftism.
2. See the theses of the Central Executive of PTE (Polish Economic Association) on a Conference in Jadwisin (held 11–13 September 1989), on the subject, 'Perspektywy polskiej polityki spolecznej'.
3. The followers of the paternalistic state are decisively rejecting the claim of the neo-liberals that the Polish state is or ever was overprotective. This is a myth, according to them, widely spread by those who want to dismantle the welfare state. In reality they argue, the share of social benefits in the national income is smaller than in all East European countries; moreover, its share has actually declined in time, never once surpassing 24 per cent. The structure of social benefits has also undergone changes which are going in the opposite direction from those in other socialist countries. The share of social benefits in kind has a pronounced tendency to decline in the national income and in the total amount of social benefits (see Winiewski, 1988, table 12).
4. A similar point of view about the conflict between efficiency and equality is expressed by Okun (1975).
5. A variant for reducing the scope of the state welfare system, which has actually found its way into the programme of Mazowiecki's government, is the idea that public consumption funds should cover only basic needs on a low level. All needs above this standard should be provided by individuals themselves.
6. The more extreme liberal minded are even against this modest role of the state. State financing, according to them, leads to bureaucratisation and

ideological corruption of the system. The state should play no role in the welfare system even in a limited capacity.

7. It merits attention that many officials dealing with social policies, not only in Poland but in other socialist countries, lately support the idea, albeit reticently, that informal structures should play a larger role in social services. Their approach is motivated more by expediency than by ideology. The state bureaucrats, in view of a lack of means which does not allow them to cope with the problem, see this as a tool to reduce the burden of the state. At an International Conference of Research Institutes of Labour and Social Problems, in Moscow, in which all COMECON countries took part in 1988, a common view was expressed that supplementary benefit systems based on private and group insurance should not be excluded.
8. Soviet economists, during my recent visit in the Soviet Union, have admitted that their social programmes in fighting poverty and social pathology are ineffective, because they are too centralised and not geared to the particular community.
9. According to Mech's calculation, 28 per cent of the total amount of expenditures goes on housing. The next in line with 26 per cent are subsidies to maintain cafeterias and other forms of public feeding (see Mech, 1989).
10. This would not be the case if increases in differentials could be achieved by reducing the wages of the unskilled low performing workers and adding those funds to the highly skilled workers. However, that is not possible to do. For social reasons, this cannot be a zero sum game.
11. It should be stressed that according to the targets of the Central Planning Committee, established in 1988, for the next three years the total consumption fund will grow slower than the national income, and collective consumption slower than individual consumption. It is unlikely that the Mazowiecki government will change these proportions. We can expect that if any changes take place by comparison with the previous administration they will not be in favour of collective consumption.
12. Considering that intersectoral and interbranch differentials have declined in the 1970s, the overall increase in relative dispersion of wages in the socialised sector was mainly the result of an increase in skill differentials (see Flakierski, 1986, chapter 2).
13. In 1971, the minimal wage constituted 42.5 per cent of the average wage, in 1976 only 31 per cent, rising to 38 per cent in 1980, but still below the 1971 level (see Spotan 1982).
14. The Interfactory Strike Committee in Gdansk was the nucleus from which the Solidarity Independent Trade Union emerged in October 1980, a month after the end of the strike in Gdansk.
15. It is worthwhile to note that in 1970 this indicator was only 5 per cent, jumping to 22 per cent in 1981 (Krasinski, Mruk and Szulce, 1985, p. 62).
16. The highest possible increase in meat prices expected by the government in August, in comparison with July, was 316 per cent. But the actual increase was above 500 per cent and up to 10 September – 800 per cent. For all 1989 the increase in prices of basic foodstuffs was over 500 per cent in comparison with 1988.

17. See Program Gospodarczy, glowne zalozenia i kierunki, Warsaw, October 1989.

REFERENCES

ADAM, J. (1984) *Employment and Wage Policies in Poland Czechoslovakia and Hungary since 1950* (London: Macmillan).

BRUS, W. and KOWALIK, T. (1983) 'Socialism and Development', in *Cambridge Journal of Economics*, nos 2–3, pp. 243–55.

CZAJKA, S. (1989) 'Zalozenia do strategii polityki spolecznej w latach 90-tych, in Czajka. S (ed.) *Polityka społeczna w krajach socialistycznychw warunkach zmian systemu funkcjonowania gospodarki* (Warsaw: ANS).

DAHL, R.A. and LINDBLOM, C.E. (1953) *Politics, Economics and Welfare*, (New York: Harper).

FILAR, D. (1989) 'Wizja Ladu produkcyjno-dystrybucyjnego jako uwarunkowanie koncepcji polityki spotecznej', a conference held in September 1989 in Jadwisin: Perspektywy Polskiej Polityki Spolecznej.

FLAKIERSKI. H. (1986) *Economic Reform and Income Distribution: A case Study of Hungary and Poland*, (Armond, NY: M. Sharpe).

FLAKIERSKI, H. (1989) *The Economic System and Income Distribution in Yugoslavia*, (Armond, NY: M. Sharpe).

GORALSKA, H. and WIKTOROW, A. (1985) *Zycie Gospodarcze*, no. 8.

GORALSKA, H. and WIKTOROW, A. (1988) *Ubezpieczenia społeczne w krajach socialistycznych* (Warsaw: IPISS).

HAYEK, F. (1988) *The Fatal Conceit* (London: Routledge) p. 73.

JENDRYCHOWSKI, S. (1986) *Gospodarka Planowa*, nos 1, 2.

JUHASZ, T. (1979) 'Impact of the Consumer Price System on the Income and Consumption Patterns in Hungary' *Acta Oeconomica*', vol. 22, nos. 1–2.

KALECKI, M. (1964) *Z zagadnien gospodarczo-społecznych Polski Ludowej* (Warsaw).

KISIELEWSKI, S. (1988) *Tygodnik Powszechny*, 22 January.

KOLODKO, G. (1987) *Gospodarka Planowa*, no. 12.

KRG (KONSULTACYJNA RADA GOSPODARCZA) (1982) *Zycie Gospodarcze*, no. 15.

KRG (KONSULTACYJNA RADA GOSPODARCZA) (1989) *Zycie Gospodarcze*, nos 12, 14.

KORNAI, J. (1980) 'The Dilemmas of a Socialist Economy: The Hungarian Experience', in *Cambridge Journal of Economics*, no. 4, p. 150.

KRASINSKI, Z. (1981) *Reforma cen detalicznych-dlaczego, jaka, kiedy* (Warsaw: PKC).

KRASINSKI, Z., MRUK, H. and SZULCE, H. (1985) *Ceny a rynek* (Warsaw: PWE).

KRENCIK, W. (1987) *Praca i Zabezpieczenie Społeczne*, no. 9.

KRENCIK, W. (1989) *Praca i Zabezpieczenie Społeczne*, no. 3.

KRENCIK, H. (1990) *Polityka płac w Polsce w Latach 1981–1985*, (to be published in 1990).

KSIEZOPOLSKI, M. (1988) *Systemy zabezpieczenia społecznego w krajach Nordyckich* (Warsaw: Studia i materialy IPISS).
KSIEZOPOLSKI, M. (1989) 'Sektor niepanstwowy w polityce spolecznej krajow skandynawskich', in PTE (ed.) *Panstwo i spoteczenstwo w polityce spolecznej* (Warsaw). The book is a collection of materials from a Conference in Lucznica, September, 1988.
KWASNIEWSKI, T. (1989) *Polityka Społeczna*, nos. 5–6.
LIPINSKI, J. (1977) *Studia z teori i polityki cen* (Warsaw: PWE).
LIPOWSKI, A. (1989) *Ceny detaliczne w Polsce; Mity i rzeczywistosc* (unpublished).
MAKOWIECKI, M. (1989) *Zycie Gospodarcze*, no. 38.
MECH, C. (1989) *Polityka Społeczna*, no. 3.
MORECKA, Z. (1989) *Panstwo i spoleczenstwo w polityce społecznej* (Warsaw: PTE).
OKUN, A. M. (1975) *Equality and Efficiency: The Big Trade Off* (Washington, DC: Brookings Institution).
PIATEK, K. (1988) *Polityka Społeczna*, no. 7.
PODKAMINER, L. (1988) 'Inequality Effects of Disequilibrium in Poland's Consumer Markets, 1965–1986: Evidence from Households' Budgets', in *Forschungsberichte*, no. 146 (Vienna: Institute for Comparative Economic Studies).
POHORILLE, M. (1975) *Spozycie zbiorowe: swiadczenia społeczne* (Warsaw: PWE).
PRYOR F. (1973) *Property and Industrial Organizations in Communist and Capitalist Nations* (Bloomington: Indiana University Press).
RAJKIEWICZ, A. (ed.) (1979) *Polityka Społeczna* (Warsaw: PWE).
ROSNER, J. (1989) 'Panstwo i sily społeczne w ksztaltowaniu polityki społecznej', in PTE (ed.) *Panstwo i społeczenstwo w polityce społecznej* (Warsaw).
ROUNDTABLE DEBATE ABOUT PRICES (1982) and (1989) *Zycie Gospodarcze*, nos 1, 11.
SADOWSKI, Z. (1988) *Gospodarka Planowa*, no. 2.
SPOTAN, Z. (1982) *Ekonomika i Organizacja Pracy*, no. 7.
SZTANDERSKA, U. (1989) *Panstwo i społeczenstwo w polityce społecznej*, (Warsaw: PTE).
SZTYBER, W. (1978) *System cen w gospodarce socialistycznej* (Warsaw: PWE).
TOCZYNSKI, W. (1989) 'Ostrogi wlasnego domu', a conference held in September 1989 in Jadwisin: Perspektywy polskiej polityki społecznej.
TYMOWSKI. A. (1979) 'Warunki bytu rodzin', in Rajkiewicz, A. (ed.) *Polityka Społeczna* (Warsaw: PWE).
TYMOWSKI, A. and RAJKIEWICZ, A. (1988) *Rzeczypospolita*, 2/X.
WALICKI, A. (1988) 'Liberalism in Poland', *Critical Review*, Winter.
WINIEWSKI, M. (1988) *Polityka społeczna Polski Ludowej* (Warsaw: Akademia Nauk Społecznych PZPR).
WISNIEWSKA, K. (1985) *Dzialalnosc socjalno-bytowa przedsiebiotstw w warunkach reformy gospodarczej* (Warsaw: Studia i Marteriaty N5, IPISS).

6 Economic Reform and Changes in the Welfare System in Poland

Zbigniew M. Fallenbuchl

6.1 ECONOMIC SITUATION

Economic reform is one of three major factors which at present strongly affect the welfare system in Poland. The other two are the current economic situation and political developments.

A very deep economic crisis reduced national product by a quarter between 1978 and 1982 and resulted in a drastic decline in the standard of living (Fallenbuchl, 1982, 1986a). It was followed by a prolonged stagnation combined with a continuing balance-of-payments disequilibrium and an accelerating inflation (Fallenbuchl, 1988a, 1989a, b). Attempts to service at least part of the foreign debt reduced the aggregate supply available for domestic absorption. A big deficit in the state budget, created mainly by subsidies for inefficient enterprises and for keeping the retail prices of basic consumption goods relatively low, required drastic cuts.

In 1989, the economic crisis deepened again. Production in the socialist industry declined by 2.5 per cent and, although the output of private industry increased by 11–12 per cent, bottlenecks in production became more pronounced and shortages of consumption goods more acute. Average nominal wages increased by 473 per cent but retail prices rose by 640 per cent. Foreign trade volume declined and the balance-of-payments deficit deteriorated. The new Solidarity-led government took power in a very difficult economic situation and had to give priority to stabilisation and fight against inflation.

The 1978 level of Net Material Product (NMP) was regained in 1988 and declined again in 1989. However, the real wage level in 1988 was still about 20 per cent below the 1980 level. It has been calculated that in that year the social minimum level was about 95 000 zl. (Brach, 1989a). The average wage in the economy was 53.1 thousand zloty, the average wage in all services 42.9 thousand zloty, and in education, which has the lowest wages in the entire economy, 37.8 thousand zloty (Misiak, 1989). The average wage in the economy was, therefore, below the poverty line and the average wage in education was about 60 per cent below that. Families needed multiple wages, additional earnings and various social benefits in monetary form and in kind, including free medical services and subsidised housing, simply to survive. Pensions and welfare payments were not keeping pace with wages. Half of the recipients received payments below 45 000 zl., which often had to cover two persons when the wife did not have her own pension (Brach, 1989c). Despite government and party declarations about the protection for the weakest groups of society, the material situation of the low income families and pensioners became very difficult.

Since the new government took office, the material situation of the population has deteriorated even further. At a time when the welfare services are desperately needed by large groups of the population, the economic stabilisation and recovery programme requires keeping incomes restricted and the budgetary deficit reduced. The level of aggregate demand must be adjusted to the limited level of aggregate supply that the economy is able to produce. That level is limited by the existing system, which cannot be changed overnight, the industrial structure that has been inherited from the past, forced industrialisation drives, and by an insufficient volume of imports which cannot be increased without new credits because of obstacles encountered, mostly but not solely on the supply side, in attempts to expand exports (Fallenbuchl, 1985, 1986b, 1989c).

6.2 POLITICAL DEVELOPMENTS

In the political field, the shock of martial law, imposed in December 1981, was followed by seven years of a potentially explosive situation and two waves of strikes in 1988. The deadlock ended with the 'roundtable' agreements, recognition of Solidarity and a partially free election. The first non-Communist Prime Minister, Tadeusz Mazowiecki, is committed to far-reaching political changes, to the removal of bureaucratic barriers and nomenclature, to economic reform and to the reorganisation of the welfare system. In his inaugural address in the Sejm (the lower house of the parliament), he declared that the aim of his government is 'to create a state which guarantees us security in our individual and collective lives' and which 'while recognising the value of human action, does not leave the weak and destitute unprotected'. He stressed that there were two immediate major tasks: 'the political rebuilding of the country and its recovery from the economic crisis'. He warned that the government would be acting under a considerable pressure 'because at any moment the work of building democracy in Poland, which has scarcely begun, may collapse in economic bankruptcy'. Inflation must be stopped and the revival of economic activity must be accelerated, otherwise 'the society would view the democratic institutions as useless if appreciable changes were not made in day-to-day life' (*Program gospodarczy*, 1989).

The pace and the shape of both economic reform and changes in the welfare system will depend, to a considerable extent, on the future political developments, including the success and durability of the new government. However, society and Solidarity seem to be split as to the changes in the welfare system. Moreover, under the presently accepted labour union pluralism, the unions which were established by the Communist government after Solidarity had been abolished (OPZZ)[1] try to outbid Solidarity in demanding improvements in wages and social services.

6.3 ECONOMIC REFORM

Under the previous governments economic reform was implemented in a confused and half-hearted manner. Its pace was slow and uneven. The proposal that was accepted by the Party Congress in July 1981 and was embodied in two acts of parliament, enacted in September of that year, was based on the autonomy of the enterprises, their self-financing and self-government. It was introduced under matial law in January 1982 in a partial form. After a slow implementation and occasional regressions, it was supposed to enter the so called 'second stage' in 1987 which was inconsistent internally and was not clear as to its final objective.

The reform has not resulted in the establishment of a self-regulatory economic mechanism. The old centrally planned system has been modified as the result of a mass of legislation, administrative regulations and discretionary decisions of the central administrators. The system that had emerged was not the traditional command system but it was not a socialist market system either. It could be called a 'manipulative system' in which the central authorities tried to manipulate the decisions of the formerly autonomous enterprises with the help of financial and direct administrative measures. On their part, the enterprises tried to manipulate the decisions of the central authorities which affected them by bargaining for various exemptions, more favourable treatment and allocation of scarce resources (Fallenbuchl, 1988b).

When, contrary to the party leadership's expectations, no clear recovery was taking place and stagnation continued, a shift in the discussions concerning the future shape of the reform appeared from the system of central parametric planning to a controlled socialist market economy (Fallenbuchl, 1988c). It appeared that the reform would be moving further in the direction of marketisation and privatisation. In summer 1989, the government of Mieczyslaw Rakowski suddenly and without proper preparation removed price controls in agriculture. Food prices increased by 878 per cent in 1989. However, the prices of inputs for agriculture also rose drastically. Animal production became less profitable and livestock declined. Inflationary expectations reduced deliveries of agriculture and shortages increased (Leopold, 1989).

Prime Minister Mazowiecki has declared that his objective is not an improvement of the socialist system, as was the case in the past reforms, but its change into a market economy similar to that which exists in the West. Various systemic changes are to be introduced gradually but in a quick succession in 1990 and 1991. They include privatisation, the establishment of a stock exchange and the creation of a capital market. There will be full autonomy and self-financing for all state-owned enterprises which for the time being would not be privatised. The government will deregulate prices, eliminate most of the subsidies, administrative allocations, obligatory intermediaries and other vestiges of the command economy. In order to stimulate domestic competition anti-combine legislation will be introduced, freedom of entry will be granted for all enterprises, while full convertibility should allow international competition and encourage foreign direct investment and joint ventures. The entire taxation system will be overhauled and the banking system reformed. A real labour market will be established in which wages will be determined with the help of collective agreements between the labour unions and the private and state-owned enterprises. At the same time, the social security system will be adjusted to the needs of a market economy, unemployment insurance will be created and the indexation of pensions and social benefits will provide protection for the needy (*Program gospodarczy, 1989*).

Mazowiecki insists that his government wishes to create a 'social market economy'. The term has been borrowed from Konrad Adenauer's Christian Democrats and the objective is to establish 'capitalism with a human face' rather than an uncontrolled *laissez-faire* system. Solidarity may not, however, be unanimous in this respect. It includes various groups, including conservatives, liberals, Christian Democrats and Social Democrats. It is too early to say which would have a dominant position in the future.

The economic situation makes modifications in the welfare system difficult but necessary. The political situation has facilitated the introduction of far-reaching changes. The progress of economic reform will make them more urgently needed. As one of the leading Solidarity activists who is now Minister of Labour and Social Policy, Jacek Kuron, has observed it is necessary to ensure protection from the worst effects of economic reform, but so far 'Poland has practically no sensible social welfare system'.

6.4 STATE ENTERPRISE'S SOCIAL AND HOUSING FUNDS

The most important feature of the economic reform is the change in the role of the socialist enterprises in the economy. They are expected to become efficient autonomous economic units maximising profits. In the Soviet-type economy, these enterprises are not only the production units but also the basic units of political indoctrination and control, and they have responsibilities for providing various social services for their workers, pensioners and workers' families (*Zakladowe fundusze*, 1988). Now their role as political units has been abolished in Poland, as it had already happened earlier in Hungary. Their role as units of the welfare system has been questioned for some time on several grounds.

First, of all, there is inequality in the workers' accessibility to social services which depends on the place of work. For thirty years after the end of the Second World War social welfare activities of the enterprises developed in a spontaneous and uneven way. The state regulations were vague and very general. Some enterprises were able to build considerable social welfare funds. Others had restricted funds for this purpose or did not have them at all. Some enterprises invested in a full scale of amenities: day care centres, kindergartens, libraries, sport fields, cafeterias, summer and/or winter camps for children and vacation hotels in choice locations. Others were able to establish only one or two items from this list, and to provide services of clearly inferior standards, or were too small to support any of them. Usually, the biggest enterprises in the priority sectors of the economy, such as coal mining or the steel industry, were able to develop a full-scale social infrastructure and this tendency further strengthened the wage differentials which operated in their favour. In the middle of the 1960s, differences in the value of social services between the average level in the fuel and power generation industry, on one hand, and the average level in the food processing industry, on the other, represented 500–550 per cent (Smulska, 1988b).

In 1973, an attempt was made to reduce the most drastic discrepancies by a decree which required the establishment of a social fund[2] in all enterprises, financed from a 2 per cent deduction from the enterprise's total wage bill. The already established differences could not have been eliminated. On the contrary, they continue to grow. Similarly unsuccessful was the creation of a Central Fund of Social Investments which operated in the years 1974–82 on the basis of depreciation accounts of all enterprises. It created room for arbitrary decisions by the central authorities and for pressures by various industrial lobbies, especially the strongest of them in the priority sectors (ibid.).

This was the situation at the time when the 1981 economic reform was introduced. Its programme stated as one of the objectives 'a reduction in the disparities in the levels of social funds per employee as between various industries and enterprises' (*Kierunki*, 1981). According to the decree on the state enterprise's finances that was introduced in 1982, all state enterprises are required to create a social fund from annual deductions from the wage fund equal to 50 per cent of the minimum wage multiplied by the number of employees. Moreover, the enterprises are allowed to supplement the fund from profits (*Zakladowe fundusze*, 1988, pp. 61–4). Similar provisions were introduced, with some exceptions, in the cooperatives (ibid., pp. 65–7), while the 1973 decree remained in force in respect of the institutions financed from the state budget. The possibility of using profits to enhance the enterprise's social funds was regarded as a measure strengthening the motivation to improve the efficiency of operations in accordance with the logic of the reform. It was based on the assumption that both the management and the workers would like to see the expansion of social amenities that the enterprise could offer. It was also regarded as a device to reduce an excessive turnover in employment and a measure to attract better workers (Smulska, 1988b).

The reform has not removed distortions in prices. The profitability of the enterprises still does not depend on their own efforts. It is affected by the state of their capital stock, which has been allowed to run down because a major part of depreciation allowances was transferred to the central budget and replacements depended often on the administrative allocation of hard currencies and permissions to import. Profits depended less on increasing efficiency than on the ability of the enterprise to convince the authorities that it should be allowed to raise prices, to obtain scarce materials from administrative allocations, to negotiate successfully for tax deductions, subsidies, subsidised credit and grants. As the biggest enterprises were in the strongest negotiating position *vis-à-vis* the centrally authorities, they were able to improve their position even further at the expense of the rest of the society.

In this situation, the continuation of discrepancies in social funds and in the social infrastructure is regarded as unjust and it is clearly seen that the system does not provide a satisfactory social protection, especially taking into consideration that the majority of outlays from the enteprises' social funds are allocated for the modernisation and development of the enterprises' own vacation facilities, and that these investments are made by relatively big enterprises which are already better equipped in this respect than the rest (ibid.).

This is taking place at a time when there is a drastic shortage of hospitals, accommodation for the elderly and schools, when the pensions and welfare allowances are at a fraction of the social minimum (ibid.). There are many cries that the system of social welfare based on the enterprises has failed, that the enterprises should provide only those amenities which are directly connected with the quality of the working place. All other amenities, especially the vacation facilities, camps for children, health services and continuing education, should be transferred to some specialised agencies or enterprises (Smulska, 1989).

The enterprises have not followed any clearly defined rational social policy. They have allocated social funds in an arbitrary and haphazard way. Moreover, the allocation was subject to intervention by the Communist Party and various other institutions associated with it (ibid.). It is a major task for Solidarity to break this link and to revise the whole system, introducing, for example, vacation pay instead of the enterprise's own vacation facilities. It is not easy, however, to effect the switch when those who have relatively good facilities will object to losing them, when the overall social infrastructure in the country is very poor, and when under the current economic situation it is impossible to allocate more funds for investment in this field.

6.5 NATIONAL HEALTH POLICY

There is a considerable concern in Poland about the state of health of the population and about the excessively high mortality, especially among the male population in certain age groups (Smulska, 1988a). Between 1970 and 1986 the number of cases of death per 1000 inhabitants increased from 8.1 to 10.1 for the total population, from 8.8 to 10.9 for the male population and from 7.5 to 9.2 for the female population. Among the male population the increases were from 3.7 to 4.2 in the age group 35–44 years, from 7.6 to 11.2 in the age group 45–54, from 15.6 to 20.0 in the age group 55–59 and from 25.5 to 29.4 in the age group 60–64. During the same period, the total number of working days per 100 employed in the national economy which were lost as the result of illness or accidents increased from 1301 to 1886 (GUS, 1987).

Various explanations have been suggested. To a great extent, they are related to certain features of the operation of the political and economic system and to the prolonged economic crisis. They include a very high degree of air and water pollution by industrial chemicals, unsatisfactory work conditions, poor and overcrowded housing, frustration and depression caused by the existing economic conditions and fears about the future, malnutrition or one-sided diet, alcoholism and, above all, deterioration in the health services.

The national health policy was discussed at a special subcommittee at the 'roundtable' conference and the representatives of Solidarity and of OPZZ shared similar views as to the catastrophic situation in this field.

Solidarity's representative characterised it as follows:

> in respect of health protection the situation was bad for years and now it has become truly tragic. The obsolete physical base, difficulties with accessibility to a medical doctor and to a health care

> centre, very bad organization, an increasingly inefficient system . . . The problems of health were neglected by the political authorities for years and now we have found ourselves in a hopeless situation without a way out . . . We are aware that we have to change it because it leads to a biological destruction, but it is not clear how to do it now when we do not have means at our disposal . . . A free national health service was established as one of the basic principles at the time when the People's Republic of Poland was created. However, a long time ago it ceased to be free and accessible for all . . . To an increasing extent it depends on whom you know and who recommends you. (Brach, 1989)

The representative of the other labour unions was equally critical:

> The state of health of society is deteriorating; there are such depressing phenomena as the excessive mortality of the male population and an increased mortality of women at the working age, one of the highest European ratios of death is caused by contagious illnesses and in some regions pathological pregnancy and birth have become a rule . . . There is an outflow of personnel from the health protection professions . . . there is an acute shortage of medications and equipment . . . The state of the health services may have an adverse impact on economic reform and on the future development of the country. (ibid.)

Both agreed that it was necessary to allocate larger funds for medical services from the state budget immediately and that a fundamental reform of these services was needed on the basis of the health insurance principles, as the budget would not be able to take the whole burden of the necessary expenditures. Already the Rakowski government had come up with a similar proposal which would replace free medical services by national health insurance. The Solidarity representative was not, however, prepared to support that particular proposal as it was regarded as internally inconsistent. He stressed that a new plan of reform should be formulated which would: (i) reduce the extremely high degree of bureaucratisation of medical services; (ii) establish self-governing bodies for the medical profession; and (iii) try to establish the actual costs of various services, medications and equipment which are at present unknown and, therefore, not taken into consideration (ibid.).

It appears that at present all political groups support the replacement of free medical services by health insurance with obligatory contributions which would cover essential services and additional individual payments for an 'extended coverage', and for the introduction of pricing for some medical services and medications.[3] The population is not, however, convinced of the merits of the proposed new system. There seems to be a widespread view that 'it will be necessary to pay more for services which will remain equally bad as they are now' (ibid.).

Some far-reaching differences have appeared between those who maintain that a considerable degree of state involvement would be necessary in health care and the believers in the ability of the market forces to provide the best solution also in this sector. Both groups wish to construct a Western type of health care but each accepts different Western countries as their model[4] (Golinowska, 1989).

The government of Tadeusz Mazowiecki is, therefore, faced with two very difficult tasks in this field:

1. It will not be able to increase the allocation of funds for health services from the state budget in the present economic situation, and it will have to depend solely on a reduction in the degree of bureaucratisation and on self-government of medical profession for an improvement in the efficient use of the same volume of resources;
2. It will have to prepare an improved proposal for national health insurance and it will also have to convince the population that a reform of health services along these lines is necessary.

Both tasks require not only considerable administrative and political talents but also a big dose of luck. The first step has been made when the Sejm enacted legislation establishing self-governing medical councils. The pre-war councils, despite their long tradition of social consciousness, were abolished on 1 January 1951 as they were regarded as incompatible with the system of state medicine. They have been re-established from 1 January 1990 in the hope that they would be able to improve the efficiency of medical services in an almost hopeless situation (Dryll, 1989).

A lot will, however, also depend not only on reducing the extent of centralisation and bureaucracy, but also on whether the medical administration would be able to change its attitude towards the medical profession and patients from that of the masters and to become the servants. This implies a process of re-education which will require some time. In the meantime, whatever changes will be enacted they will be implemented by the existing administrative personnel which will be able to frustrate even the best reform.

6.6 SOCIAL INSURANCE

The principle of social insurance has also been accepted by experts and by various political groups as a basis for the reform of the social security system.[5] A proposal of the reform was introduced, after a series of delays, by the government of Zbigniew Messner in July 1988 and it was discussed by the Sejm Committee on Social Policy, Health and Physical Education on 19 October of that year. The Minister of Labour and Social Policy, who presented the proposal, admitted a very unsatisfactory state of social policy in Poland. In his view what is in existence cannot be regarded as a system. It is not comprehensive and internally consistent. He pointed out that as a new economic system was introduced which would stress the importance of economic calculations, the new social security system should be based on the same logic.

The 'economisation' of the social security system is, therefore, based on the rule that 'the size of benefits depends on the length of time during which contributions were paid'. The proposal includes also a mechanism of automatic indexation, makes family allowances independent from the criterion of family income and transfers family welfare payments from the enterprises to the territorial social services, which are to be expanded in order to be able to cope with the new tasks, and some social amenities from the enterprises to specialised agencies (Brach, 1988a).

The committee approved the proposal and expressed support for the liquidation of anti-motivational functions of several existing welfare allowances. It was pointed out that, for example, under the old system, a low income family could more easily increase its income by collecting a large number of child allowances than by looking for a better payed job or working overtime which would lead to the loss of the allowances. The committee also accepted the rule that the pension is not a welfare payment but a part of income that has been earned earlier in life and that the size of benefits must therefore reflect the size of contributions made. It also instructed government to start immediately the necessary organisational preparations which would enable the territorial social services to cope with the new tasks. At the same time, some concern was expressed whether this move would not lead to an expansion of territorial bureaucracy (Brach, 1988b).

At the meeting the minister agreed that the reform would be 'a painful process' and that for this reason 'it requires a social acceptance'. As neither the government of Messner nor that of Mieczyslaw Rakowski that followed it were able to obtain confidence of the population, no further action has taken place until now.

In the meantime, the situation of pensioners has deteriorated. The average pension paid by the Office of Social Insurance (ZUS) represented 58 per cent of the average wage in 1987, 52 per cent at the end of 1988, 48 per cent at the end of the first quarter of 1989 and 36 per cent after the first six months. When the government of Rakowski announced that a new pension law could not be introduced before 1991, the pensioners organised a massive demonstration in Warsaw on 13 April 1989 (Brach, 1989c). This is another problem that has been inherited by the present government.

The Second Congress of Solidarity, which was held in Gdansk in April 1990, declared that the retirement pensions and workers' compensations require some fundamental changes. Various privileges connected with the type of work, state decorations and honorary titles, usually obtained by the high party and state officials, should be eliminated and the payments should depend on the years of employment (Uchwala Programowa, 1990).

The Mazowiecki government has found it very difficult to formulate a retirement pensions and workers compensation act which would be acceptable to the parliament and to the representatives of various interested groups. Minister Kuron was forced to withdraw his ministry's proposal in November 1990 and the work had to start from the beginnings on a new bill.

6.7 LABOUR LAW

Before the Second World War Poland had not only a relatively well-developed system of social insurance that was administered by the Office of Social Insurance (ZUS), but also a progressive labour law. The system included the obligatory health and accident insurance for blue- and white-collar workers, including agricultural workers, that was introduced in the first years of the newly established state and unemployment insurance system which was introduced in 1924. A large part of social security provisions even now is still based on the 1923 law. Similarly, Poland had one of the most progressive labour legislations in Europe. The labour law secured the right to form labour unions, the forty-six-hour working week, paid vacations, rigorous requirements concerning the conditions of work with inspections by a specialised personnel from the ministry of labour (Landau, 1988).

Many of the provisions of the labour law were changed or became inoperative when the Soviet-type economic system was introduced at the end of the 1940s. The work protection and workmen compensation was one of the subjects that are included in the 'roundtable' agreement. It accepts that in the market economy, which will now be established, the state must retain its responsibility for the introduction and implementation of the necessary labour legislation, and that the international convention of the International Labour Office dealing with these matters should be ratified and implemented.

There will be a reduction, starting in 1990, in the maximum number of involuntary overtime hours in transportation, communications and in the enterprises designated as of special importance for the national economy. The norms established by the labour law should apply to these fields as well. There will be a programme of gradual elimination of work by women on night shifts and the application of specific ILO standards in this respect. Another programme will attempt to improve physical conditions of work, gradually eliminate features that are harmful to health and improve protection of health and life of workers in all sectors of the economy, including agriculture and the non-agricultural private sector. Bonuses should not be subject to the condition of no or low absenteeism, irrespective of whether the absence was caused by illness or other justified reasons. There should be great flexibility in regulations concerning change of work, including shifts from the state to the private sector. Finally, there is concern about alcoholism and other pathological behaviour which destroy working patterns, endanger health and destroy human dignity (Baka and Trzeciakowski, 1989).

With the strong pressure from both the Solidarity and the other labour unions (OPZZ), and a high degree of competition between them for support by the workers, it can be expected that a very progressive revision of the labour law will be effected within the shortest possible time. The new system will be fully consistent with the ILO conventions and it will represent a clear switch from the Soviet-type to the Western system of labour legislation.

6.8 UNEMPLOYMENT INSURANCE

It is the essence of economic reform that the enterprises should base their activities on the profit maximisation principle. In this situation some of them will be forced to reduced excessively large numbers of employees while others, which are unable to become profitable, will have to be liquidated and their workers will therefore lose employment. From the very first document on economic reform of 1981, it has been accepted that rationalisation of employment will result in some unemployment. Indeed, the very fact that the Polish economy has experienced continued shortages of labour rather than a degree of unemployment may be accepted as the best proof that the pre-Solidarity economic reform was not implemented to a significant extent.

From the very beginning Solidarity insisted that economic reform was necessary and in April 1981 its Centre for Social and Labour Tasks prepared a proposal for the programme of social renewal (*Program Odnowy Społecznej*, 1981), which subsequently served as a basis for the programme that was adopted by the First National Congress in Gdansk in September–October 1981. For a movement that was created almost overnight from below as the result of workers' protest and demands for improvements in the standard of living, these two documents reflect a surprisingly mature, responsible and restrained attitude, although it is, of course, unknown whether the leaders of Solidarity would have been able at that time to secure sufficient support of the rank and file for the implementation of various austerity measures that the programme accepted as necessary.

The programme accepted that some unemployment would probably occur as the result of the rationalisation of employment, restructuring of the economy, and increasing the efficiency of production. It demanded, however, that the government should provide retraining and should facilitate transfer of labour in order to ensure full employment in the economy as a whole, although it may not be possible to avoid unemployment among some specific groups of people. This position was repeated in an underground statement on economic reform that was issued in April 1987. It accepted some unemployment as unavoidable but insisted that some preparatory measures should be taken in advance in order 'to assist employees in changing jobs and place of residence, as well as helping them to acquire new employment qualifications through retraining programmes'. It also pointed out that it is 'necessary to markedly improve the effectiveness of employment agencies' (NSZZ 'Solidarnosc', 1987). This is the position with which Solidarity entered the 'roundtable' discussions and it is reflected in the agreement that was reached during these negotiations.

The agreement accepts the objective of maintaining full employment in the sense that there will be a policy facilitating the creation of new places of work. It will not mean that the state should guarantee to everyone a job in a given trade or profession and in a given place. It is hoped, however, that economic reform and a more efficient use of economic mechanisms will create adjustment processes in the labour market.

It is necessary to reconstruct the territorial employment service in such a way that it would, above all, serve to provide assistance to those who are searching for a job. At the same time, the law on punishment for those who avoid employment should be withdrawn immediately. Special efforts should be made to provide jobs for the handicapped and elderly if they wish to work. Unemployment benefits for those who are looking for employment should be accepted as a necessity. When the enterprises are liquidated and whole groups of workers are laid off, conditions must be created for their retraining. There should be special legislation controlling conditions under which groups of workers could be dismissed with at least one month warning (both Solidarity and the OPZZ registered their wish to extend this period to three months). The workers who are retrained should receive an allowance equal to their last pay, retraining should be free and it should be counted as period of employment.

Transfer to another job or the selection of a new trade or profession must be effected with the approval of the person involved. Those who decide to open businesses or work as self-employed should have an access to credit. There will also be an opportunity to select early retirement in the case of workers who are employed in the establishments subject to liquidation.

Differences of opinion were registered between the representatives of the government, on one hand, and the representatives of both labour unions, on another, as to the period during which those workers who have an accommodation provided by their enterprise should have the right to keep it when the enterprise is liquidated or there is a group reduction in employment – i.e. until an equivalent accommodation is found (the unions) or only during the period of liquidation of the enterprise (the government). Similar differences were registered in connection with specific provisions which cover those who live in workers' hostels or who rent private accommodation which is paid for by the enterprise. There were also differences as to the conditions under which a worker could sue for an unlawful dismissal (Baka and Trzeciakowski, 1989).

Two bills were soon introduced by the government in December 1989: (i) on employment and (ii) on group dismissal for work. They embody the provisions agreed upon during the 'roundtable' discussions. The former defines unemployment in accordance with the standard Western definition and introduces an obligatory registration of the unemployed. A network of regional and county (*wojewodztwo*) employment offices is created as well as employment councils at the county level as social advisory bodies composed of the representatives of employers, labour unions, state administration and local authorities. The employment offices are responsible for the registration of the unemployed and for directing them to available jobs or for retraining. They can also create an additional employment position in cooperation with the interested enterprises. To finance these activities and unemployment benefits a new Employment Fund has been created. It replaces the former Fund of Employment Activisation (PFAZ) and is established from obligatory contributions by all private, cooperative and state enterprises. The unemployment benefits for those registered and periodically reporting to the employment offices has been determined at the level of 70 per cent of the last remuneration paid during the first three months of unemployment, 50 per cent during the following six months and 40 per cent afterwards without any time limit. Young people entering the labour market who are unable to find employment are entitled to unemployment benefits and so are those who worked outside the country if they paid unemployment contributions (I.D., 1990).

The second bill concerns the conditions which must be met before an enterprise can dismiss all or large groups of workers for economic reasons. The labour unions must be notified about the proposed dismissal at least forty-five days earlier and an agreement must be reached between the management and the union as to the procedure to be followed. However, if the agreement cannot be reached, the management can act unilaterally. The size of compensation has been determined at the level of a monthly remuneration for those who worked for less than ten years, two monthly remunerations for those who worked from ten to twenty years and three monthly remunerations for those who worked for more than twenty years. This bill proved to be controversial and was sent by the parliament back to the government which was instructed to define the role of workers' self-management in the process and to re-examine the formula for compensations (I.D., 1990).

Almost overnight an entire network of employment offices was created on the territory of the whole country in the first half of 1990. They register the unemployed, pay unemployment benefits, list available openings, try to find jobs for the registered unemployed and to provide for them retraining. Considerable administrative efforts were needed to train the staff and to find appropriate office space. The greatest obstacle was a complete lack of experience in this field.

At the moment, the labour unions have accepted the unavoidability of unemployment and concentrate on watching the government's efforts to cope with the growing unemployment which had reached one million persons, or 7.5 per cent of the labour force, at the end of October 1990. Both the further acceptance of unemployment and the adequacy of provisions would, however, depend on the size of unemployment.

6.9 HOUSING

A particularly difficult situation exists in housing. There has been an acute shortage of accommodation since the Second World War and the situation is deteriorating. Poland compares unfavourably not only with countries in Western but also in Eastern Europe. In 1988, there were 284 dwellings per 1000 inhabitants in Poland as compared with 417 in Austria, 446 in Denmark or 477 in the Federal Republic of Germany. In Eastern Europe the comparative figures are 359 for Bulgaria, 366 for Hungary, 370 for Czechoslovakia and 417 for the German Democratic Republic (Zarski, 1989).

Despite this situation the production of accommodation has declined since the beginning of this decade. In 1988, the socialist construction industry produced 22 per cent dwellings less than in 1980 (126.5 thousand as compared with 151.4 thousand). This was 4.1 thousand less than in 1987 and 6.8 thousand less than the plan. At the same time, the output of the private construction industry has not been expanding because of shortages of building materials and of the land that is prepared for development. Taking both sectors together in 1979–88, the average annual construction of dwellings was 202 000 per year, or 17 per cent less than the average for 1971–8 (242 000) (ibid.). The plan for 1989 envisaged that the socialist construction industry would build 130 000 dwellings and the private sector would contribute another 65 000. The actual numbers constructed were, however, only 100 000 and 35 000 respectively. The two sectors produced jointly in that year less accommodation than the 1960s' level which had been recognised as very unsatisfactory (Gornicka, 1989b).

At the same time, when an insufficient amount of new accommodation is constructed the older existing houses have been deteriorating because of unsatisfactory maintenance. This is particularly true in the case of the privately owned apartment houses. Ever since the introduction of a decree concerning 'public allocation of housing' immediately after the war, the owners have lost control over the renting of a accommodation in their houses. All dwellings have been allocated administratively at centrally fixed rents. The owners have, however, been responsible for cleaning, garbage removal and repairs. The rents have been kept artificially low. Even when they were raised in 1989, they could cover only a fraction of current operating costs. As a result, all privately owned buildings were left without proper repairs. The problem was recognised at the beginning of the 1980s when exemptions from taxation were allowed for the owners who had to face costly repairs and subsidies even were offered. However, the rapidly progressing inflation and shortages of materials prevented these measures having any effect.

So far the Mazowiecki government has not decided to abolish the heavily bureaucratic administrative allocation of housing. It is, of course, difficult to introduce any changes at a time when there is an acute shortage of housing, the construction of houses is in decline and real incomes are drastically cut.

The years of administrative allocation of accommodation according to changing priorities, political and even private connections and simple bribery, with rent controls at very low historical levels, and the lack of allocation of resources for maintenance have resulted in complete chaos. The majority of the population lives in overcrowded and often substandard conditions and the waiting list for accommodation exceeds ten years, while a chosen few enjoy very comfortable living. It very often happens that those who have relatively high incomes pay very low rents and that the size of the rent is not correlated with the quality of the accommodation. It has been recognised that often the level of rent, which depends on the year when the accommodation was allocated, is more important than wages in determining the financial situation of families (Brach, 1988a).

For a while the government of Mieczyslaw Rakowski seemed to recommend a plan for 'treating accommodation as commodities', i.e. rents that would fully cover investment outlays, operating costs, repairs and maintenance. These rents were to be introduced by stages by consecutive reductions in subsidies from the state budget which were 320 billion zloty in 1988, or 1.8 per cent of the total money income of the population in that year, and 520 billion zloty according to the plan for 1989 (Gornicka, 1989a).

When the problem of housing was discussed in a special subcommittee at the 'roundtable' negotiations, the government representative opted for the retention of the 'protective' role of the state at present and so far in the future as it can be predicted. The stress was on the establishment of a special bank for housing which would advance credit for those wishing to buy dwelling or build it, on the creation of better conditions for the expansion of the private construction industry, the development of the building materials industry and better preparation of building lots by local authorities.

The official labour unions (OPZZ) supported the plan that rents and prices of housing should be sufficient to enable self-financing of this sector of the economy. They would introduce 'housing allowances' for those with low incomes instead of subsidised housing. They feel that the whole field should first be put in order (ibid.).

Solidarity supports the creation of a specialised bank, the use of credit and housing allowances in order to move in the direction of the marketisation of this sector of the economy as soon as possible (ibid.).

It seems that the majority of Polish experts believe that an upward revision of prices for housing and rents is necessary, and the existing historical differences depending on when the accommodation was obtained should be eliminated, with a considerable degree of state support for low income families and credit and housing allowances for others.

In January 1990, the Mazowiecki government proposed to increase rents paid for those accommodation in state-, city- and privately owned houses, which are at present subject to the administrative rent and allocation control, in two stages. From 1 July 1990 the new rents were to be sufficient to cover current operating costs and small repairs, and from 1 January 1995 they are also expected to cover capital costs (Starkowska, 1990).

Because of the existence of various vested interests, any reform in this field is difficult to implement. It has to be carefully prepared and introduced by stages rather than in the form of major surgery. It is likely that in the meantime a substantial dose of inefficiency and inequity would remain.

6.10 PROSPECTS FOR CHANGE

The present open discussion of the Soviet-type welfare system as applied in Poland during the last forty four years has revealed not only its inefficiency but also the basic inequity that it creates in practice. Moreover, it is not compatible with the logic of marketisation which is expected to be introduced as the result of the implementation of economic reform. There is no political group which would not agree that it must be changed. There also seems to be an agreement as to the main directions of the necessary changes. The problem is, however, that these changes are very difficult and the operation would have a very uneven impact on various groups.

The state administration may have vested interests to defend the status quo. The OPZZ are now fighting for their life. They have assumed a populist position and make changes in the welfare system difficult by refusing to accept the costs involved in the process. Solidarity is also in a difficult situation. It is now paying for being a labour union and not a political party. It is paradoxical that its main supporters are employed in the biggest enterprises in the sectors that were regarded as priority sectors in the past, such as coal mining, steel metallurgy, ship-building. They are the very people in favour of whom the welfare system has been biased. For example, they enjoy better amenities and social services in their enterprises which they would lose if these were transferred to specialised agencies or enterprises. It is unlikely that the government supported by Solidarity would be able to withdraw this bias without offering at the same time significant benefits from the new welfare system. Taking into consideration the enormous difficulties that would be encountered in the process of changing the welfare system, it is unlikely that the benefits could appear immediately.

Considering all these elements, it is doubtful that quick changes on a wide front would take place in the welfare state in the near future in Poland, irrespective of the degree to which the economic reform would be implemented.

NOTES

1. Ogolnospolskie Porozumienie Zwiazkow Zawodowych (National Coalition of Labour Unions).
2. The enterprise social fund was the source of financing vacation, cultural and sport facilities, social welfare payments and retirement pensions.
3. This would not be unlike, for example, the obligatory Ontario Health Insurance Plan which covers basic medical services and can be supplemented, on voluntary basis, by an additional extended coverage insurance.
4. The discussion is between the advocates of the market-determined private medical services, as exemplified by the American system, and various obligatory state-financed health insurance plans which are in existence in Western Europe or Canada.
5. Family allowances, pensions, workers' compensation and welfare payments for the poor, sick and invalids.

REFERENCES

BAKA, W. and TRZECIAKOWSKI, W. (1989) *ZG*, no. 16.
BRACH, B. (1988a) *ZG*, no. 40. (*ZG* stands for *Zycie Gaspodarcze*)
BRACH, B. (1988b) *ZG*, no. 44.
BRACH, B. (1989a) *ZG*, no. 7.
BRACH, B. (1989b) *ZG*, no. 15.
BRACH, B. (1989c) *ZG*, no. 17.
DRYLL, I. (1989) *ZG*, no. 22.
FALLENBUCHL, Z. M. (1982) 'Poland's Economic Crisis', *Problems of Communism*, no. 2.
FALLENBUCHL, Z. M. (1985), 'The Balance of Payments Problem and the Economic Crisis in Poland', *The Carl Beck Papers*, no. 406.
FALLENBUCHL, Z. M. (1986a) 'The Economic Crisis in Poland and Prospects for Recovery', in *East European Economies: Slow Growth in the 1980s*, US Congress, vol. 3 (Washington).
FALLENBUCHL, Z. M. (1986b) 'Poland: Internal Economic Development', in P. Joseph (ed.) *The Economies of Eastern Europe and Their Foreign Economic Relations* (Brussels: NATO).
FALLENBUCHL, Z. M. (1988a) 'The Polish Economy in the Year 2000', The Carl Beck Papers, no. 607.
FALLENBUCHL, Z. M. (1988b) 'The Present State of Economic Reform', in P. Marer and W. Siwinski (eds) *Creditworthiness and Reform in Poland* (Bloomington).
FALLENBUCHL, Z. M. (1988c) 'Plan and Market in the Light of Experience and Current Discussions in Poland', paper presented at AAASS Convention.
FALLENBUCHL, Z. M. (1989a) 'Poland: The Anatomy of Stagnation', in

Pressure for Reform in the East European Economies, US Congress, vol. 3 (Washington).
FALLENBUCHL, Z. M. (1989b) 'Socio-economic Instability in Poland at the End of the 1980s', paper presented at a conference on 'Instability in Poland', Pennsylvania State University.
FALLENBUCHL, Z. M. (1989c) 'Obstacles to Trade with the West: The Case of Poland', paper presented at the Atlantic Economic Convention in Montreal.
GLÓWNY URZAD STATYSTYCZNY (1987) *Rocznik statystyczny* (Warsaw).
GLÓWNY URZAD STATYSTYCZNY (1989) *Rocznik statystyczny* (Warsaw).
GOLINOWSKA, S. (1989) *ZG*, no. 1.
GORNICKA, T. (1989a) *ZG*, no. 12.
GORNICKA, T. (1989b) *ZG*, no. 48.
I. D. (1990) *ZG*, no. 1.
JOSEPH, P. (1986) (ed.) *The Economies of Eastern Europe and Their Foreign Economic Relations* (Brussels: NATO).
Kierunki Reformy Gospodarczej (1981) (Warsaw: Trybuna Ludu).
LANDAU, Z. (1988) *ZG*, no. 46.
LEOPOLD, A. (1989) *ZG*, no. 46.
MARER, P. and SIWINSKI, W. (1988) (eds) *Creditworthiness and Reform in Poland* (Bloomington: Indiana University Press).
MISIAK, M. (1989) *ZG*, no. 6.
NSZZ 'Solidarnosc' (1987) *On Reforming the Polish Economy* (Brussels: Coordinating Office Abroad of NSZZ 'Solidarnosc').
Program gospodarczy-Glowne zalozenia i kierunki (1989) (Warsaw: Rzeczpospolita).
SMULSKA, G. (1988a) *ZG*, no. 6.
SMULSKA, G. (1988b) *ZG*, no. 35.
SMULSKA, G. (1989) *ZG*, no. 4.
STARKOWSKA, M. (1990) *Lad*, no. 5.
Uchwala Programowa II Krajowego Zjazdu Delegatow NSZZ 'Solidarnosc' (1990), Gdansk.
Zakladowe fundusze socjalny i mieszkaniowy (1988) (Warsaw: Instytut Wydawniczy Zwiazkow Zawodowych).
ZARSKI, T. (1989) *ZG*, no. 27.

7 Recent Trends in Social Policy in Hungary

Zsuzsa Ferge

7.1 BACKGROUND CONSIDERATIONS

7.1.1 The New Political Framework of Social Policy

Before turning to details, the *political* essence of the new trends should be briefly summarised. By now the collapse of the 'socialist systems' is a fact, even though there are considerable differences between the countries.

The Hungarian Kádár-system was a 'mild dictatorship'. Quite a few reforms were started by the 'reform wing' of the then ruling party. Hence the process of structural change, or 'de-Stalinisation', has been slower and less violent here than elsewhere. None the less, the elections on 25 March 1990 have shown that the overwhelming majority opted for a clean break with the past: a non-socialist system, with parliamentary democracy and a market economy.

Of the new dominant trends, political liberalism and economic neo-liberalism seem to be the most important. The real issue is – and not only in Hungary – whether political democracy will be a partner of, or dominated by, economic democracy, or, in other words, whether the newly liberated political forces, the new freedoms of organisation and self-defence will be able to check to some extent the newly liberated economic forces. Otherwise – especially because of the dire economic conditions of the country – it may happen that *the trade-off between the newly acquired freedoms and the weakening existential securities* (job security, income security, etc.) *will be negative for large segments of the population.*

7.1.2 The Social Policy Background

Before turning to recent trends and current changes, some elements of the social or welfare policy of the East European totalitarian systems need to be highlighted.

The ideological starting point of these systems, Hungary's included, was originally that in a socialist system the economy – operating without exploitation and the profit motive – would automatically take care of all social problems. Hence there was no need for a separate and autonomous social policy. This position did not imply a complete absence of welfare institutions. The ideological view on social policy entailed, though, a number of peculiar features.

The *first* characteristic was the strong, almost organic connection between economic and social policy. One of the tenets of socialist ideology emphasised the role of work, the legitimacy of 'distribution according to work' – and the non-legitimacy of any other access to income. The corollaries were manifold. One of them was a peculiar employment policy aiming at formal full employment at the expense of economic rationality, assuring full control over the whole labour force by the totalitarian power. The second corollary was that all *social* incomes (pension, sick pay, family allowance and such like) had to be *work related*. The emphasis was not on contributions, but on the fact of having a job, preferably employment in the state sector. Those having no employment, *and their family members*, had no right to any income (including family allowances). (This rule served, in varying degrees at different periods, to discriminate against politically undesirable groups, from political dissidents to all those who worked outside the state sector, including, up to the mid-1970s, members of cooperatives, too.)

Elements of 'distributional justice' were also built into economic policy. Hence the relatively levelled wage distribution, and a so-called anti-rich price system. The price system also ignored economic rationality, but enabled even the majority of the poor to cover their basic necessities.

Despite some of the positive sides of the above mentioned solutions (existential security, the preventive role of employment policy, etc.) a *second* particular feature followed from the emphasis on work. This implied not only the single-minded accent on 'distribution according to work', but also the acceptance of the Bible's command that 'those who do not work, should not eat'. As a matter of fact, all forms of social assistance were abolished in Hungary in 1950, whatever the reason for destitution. Politics decided that poverty could not exist under socialism. Therefore, its existence was absolutely denied, and the expression itself became for long taboo.

Some forms of assistance slowly crept back from 1960 on, first for the elderly, and later, from 1974 on, for families with children. But up to 1989, social assistance remained bureaucratic and discretionary, quantitatively inadequate, and excluded the 'undeserving' poor. It was also assumed (contrary to reality) that those who work can manage to cover their needs on a socially acceptable level. If not, their inadequacy stems from a 'fault of their own'. This judgement was applied not only in the case of income deficiencies, but also, for instance, in the case of inadequate housing. As a consequence, the fact of homelessness was, similarly to poverty, denied, and practically no solution existed for those having no shelter.

A *third feature* of welfare policy within totalitarian politics was its total domination by the politics of the party state, with a two-fold consequence. *On the one hand*, it was handled *residually*. Resources were concentrated on so-called productive branches, fully neglecting the 'non-productive' spheres, including housing, health, education and so on. (Obviously, economic policy itself was under the domination of politics. As a consequence, economic investments were misdirected, and ignored both economic and social rationality.) *On the other hand*, the only omnipotent agency, deciding about the forms, the contents, the levels of benefits as well as about all organisational aspects of the institutions, etc. in the welfare field, was the state, or, rather, the party. Hence, welfare redistribution was always presented as the sign and the outcome of the benevolence of the state, and social benefits as gifts.

Under these conditions, the citizens could not directly participate in any way in shaping the welfare system. The notion of *social rights* was practically banned from the vocabulary of social policy.

A *fourth characteristic* – an inevitable consequence of the power logic – was the total neglect of the individual. Social policy had, as in all systems, a legitimating role. But the needs to be covered by social policy were always defined by the central power. And this power was interested only in its image as reflected in macrostatistics. Hence the big (near universal) systems, which could be handled by central legislation in a uniform way, progressed quite rapidly. But the central power remained for long totally insensitive to the particular situations and needs of families, of individuals or of groups. This explains the neglect of the indexation of pensions, or social assistance, or of personal social services (various forms of social work) in general.

To sum up: the totalitarian system has built up some important welfare institutions (social insurance, public health), formally similar to those emerging in Western welfare states. While these institutions, operating on a large scale, have been instrumental in reducing massive poverty and some inequalities, their *mode of operation* has followed the totalitarian logic: their importance has always been secondary to the so-called productive sphere; they have operated in an uncontrolled, undemocratic way; they have remained insensitive to most minorities and individual needs; instead of becoming institutions of public service, they have become agents of political domination.

The present widespread dissatisfaction with the welfare policy of the last decades and the wild search for new solutions have to be seen against this background.

7.2 CURRENT TRENDS IN SOCIAL POLICY

The prevailing trends reflect both the dissatisfaction with the past, the impact of the economic crisis aggravated by heavy foreign debts, and also new political opportunities. The welfare system is affected partly adversely, partly beneficially. The developments which, in the assessment of the author, *adversely* affect the welfare of citizens, are the following:

1. It is widely recognised that the former 'organic' relationship between economy and social policy, stifling both spheres, has to be ended. The withdrawal of the state is a necessary corollary. This implies, among other things, the replacement of direct state intervention with fiscal and monetary measures. One consequence is the decline or bankruptcy of ineffective firms, and the increase of open unemployment. Another outcome, directly following from the elimination of price subsidies, and due also to the endeavours to reduce budget deficits by lowering private consumption, is a two-digit inflation rate. Both trends are redistributing income and opportunities from the poorer to the better-off segments of the population. Almost all these consequences are inevitable. It is worrying, though, that the instruments of counteracting the negative social consequences of unemployment and inflation have not been properly dealt with (at least up to the elections).

2. Market and private solutions are advocated and officially supported not only in the 'economy proper', but also in health, housing, education, social security, social and human services. As a matter of fact, market solutions have started in the sphere of welfare services: resistance has been weaker there than in the case of the managerial

lobbies of the highly subsidised state industries. Marketisation goes together with a shift of former public burdens to the population at large, and to the weaker groups in particular.

3. The withdrawal of the state from its former responsibilities is lowering the standards (which were initially on a relatively low level in most cases) in social insurance, the health services, etc. The appeal for private solutions is thereby increasing, further weakening the support for general schemes.

4. With market or private solutions spreading, the danger of replacing the currently existing universal (or near-universal) and integrative systems with segmented (health, insurance, etc.) systems, with a means-tested, selective subsystem for the 'truly needy', is quite real.

5. On the whole, income inequalities are increasing, entailing the threat of existential insecurity and poverty in case of large segments of the population. The present government as well as most opposition parties see as the only remedy the expansion of selective, discretionary assistance.

The radical political change has also opened up new opportunities in shaping the welfare system. Some of the expected *positive* outcomes are the following:

(a) There are new possibilities of organising pressure groups, groups of self-defence, etc. for promoting in the political arena the interests of the poor, the elderly, the handicapped.

(b) The possibility of pluralisation of the welfare system is appearing. The actors known elsewhere – voluntary agencies, private non-profit organisations, market-oriented agencies, local self-help groups – are all slowly emerging. The Church is regaining its independence and is reviving the traditions of charity. Private foundations are created, promoting various humanitarian concerns. Even within the state sector, there is more scope for new initiatives and innovative practice. No doubt, the 'welfare mix' has flaws which are being slowly recognised in the developed countries. However, after an overcentralised state-organised system the mix is appealing.

(c) With mounting poverty and a more open political field, there is more sensitivity towards individual needs. The legitimacy and necessity of personal social services has been slowly accepted. (Some specialised services, such as, for instance, child counselling agencies (financed by the budget) emerged in the mid-1970s.) Social work acquired official acceptance only in the mid-1980s. Social work centres, operated by the local councils, are expanding relatively rapidly. (It may be worth mentioning that the education and training of professional social workers started only in 1990.)

(d) The importance of local self-government is gradually being recognised and the enactment of the legal basis of this institutional change is under way. Local self-government and its popular control may radically change many former, rigid and bureaucratic institutions.

7.3 THE SYSTEM OF SOCIAL SECURITY

In Hungary, the concept of (work-related and contributory) *social insurance* is widely accepted, that of a *social security* system (integrating social insurance and basic security for all) far less. The system of social insurance has included both flat-rate and earnings-related social benefits in cash related to employment, and some universal benefits also in cash, such as the maternity grant at childbirth. Social assistance in cash has been the responsibility of local government.

The *health system* (similarly to education) has been financed from the budget as a public service.

From January 1990, this system is changing. The logic of the change is to make a clear distinction between benefits and services covered from general taxation (the budget) and from (payroll) contributions of employers and employees. The first provisions will be called 'social policy' benefits, the second ones social insurance benefits.

In the case of social insurance benefits, the 'equivalence principle' (equivalence between contributions and benefits) will be applied more strictly. Of the present schemes, contributory pensions, maternity leave and sick pay should remain within the existing social insurance system. The health service should also become insurance based. The first move is already completed: the parliament adopted a Law in December 1989 according to which the financing of the health service has passed from the state budget to the budget of social insurance. The same is planned for unemployment benefits.

Benefits based on a citizen's right (which are flat rate) have to be moved out of the social insurance system. From April 1990, family allowances and flat-rate maternity grants, child care grants, and so on will be financed directly by the state budget, and will not be considered part of the social security or social insurance system.

Social assistance will remain the responsibility of local government. Assistance will mostly retain its discretionary character, even if certain normative, legally enforceable elements are built into it. (A recent example is the housing assistance. Because of the significant increase in rents and charges from February 1990, 20 to 30 per cent of families will be unable to meet the new costs. Hence the parliament adopted a new form of – partly income-tested, partly discretionary – assistance to help the most needy families, such as families with children, or the aged with a low pension.)

In the view of the present author, the arguments advanced in favour of the above changes are not very reassuring. If access to health services should remain, as declared, universal, then the new arrangement is not making the profile clearer. If the national health insurance principle is followed, then the present financing by employers will soon be questioned. The unemployment insurance scheme without state support is unlikely to be satisfactory. In the case of the family allowance, the budget is less likely to preserve its value than would a self-governing social insurance system. It is uncertain what will happen to the solidaristic elements – for instance, an acceptable minimum pension – currently built into the pension system if the equivalence principle is emphasised.

Because the new arrangements are as yet very fluid, this account will hereafter present the system of social insurance as it operated before January 1990.

7.3.1 Facts About the Social Insurance System

The Hungarian social insurance system was built up on Bismarckian lines between 1890 and 1930. This was gradually changed, especially from 1965 on, from a fully funded to a pay-as-you-go system, with more solidaristic elements built into it. Up to the end of 1989, the social insurance system included:

(a) a pension system, covering about 95 per cent of the elderly over the pensionable age limits (60 for men, 55 for women);
(b) a sickness benefits scheme similar to that of most countries;
(c) a relatively generous package related to maternity (twenty weeks paid leave after delivery; right to a child care allowance about 70

per cent of the former wage until the child is 2 years old, plus one year's flat-vote grant, both payable also to the father; long periods of paid leave if the child is sick, etc.). Some of these benefits – a single payment on delivery, for instance – are not related to employment, but are offered as a citizen's right;
(d) family allowances now from the first child, with higher than average sums for handicapped children, for families with more than three children, and for single parents;
(e) other miscellaneous benefits (e.g. in the case of funerals, etc.);

The mostly work-related provisions of social insurance have been complemented by some forms of social assistance. From January 1988, an unemployment benefit scheme financed by the state has been introduced. A public health service and many other services (child care institutions, etc.) completed the system.

The statistical trends present a relatively favourable picture as shown by some examples: the ratio of social security and health expenditures to the GDP went up from under 10 per cent in 1970 to 14 per cent in 1980, and to 16 per cent both in 1985 and 1987. The West European average – according to ILO data – was around 14 per cent in 1970 and 21 per cent in 1980. The distance between Hungary and Western Europe has somewhat increased, but there has been no decrease in expenditure in Hungary even in the last, economically declining years.

The coverage of social insurance has increased rapidly. The number of pensioners was 534 000 in 1950, 810 000 in 1960, 1 452 000 in 1970, and 2 337 000 in 1988. About 95 per cent of those over the pensionable age limit have a pension. The number of children getting family allowances was 1 094 000 in 1950, 1 422 000 in 1960, 1 597 000 in 1970, and 2 320 000 in 1987. From April 1990 the access to family allowance will be a citizen's right.

The replacement rate (the ratio of average pensions to average wages) has gone up from 22 per cent in 1950 to over 55 per cent in 1988. The average amount of the family allowance per child is currently about 12 to 15 per cent of the average wage, as compared to 3 or 5 per cent before the mid-1960s.

The total pensions amount currently to 9 per cent of the GDP – instead of 2 or 5 per cent some decades ago.

The number of mothers on child care grants, collected during prolonged maternity leave, introduced in 1967 and improved since then, is yearly over 200 000, which means that between 4 and 5 per cent of the total labour force are constantly on subsidised child care leave (see *Hungarian Statistical Yearbooks*).

The main flaws of the system are the following:

1. Relatively low levels in the case of most benefits. This is true despite comparatively high replacement rates. The reason is the relatively very low level of wages.
2. The absence of proper indexation. Despite the high rate of inflation (between 10 and 20 per cent) in the last three years, compensations have remained belated, non-automatic and inadequate. True, the real value of very low pensions has been almost maintained. But the loss of the other beneficiaries is very significant.
3. The absence of a genuine 'safety net' because of the absence of some universal schemes and the defects of the assistance schemes.
4. The absence of self-government within the system.
5. From the perspective of the state, the problem is the threat of a serious disequilibrium of the system in the near future. (The reasons are similar to those in many countries: aging, the slow maturation of the system, etc.).
6. From the perspective of the employers, the problem is the high rate of contribution. (From 1987 on, the contribution paid by the employers amounts to 43 per cent of the wage fund, and that paid by the employees to 10 per cent of the gross wage.)

7.3.2 The Controversial Issues

There are many different proposals for reforms, prepared mainly by various government agencies, and sometimes by the new parties. Most of them concentrate on the organisational issues of the whole system, and on the pension system, the largest item within social insurance.

In the case of the pension system, one of the major questions is the *number of the necessary tiers*. The current system consists of one tier – a compulsory, earnings related scheme. It can be complemented by optional, individually contracted private schemes. There are proposals for a two- or three-tier system. The first tier would consist of a universal, flat-rate basic pension financed by taxation. The second tier would cover the earnings-related benefits financed by compulsory contributions. The third tier would be built up of voluntary insurance schemes, contracted individually or, in most plans, in a corporative way (pension schemes organised by firms or professions).

Most political actors accept (at least on paper) the first tier. Unfortunately, there is no strong constituency supporting this scheme. (Alongside the 2.4 million pensioners, the number of those who are unprovided for above the pensionable age limit is around 200 000, and this is a very weak and scattered group.) Also, partly because of the weak support, the lack of funds seems to justify the indefinite postponement of a universal pension scheme.

The relationship between the second (compulsory) and the third (optional, private) tier is more controversial. Most vocal groups argue for low or very low compulsory coverage. By contrast, private pension schemes should have a major role. The debate is as yet very lopsided. Those in favour of private schemes emphasise only their advantages, including freedom of choice, lower compulsory contribution of employers, a complete match between contributions and benefits, and so on. The international experiences are not analysed, nor the problems of the transition from the current system to a new one, nor again the problems of a 'dual welfare state' emerging under these conditions. If no resistance is built up after the elections, the recent changes may be pushed to their logical conclusion, which is the dismantling of the existing near-universal system.

Another debated question is, *who will govern social insurance*? With the political changes of the last years, the Directorate of Social Insurance has become an autonomous and, in principle, *self-governing* body from 1 January 1989. However, the self-government has not been enacted – because of the hidden resistance of the former power groups.

There are several open questions relating to *the financing of social insurance*. It is generally agreed that social insurance needs reserve funds alongside a pay-as-you-go system. Some vocal groups working within the social security system, together with the major parties, advocate full funding and require the state to build up the funds. The international experiences with funding are not taken into account in the funding proposals. Another controversial issue is the contribution rate. The rate paid by the employers is excessively high (43 per cent of the wage fund). With the current burdens of the social insurance system, this rate can hardly be lowered. Change is warranted, though, not only because of the understandable resistance of the employers, but also because this arrangement almost prohibits the creation of new jobs in the – as yet very weak – small private firms.

In the case of pensions, there are contrasting views in connection with the *pensionable age limit* (which is very low), the *ceiling* on salaries covered (there was no ceiling up to December 1989. The parliament accepted one which is about five times the average pension), and the *taxation* of pensions (at present untaxed).

There is no due attention paid to some basic issues. The problems of adequacy versus equity, or of solidarity versus the equivalence principle are not treated either in professional or in public debates. The huge problems connected with changing lifestyles and family patterns have not yet been faced. The difficulties of indexation, including the valorisation of past earnings, are almost ignored. The list of gaps could be lengthened.

To sum up: it seems that those issues which are connected with the immediate interests of those in favour of private (occupational or other) insurance occupy the forefront. The fate of the traditional scheme, or of universal schemes in general, is rather uncertain.

7.4 THE CASE OF THE HEALTH SYSTEM

7.4.1 The State of the Health System

Hungary has gradually transformed the pre-war insurance-based and fragmented health system into a public health system – a common pattern in all East European countries. Universal access to health was adopted in 1974. As usual, the statistics portraying the development of the health system are impressive (Table 7.1).

Despite quantitative growth, the health system is in crisis. Patients, doctors and health personnel in general are all frustrated. The reasons for and the signs of this crisis are manifold. The health system has been chronically underfinanced. Investments in the health system were almost absent for about three decades. During the whole period since 1945, between 3 to 4 per cent of the GDP have been allocated to run the health system. This ratio is one of the lowest in Europe. (Only Rumania and the Soviet Union have similar or lower rates.)

The medical profession and the health service in general were, like all other spheres in the domain of welfare, dominated by political, and politically dominated economic interests. Medical personnel have continually had a disciplinary function in blatant clash with medical interests. The most important case in point is that of sick pay. Sick pay has always been seen as a financial loss for the state, which is – at least partly – caused by the poor discipline of workers,

Table 7.1 Some indicators of the health system

	1970	*1980*	*1987*
Number of physicians	23 524	30 842	35 443
Per 10 000 inhabitants	22.7	28.8	33.4
Of which:			
in Budapest	46.0	55.3	59.1
in the countryside	17.1	22.5	27.1
Number of hospital beds per 10 000 inhabitants	82.9	89.2	98.6
Of which:			
in Budapest	137.7	141.9	145.4
in the countryside	69.7	76.6	87.0

Source: *Hungarian Statistical Yearbooks.*

and by lax medical practices. The consequences of this view have been – alternately – the following: the evaluation of general practitioners on the basis of the length of paid sick leave they accorded to patients; a limitation on the average number of days of sick leave a doctor could accord to his/her patients; the parallel organisation of primary care: it was assumed that company doctors could better control the patients. Therefore, the right to accord sick pay was delegated in the mid-1980s from the area general practitioner to the company doctor (if there was any). This seriously curtailed the rights and responsibilities of those working in primary health care.

The consequences of scarce resources were numerous from poor hospital care to the low pay of the staff, including doctors. The personnel have been seriously underpaid even in relation to the generally low pay level. Partly because of scarce resources, and partly for more general social reasons, access to health care has remained rather unequal, both regionally and socially. These inequalities have persisted despite the explicit pledge in the constitution 'to give the best possible medical care to all'. They are widely reflected in the health status of lower social strata and in that of the inhabitants of less developed regions.

The moral state of the personnel has become critical. Low pay has entailed dire consequences. Doctors and nurses (especially specialists and surgeons) are heavily tipped by the patients. These payments, called 'money of gratefulness', have many functions. Originally, they were meant partly to assure extra good care, and also to 'make good' the state's mistake in not paying the doctors adequately. (In all opinion research surveys asking about 'the just pay one should get', doctors always came out at the top of the list. Their low pay was consequently seen as a disgrace.) In the last ten years or so, this payment has become a sort of compulsion for patients, even though it has remained non-legal, if not outright illegal. The final blow fell on morals in 1989, when the Ministry of Finance made these tips taxable.

Low pay is distorting the whole structure of the health service: in posts where no tips can be expected, there is a scarcity of labour (from anaesthesiologists to the cleaning staff).

The health status of the population is deteriorating either absolutely or relatively (as compared to more developed countries). Infant mortality decreased for instance between 1960 and 1987 from 47.6 per thousand to 17.4 per thousand – but it is still one of the highest in Europe, and Hungary has shifted down in the rank order of countries. (In 1987, this ratio was worse only in Yugoslavia, Rumania and the USSR.) The mortality rate (13.4) is the worst in Europe, and it is especially high and increasing in the relatively young age groups. Life expectancy at birth is the lowest in Europe in the case of men, and in the case of women only Rumania has a lower figure. Hungary is leading in Europe in cases of heart and artery diseases, fatal accidents and suicides.

Despite high morbidity rates and the frequency of physical handicaps, rehabilitative medicine is on a very low level; hence a relatively high rate of retirement for health reasons, which, again, is a factor increasing the costs.

The infrastructure of the system, especially hospital buildings, is in a desolate state, the technical level (instruments, appliances, etc.) of medicine is low and obsolete.

The system is very inefficiently organised. Despite the relatively high number of physicians, the time spent on patients is excessively short: around two minutes in the case of general practitioners, and seven minutes in outpatient clinics. Simultaneously, the number of visits to doctors is inordinately high. At outpatient clinics alone, there were 77 million visits in 1987, i.e. eight per inhabitant. The number of hospital patients was 2.2 million in the same year (see *Hungarian Statistical Yearbooks*).

These indicators imply that general practice is very inadequate. It does not assure any definitive care, and preventive medicine is practically unknown there (or elsewhere). The most expensive solution, hospital care, is too extensively used. Also, because of the absence of nursing homes and the shortage of places in 'social homes', costly hospital beds are used for chronic diseases.

No doubt, the dire health status of the population cannot be blamed solely on the health system. Rapid and drastic historical changes, high mobility rates entailing adjustment problems, all sorts of material and emotional losses together with endemic fear of the political powers have contributed to an exceptionally high rate of neurotic and psychic diseases and to self-destructive tendencies, from excessive alcoholism to suicide. One of the most commonly invoked reasons is overwork in general, connected to low pay and the necessity of working extra hours in the first, the second, or the household economy. (Extra work is a must if one wants to make ends meet, and vital if one wants to cover needs like acceptable housing.) According to statistics, Hungarians have the longest working hours in Europe. Obsolete, unhealthy or dangerous working conditions constitute another reason, leading to a high rate of industrial accidents. Pollution of all sorts is also an important cause of morbidity and probably also of mortality.

Nevertheless, besides social and historical reasons, the health system is also accountable for the almost tragic health conditions of the country. The necessity of its reform is urgent.

7.4.2 Proposals for Reform

Several reform proposals or scenarios have been worked out in the last few years. Some of their components have already been adopted. The motivations behind the proposals are mixed. While each and every reform plan wants, no doubt, to improve the health service in general, plans may also serve other interests. The three strongest and most visible interests are that of the state budget to save money and/or raise more funds; that of the medical profession to improve its financial and social standing; and that of the best-off groups within society, which would like to get better medical care in the short run even if they have to pay for it. The not very solvent majority is as yet silent.

Of the proposals of general interest, serving the improvement of the whole service, the most important is the *change of the structure of medical care*. The idea of structural change implies the following elements: the radical improvement of preventive medicine, by aiming at the earliest possible detection of sickness and assuring that all detected medical conditions are adequately taken care of. This presupposes the significant improvement of general care. The objective conditions (diagnostic facilities, etc.) and the professional responsibilities of primary health care, and of the general practitioner working there, should be considerably improved. It is suggested that the idea of the 'family doctor', closely following the patient's medical needs and aiming at definitive treatment in all possible cases, be (re)introduced. There are proposals for, and some experiments with, community health centres, by means of which primary care could be rapidly ameliorated. If primary health care were improved, then the present outpatient clinics could change their role. Instead of complementing primary care, they could fulfil the role of hospitals, reducing thereby the burden of the present hospitals (for example, in post-operational care). Also, if the responsibility of primary health care were increased, then the profile of company health care could change. The current parallelism between company doctors and general practitioners could be abolished, and company doctors could focus more on the particular health risks of the work place and the workers.

The general interest may also be served by some other, often mentioned reform proposals. One of them is the rapid development of community social care to free the health system from this duty, and also in order to give more adequate care to clients. Another reform widely approved of concerns the weakening of the present, almost feudal, hierarchy within the medical profession, and the strengthening of the participation and control of the population.

The restructuring of the health service from a top-heavy to a more balanced one would diminish the need for hospital care, the most costly form of care. However, this is not necessarily a money-saving method. (More conscientious screening could multiply the number of cases to be treated, for instance.) Therefore the question of resources and methods of financing are crucial. Also, the reorganisation of the service is a major issue, especially because of the current power relations within the profession, and of those between the profession and the laity.

The various organisational reform proposals try to solve at least part of these problems. The major models proposed are the following:

(a) An insurance model financed predominantly by the population. Insurance would be compulsory for everybody, paid by the insured person from an income which should be increased by the amount of payable premium. The payment of the contribution of destitute people should probably fall to the state. This model is similar to that of West Germany, but introduced in a much poorer country. Therefore, it is proposed to limit the care, paid for by compulsory insurance, to a 'minimum level'. Complementary private schemes are assumed to play a major role in this system.

The lobby in favour of private insurance being relatively strong, some preparations have already been made to encourage this model. One of the large insurance companies is already cooperating with a West German company to form insurance agents and experts, and probably to build up a Hungarian company. Also, private medical practice is strongly encouraged by the market lobby, largely represented in the Ministry of Social Affairs and Health, too. (It is interesting to note that the efforts from above to widen private practice were not matched by equal enthusiasm among the doctors. Apparently, the doctors still have 'the best interest of the client' at heart.)

(b) An insurance model financed exclusively or predominantly by the companies. There are two variants of this model:
(b1) The model suggested by the ministry proposes financing the whole health service from the contribution paid by the employers. This solution would differ from the current public health service model only in its management. The service would not be financed and run directly by the state but by the national social insurance organisation (the Directorate of Social Insurance), out of a separately managed 'health fund'.

The proponents of this model emphasise its following advantages: the insurance company would control outlays more closely; it would enforce cost-effective methods; the health fund would be better adjusted to inflation than if handled by the budget; access to health care as a citizen's right would be better ensured than in the first, market-based model.

At present, this seems to be the winning scenario. The changes in financing social insurance adopted by the parliament in December 1989 ('the switch' in the financing of family allowances and of the health fund, the first assigned to the budget, the second to the Directorate of Social Insurance) already pave the way to it. This model, like model (a), leaves a large place to private, market-type insurance.

(b2) Some of the opposition parties propose a company-based insurance system, with separate, company-managed health funds. This model has also supporters within the state administration; therefore experiments are already going on in some companies. This is clearly a market-type model. The same model is proposed on a regional basis, in the form of voluntary local health funds.

(c) The health care system, financed, managed and run by local self-governments, figures both among the models proposed by the government and by some parties in the opposition. This model follows by and large the Swedish or Finnish solutions, except that local taxes play a smaller role in Hungary than in the Scandinavian countries. Hence the financing has to be based only partly on local resources, and partly on the budget. The responsibility for hospitals is a matter of decision and bargaining in this case. It is likely that there will be area hospitals under local responsibility, and more specialised central hospitals.

This model seems to be very popular with large segments of the population, and also with local governments. Accordingly, there are already some local initiatives to prove the feasibility of this type of organisation.

(d) Finally, there is also the possibility of continuing the present, public service model. This outcome seems to be very unlikely because most powerful groups have already opted for one of the insurance models, and popular support will probably turn to the increased responsibility of local self-government.

It is a common feature of all the proposals that they spell out very clearly all the advantages of the preferred solution, but omit to draw attention to their possibly mitigating consequences. To wit: in the case of models (a) and (b), the cost-saving possibilities are heavily underlined, because it is assumed that insurance companies will be strict with tariffs and will introduce cost-saving methods of organisation, etc. In the case of method (a), accent is on the 'visibility of financing', implying that those who pay the fees will be willing and able to influence service delivery. It is also emphasised that if contributions are paid directly by the users, the 'tipping' of personnel will be automatically abolished. In all these cases, the enhanced opportunity of free choice of doctors and hospitals, and the possibly benign impact of competition between care givers is often underscored. In the case of model (c), the enhanced possibility of popular participation and control and the closer ties between the health service and the population are pointed out as attractive features. Since this model seems to be able to solve the major problems of the existing overcentralised system, without creating apparent new ones, hardly anybody sees any advantage in continuing the present system (except perhaps the most dogmatic adherents of the totalitarian system).

As for the drawbacks, no mention is made of the possible ill-effects of a market-based and profit-oriented health system. It is not even alluded to that a dual health service may be the direct consequence of the reduced responsibility of the state and the increased role of the market. It is never hinted at that these dangers can be avoided or seriously reduced either by the local self-government model, or by (a more democratically organised) public service model. All insurance-based models are presented as solving the problem of the low pay of doctors – which they obviously cannot do without additional resources. Most importantly, the well-known limitations of health insurance systems are not disclosed.

It is, for instance, often discussed abroad that insurance schemes usually do not cover 'bad risks', geriatric patients, mental patients, mentally or physically handicapped people and, sometimes, lasting and incurable diseases. The groups involved, which are usually weak and not vocal, have to fall back on an impoverished public service, or they might stay unprovided for. A similar fate threatens those who are unable to pay the insurance fees or can buy only a cheap or partial insurance.

A British analyst questions the economic arguments in these terms:

> As the dominant provider of health care and major employer of medical staff and purchaser of drugs, governments can be held accountable for rising medical costs and have an incentive to control them. The containment of medical prices and dubiously effective and expensive treatments have been more successful in Britain than in almost any other country. Insurance schemes on a fee for service basis are, by contrast, very ineffective in constraining costs. The consumer is not faced with the true price, he merely passes the bill on to the insurance company . . . The demand for medical care is unusual. It is not made by the consumer but by the suppliers, the doctors, who have a monopoly of knowledge and diagnose our need for care. Insurance companies find it very difficult to argue with the diagnosis. Escalating medical fees and insurance premiums have been the result in most countries that

finance their health schemes this way (Abel-Smith, 1976). The administrative costs in private insurance schemes are high because of the extra cost of handling claims (Glennerster, 1985, p. 142).

An additional problem arises because in a *democratic* state the citizens may find some means of controlling the standards and priorities of the public health system (especially if local self-governments have a major responsibility), but they have much less voice and less possibility of participation and control in the case of insurance schemes.

To sum up: the reform of the health system is urgently necessary. The proposed reform scenarios all have advantages. From the perspective of a more equitable and more democratic system, some seem to be more suitable than others. However, these models are not very likely to win, because the newly acquired political freedom is better used by strong and vocal groups, interested in the advantages of market solutions. However, the future after the elections is hard to predict.

7.5 THE CASE OF HOUSING

Of all the unsolved social problems of Hungary, housing seems to be both the most serious and the most intractable. It is affected in a combined way by all the ills which have – singly or in pairs – affected the coverage of other major needs. It has been simultaneously plagued by excessively high prices and scarcity; by the neglect of individual needs and the residual character of welfare provisions in general; by bureaucratic central regulations and favouritism; by ineffective management and state monopolies.

From 1945 to 1949, while the country was still a mixed economy, efforts were concentrated on the – at least partial – reconstruction of a severely damaged housing stock. In 1950, about one-third of all flats were expropriated by the state with some ideological excuses and some underlying motives. The main ideological argument was to 'rid people of the exploitation of the landlords', and to assure the better maintenance of the housing stock by the 'collective owner'. In fact nationalisation allowed the state to 'redistribute' housing scarcity by subdividing existing larger flats, or just imposing cohabitation on the former owners or tenants. It also enabled the state to lower both wages and rents: by claiming that the state would provide cheap housing for all, wages did not have to cover the real costs of housing.

As for the repair and maintenance of the housing stock, the state proved to be the worst possible master. The very obsolete and still partly damaged stock of state-owned, rented flats was hardly touched in the following decades, despite an important and continued increase in rents from the 1970s on; hence the desolate state of the majority of state-owned houses even in 1990. A large number of flats within these houses have been modernised (for instance, by adding a bathroom or installing central heating) – more often than not at the expense of the tenant.

The construction of new flats was neglected not only in the early 1950s (when it was at its lowest), but up to the 1960s. From then on, the improvement of housing conditions has become a strongly felt popular need. And due to the impact of the revolution of 1956, the state had to answer this need. The fifteen-year plan starting in 1960 projected the construction of 1 million flats, 60 per cent of them with state funding. This number of new flats was supposed to end the housing scarcity, at least quantitatively. The plan was numerically fulfilled, albeit the participation of the state was much lower than planned. (Thirty-six instead of 60 per cent of the flats were constructed by the state.) However, the shortage of flats did not end. Geographic mobility, the separation of generations and the multiplication of small families all played a part in shaping new needs, besides growing expectations. But resources have slowly diminished. The number of new flats per thousand inhabitants declined after 1980, while there are still hundreds of thousands of families queueing up for a relatively cheap (albeit not free) state-owned flat. (The waiting period is still well over five years (Table 7.2).)

State responsibility for the coverage of housing needs was still accorded lip service in the 1970s, but the objective situation had already changed: the majority of the flats were constructed by the future owners and inhabitants. This trend has continued ever since. In recent years, the state has constructed only about one-tenth of the new flats.

From the early 1980s, the state explicitly gave up its formerly acknowledged obligations and responsibilities in housing – without giving adequate support to private home builders or buyers, and without increasing wages and salaries so as to cover the real costs of housing. The production and trade of construction materials as well as the building industry itself have remained a state monopoly, with escalating prices, often poor quality, and bottlenecks in the supply.

Table 7.2 The waiting period for state-owned flats

	Years		*Years*
1951–55	3.3	1976–80	8.5
1956–60	5.7	1981–85	6.9
1961–65	5.6	1986	6.5
1966–70	6.4	1987	5.4
1971–75	8.4		

Source: *Hungarian Statistical Yearbooks*.

Table 7.3 Major characteristics of the housing conditions

Around	*1960*	*1970*	*1980*	*1988*
Number of lived-in flats, in 1000	2710	3034	3416	3923
Percentage of flats with				
— electricity	74.6	91.7	98.0	99
— running water	22.7	36.1	65.0	78.1
Inhabitants per				
100 flats	343	327	303	270
100 rooms	236	199	151	122

Source: *Hungarian Statistical Yearbooks*.

In the last ten years, the state has gradually passed over to the builders practically all the costs of public amenities (roads, electricity, water supply, and so on). As a counterpart, the conditions for getting cheap state loans have been somewhat eased, especially in favour of families with several children. Also, the total discrimination against one-family homes has been lifted. However, the loans have never covered the majority of costs.

Therefore, the spectacular improvement in housing conditions – as is shown in Table 7.3 – is almost a miracle. This evolution was made possible only by the emergence of a huge 'second economy' in housing – operating with different means in the towns and villages. In the villages, house building was almost always a family affair, without a building market and private builders. The former traditions of reciprocated labour have survived. Hence, most one-family houses have been built with the help of family, friends and colleagues – but at the price of almost inhuman physical and mental efforts. This form of self-help could not prevail in towns, with multiflat tenement houses. The mobile and flexible private entrepreuner have also disappeared, and private rented housing was prohibited anyway. Only a heavy, slow and expensive state industry has remained at the disposal of the builders, buyers or improvers.

Housing conditions in the towns could be improved in one of the following ways: by modernising the flat, partly at one's own expense; by exchanging one's flat on a semi-legal private market, with excessive costs; by having an apartment house built, in which the flats are owned by individual families; by buying a home either on the private market, or from the state (the prices being by now similar); or by applying for a rented, state-owned flat.

This last opportunity, the access to a state-owned flat, was, until the mid-1970s, biased in favour of those close to the top. Since then, the newcomers to the élite have found other ways of obtaining good housing – for instance, by using their 'political capital' to obtain at least as much 'real capital' as necessary for exclusive residences. Simultaneously, the distribution of 'social' housing has become more 'socially minded', taking into account the financial conditions of the family, the number of children, and suchlike. However, the 'social' housing stock has meanwhile shrunk.

The gap between wages/salaries and the prices of new flats (whether built or bought) has become enormous. (In 1988, the cost of the construction of a small private flat amounted to about 200 months of average wage, out of which only the smaller part could be covered by loans. The purchase price of such a flat was about three times as much, with no increase in the loan.) This explains the emergence of the above mentioned 'second economy'.

A new and grave social problem became visible late in 1989, and this is the emergence of homelessness. No doubt, this issue was never faced by those in power: they ignored it together with all facets of poverty and destitution. However, as long as police measures were easily used against 'vagrants' (for instance, by banning them from towns in general or from public places in particular), and as long as labour scarcity pushed firms to employ everybody and to offer them, if needed, a bed in the workers' dormitory, outright homelessness did not become painfully visible. At the end of 1989, the police became more restrained, and ceased to employ the former methods. More importantly, many – especially unskilled, single – workers lost their jobs and their shelter together. It was only then, after major conflicts between the homeless, the general public and the police that some public shelters have been opened. It is to be expected that with increased unemployment, criminality and poverty, the number of the homeless will increase, while the probability of finding an adequate solution for them is almost nil.

To sum up: until the late 1980s, the 'social' element in housing policy consisted of low rents, cheap loans, and a diminishing stock of housing constructed by the state. The problem of the homeless was ignored, and only very inadequate solutions were found to ease the housing misery of the poor, gypsies among them. The housing crisis is by now so deep that major steps should be taken.

Unfortunately, no political or social force has been able as yet to propose a viable solution to the crisis, least of all the present government. On the contrary: the current budgetary crisis is propelling the government towards measures which could benefit the budget at least in the short run. In accordance with the neo-liberal mood in other spheres, the current solution advocated by almost everyone is to rely more heavily on market forces in the case of housing, too. Thus, reprivatisation of the housing stock is on the agenda. (As a matter of fact, privatisation has been on the agenda for several years, but up to now it has meant that the best flats occupied by members of the élite have been sold to them at a very low price. Apparently the new prices will be much higher.) The other market element is the increase in rents. The last increase took place in February 1990 – rendering necessary a new housing assistance scheme for about one third of those living in rented flats. (Incidentally, this was the first instance when the parliament introduced an assistance scheme tied to the official poverty line.) A third measure (introduced at the same time) was a new tax levied on the cheap loans to cut the state's losses caused by the inflation. Albeit the parliament was manipulated into accepting the new tax, it is considered an unlawful breach of contract by many. It is likely that this will be the first case to be dealt with by the newly formed Supreme Court.

The new measures do not get to the root of the dismal housing conditions, neither have state monopolies in the housing industry or in the management of rented housing been touched. The interests of the citizens – whether owners, tenants or homeless – are considered secondary to those of the budget. The increasing reliance upon the market will probably solve the housing problems of the better-off, while for the majority the prospects of acquiring a first home, to improve their housing conditions, or – in many cases – to maintain themselves on the present level, are continuously worsening.

REFERENCES

ABEL-SMITH, B. (1976) *Value for Money in Health Services* (London: Heinemann).

Documents of the Ministry of Social Affairs and Health, and the Directorate of Social Insurance with proposals for the reform of the pension system, and of the system of social insurance. (Documents prepared in 1988 and 1989.)

ERNST, G. (1983) *A lakásigények hosszútávú alakulása, 1981–2000* (Long-term Housing Demands, 1981–2000) (Budapest: Építésgazdasági és Szervezési Intézet).

FERGE, ZS. (1988) 'The Trends and Functions of Social Policy in Hungary', in Jallade, J-P., *The Crisis of Distribution in European Welfare States*.

GLENNERSTER, H. (1985) *Paying for Welfare* (Oxford: Basil Blackwell).

GYŐRI, P. (1987) 'Lakásrendszerünk kialakulása, buktatókkal' (The Painful Emergence of the Present System of Housing), in Ferge, Zs. and Várnai, Gy. (eds) *Szociálpolitika ma és holnap* (Social Policy Today and Tomorrow) (Budapest: Kosuth Könyvkiadó).

HEGEDŰS, J. and Tosics, I. (1982) 'Lakásosztályok és lakáspolitika. A Budapesti lakáspiac irányításának változásai az elmúlt három évtizedben.' (Housing Classes and Housing Policy. Changes in the Management of the Housing Market in Budapest in the Last Three Decades), *Mozgó Világ*, nos 9, 10.

HUNGARIAN STATISTICAL YEARBOOK (several years) (Budapest).

INTERNATIONAL LABOUR OFFICE. *The Cost of Social Security* (Geneva).

JALLADE, J.-P. (1988) *The Crisis of Distribution in European Welfare States* (Stoke-on-Trent: Trentham Books).

LOSONCZI, A. (1989) *Ártó-védő társadalom* (Society – How It Harms, How It Protects) (Budapest: Közgazdasági és Jogi Könyvkiadó).

OECD (1987) *Financing and Delivering Health Care* (A Comparative Analysis of OECD Countries) (Paris).

OECD (1988), *Reforming Public Pensions* (Paris).

Programmes of the new Hungarian parties.

SZALAI, J. (1986) *Az egészségügy betegségei* (The Sick Health System) (Budapest: Közgazdasági és Jogi Könyvkiadó).

SZELÉNYI, I. (1983) *Urban Inequalities under State Socialism* (Oxford: Oxford University Press).

SZOCIÁLIS ÉS EGÉSZSÉGÜGYI MINISZTÉRIUM, Egészségügyi Reformtitkárság (1986), *Elgondolások az egészségügy reformjáról* (Ministry of Social Affairs and Health: Proposals for the Reform of the Health Service).

8 Economic Reform and New Employment Problems in Hungary

János Timár

8.1 ON THE ROAD TO STRENGTHENING PLURALIST DEMOCRACY AND BUILDING UP A SOCIAL MARKET ECONOMY

The Hungarian reform process[1] which has been going on for many decades overcame the impasse by the end of the 1980s. The last few years have already seen the beginning of a new period which, on the one hand, comprises the transformation of the monolithic party state into a modern pluralistic democracy, and on the other hand, entails the initial transformation of the central economic management system based on state-monopolistic ownership relations into a market economy, founded instead on mixed ownership, which also includes the growing role of private property.

The seal of legitimacy was placed on the change of the political system by the parliamentary elections of March 1990. The earlier ruling party, the Hungarian Socialist Workers' Party (HSWP), could not attain the minimum votes necessary to win any representation (4 per cent) – in spite of the personal and organisational changes implemented. The reform party of social-democratic hue, seceding from the HSWP under the name of the Hungarian Socialist Party, still carries the burden of the past and – in spite of its outstanding role in the peaceful transition – could only win fourth place and will thus be in opposition. The power of government will be wielded by a coalition representing rather conservative and Christian-democratic ideas with some national current underlying it.

The strengthening of parliamentary democracy and the development of its institutional system still demand further, persistent work. A much greater and time-consuming task will be to transform the economic system and build up a market economy, and trigger an upswing.

Reform of the Hungarian economy had already started, as a matter of fact, in the late 1950s, with the abolition of 'compulsory delivery' of agricultural products in 1957. In 1968, the planned command economy was formally abolished – and this has remained unique in East European countries – and an attempt was made to manage the state sector with market methods.

In the 1980s, a number of new government measures followed one another, legalising the private sector and the classic forms of enterprise in a market economy (joint stock company, limited liability company, etc.), transforming the entire banking system and restoring the system of commercial banks. In addition, a value-added-type tax was introduced, together with an up-to-date system of personal income tax. The road was opened for the foundation of private capitalist companies, foreign investments were granted advantageous conditions and guarantees, and foreign trade activities were liberalised.

However, the accomplishment of a much bigger and more complex task than the preceding ones has just begun: the transformation of ownership (property) relations, beginning with the working out of a new, genuine system of ownership of the big state enterprises and farming cooperatives. A similarly difficult, parallel task is to modernise the economic structure, the management of enterprises and their technical equipment.

All these experiences prove that a political regime can be overthrown in a few days by an uprising of the dissatisfied population and this can even be legalised by democratic voting as in some other East-European countries but the change of an economic system is a complex task needing a long time to complete. This is why Hungary – despite all her present difficulties – is in a more advantageous situation, because modernisation of the economy which is vital in the building of a market economy has been going on for some time, and preparations for boosting the economy are on course. This is proven not only by the visits and comments of Western political leaders, but also by imminent large investments by multinational companies in Hungary.[2]

8.2 SITUATION OF THE HUNGARIAN ECONOMY AND LABOUR MARKET EQUILIBRIUM

The results achieved in abolishing the command economy, in building up the institutional framework of a market economy and in starting the transformation of ownership relations by no means imply that the country has already overcome its economic difficulties. In fact it is likely that the graver effects of the protracted economic crisis, which also affects the population, are only now coming to the surface, and that the burdens due to delay in carrying out tasks in the past and to measures which cause conflicts are now oppressing people. The crisis can be directly traced back to the time when the current regime decided to ward off the grave international economic impact of the oil price explosion of the 1970s by considerably increasing the price subsidies of important products and consumer goods, and the subventions to loss-making state enterprises, while significantly reducing investments and thus making efforts to maintain the earlier growth rate of living standards. Behind these efforts, made with some good intentions, was the impotence of a policy afraid of changes. On the whole, the crisis was rooted in the socio-economic system based on the 'Soviet model'.

To fight the multiplying difficulties, the country raised foreign loans in increasing amounts to put off the necessary deep structural changes that were needed. The accumulated debt of itself increased the economic difficulties of the country during the 1980s. This in turn was aggravated by the significant decline in the solvent demand of other East European countries, above all the Soviet Union, and by the weak competitiveness of Hungarian products on the world market. As a consequence, the upswing of economic growth, which lasted until the mid-1970s, was halted. In the 1980s, the economy practically stagnated and the burden of servicing the country's huge foreign debts increased dramatically. Per capita real wages began to decline, and in 1989 they had already fallen below the level of 1975.

Inflation played a growing role in the decline of the real value of incomes. The annual rise of consumer prices, still only 2.8 per cent in the first half of the 1980s, jumped to 6.3 per cent in the next five-year period, then continued to rise, and reached 20 per cent by the late 1980s.

One of the causes of price increases was the price reform, in the framework of which a great number of consumer goods and services were classified as having 'free prices', that is, the central 'official' setting of prices was abolished for this category. Thus, under the conditions of good shortages, it had become possible for sellers to shift the inflationary burden of the budget deficit and debt service on to the ever widening consumer sphere. In the category of the remaining, centrally fixed or limited prices, however, it was the reduction of price subsidies, that is, the official raising of prices, that also increased the price level. The reduction of price subsidies has been accelerated with the expansion of the economic reform. With the ongoing transition to a market economy, price subsidies will be more and more limited.

In consequence of this process, the average price level of consumer goods and services increased by 55 per cent on average in the 1970s, and by about 100 per cent in the 1980s. Price rises were greatest for clothing and services, as well as for household heating and energy – and this was mainly caused by the reduction of state subsidies.[3]

In spite of the slowing and then stagnating of economic growth, the excess demand for labour has persisted right up to recent times and has in turn strengthened inflationary pressures. This is the case because the necessary requirements of efficiency have not yet asserted themselves and the mobilisation of internal labour reserves and the dismissal of superfluous labour have not yet begun. In fact the utilisation rate of the potential labour capacity – although actually diminishing because of demographic causes – has even increased (Table 8.1).

Table 8.1 Utilisation of potential manpower capacities (in thousands)

	1984[4] 1 January	*1989* 1 January	*Difference*
1. Population of working age*	6093	6068	−25
2. Economically active population below and beyond working age	142	119	−23
3. Economically active pensioners	416	406	−10
4. Inactive pensioners of working age	239**	292***	+53
5. Students of working age	395	451	+56
6. Potential manpower capacity (1 + 2 +3 − 4 − 5)	6017	5850	−165
7. Total employment	5620	5509	−111
8. Unemployment	3	16	+13
9. Economically active population, total (7 + 8)	5623	5525	−98
10. Rate of utilisation of potential manpower capacities (%) (9:6)	93.5	94.4	+0.9

* Male 15–59, female 15–54 years. **Handicapped 211.9. ***Handicapped 257.7.
Source: Own computations based on National Balances of the Labour Force for January 1984 and 1989. Published by the Central Statistical Board.

Because of the extensive growth of the economy, its insatiable demand for labour (Gábor, 1979) and the 'soft budget constraint' (Kornai, 1980), the utilisation rate of potential manpower capacity, which at the beginning of 'building socialism' (in 1949) had not even attained 70 per cent, had already risen by the mid-1970s to above 90 per cent and has grown even in recent years; in 1989, it attained an unprecedentedly high level in comparison with market economies: it rose above 95 per cent.

Table 8.1 also indicates changes, started in recent years, in the equilibrium of the labour market. This is palpably shown by the number of registered unemployed. In 1984, this figure had still been at an insignificant level, but then it increased five-fold, even though its ratio (0.3 per cent) is still negligible relative to the natural rate of unemployment in market economies. Another indication behind the statistical data is the significant growth in the number of inactive pensioners of working age compared to 1984. This growth is no longer a consequence of normal retirement or because of disability, but is rather due to the fact that the restrictions affecting budget-subsidised organisations and certain isolated areas of the economy have forced some belt tightening, and employers have thus resorted to early retirement instead of dismissals. Both phenomena are indicative of important changes, and we shall revert to them later, but they have not yet changed the extremely high activity rate of the population.

If this high economic activity rate is examined by sex and age, it may be stated that in Hungary[5] – as in other East European countries – the rates are in some respects similar to, though in others essentially different from, those in West and North European countries.[6] (See Figure 8.1.)

As regards economic activity by sex, there are no significant differences with regard to men either because of geographical regions or social position, but there are large differences in respect of women. In Eastern Europe, the economic activity of women scarcely lags behind that of men and is significantly higher than the average of North and much higher than that of West European countries. At the same time, in Hungary – and in other East European countries, too with the exception of the former GDR – the percentage share of women working part time is insignificant.

In developed market economies, the economic activity rates of men are always near to the demographic maximum. The rate for women, however, has only gradually grown under the combined impact of such factors as the rapid decline in the number of children per family, development of the education and qualifications of women, the massive suppression of small-scale farming, the effect of rising demand on the labour market, and the desire of women to

Figure 8.1 Economic activity rate of the population by sex and age groups in 1980

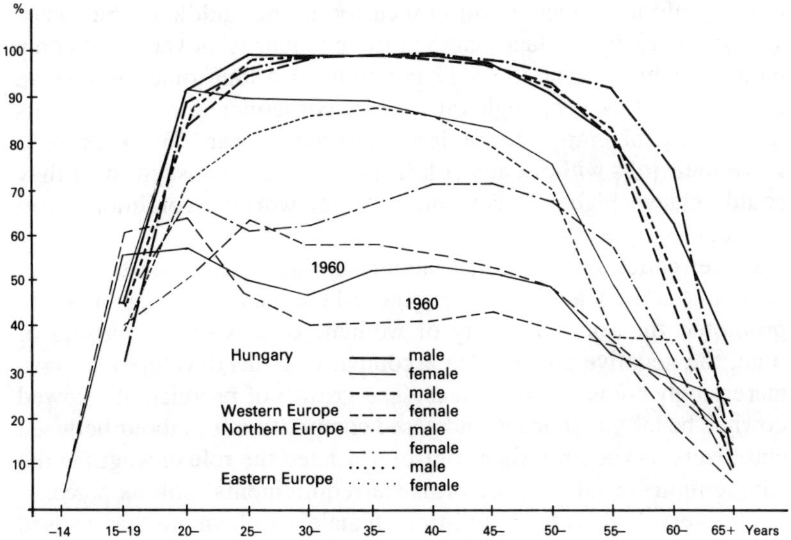

Source: Table 8.1 and ILO (1986).

contribute to the family income. Related to all these, the changes in the social role of women, in the system of values and in the way of life, has also played a role.

The growing economic activity rate of women is a general tendency, observable for many years, and accelerating in the last two or three decades. There is, however, a significant difference in the female activity rates between the Hungarian and Western economies, as indicated by Figure 8.1. According to a widespread belief in Hungary, the main reason for the rate being much higher there than in Western economies is the low level of earnings. But this assumption is only partially true. Undoubtedly the global labour shortage, developed and maintained by extensive economic growth, has made the labour market more attractive for housewives. At the same time, the relatively low living standards, as well as the demonstrative effect of higher Western consumption, has strongly increased interest in raising the income of the family. The impact of these economic factors was strengthened by the ruling ideology which puts stress on female work, as well as by the economic pressure resulting from the recent fall in real earnings.

With a continuing overheated economy and a global labour shortage, economic activity, which was nearing the demographic maximum, profoundly increased job security till the middle of the 1980s. This is proven by the fact that the rate of labour turnover moved on a national average around 15–17 per cent for a long time, and 88–92 per cent of this very high rate was a consequence of movements initiated by the employees, at least until recent years. Workers could leave their jobs without any risk if they were not satisfied, or if they could achieve higher wages and/or better working conditions elsewhere.

Under conditions of global labour shortage the increased rate of economic activity no doubt strengthened the security of existence and promoted the social equality of women. But, with the passing of time, the negative phenomena accompanying this development have increasingly come to the surface. The growth of productivity slowed down. The labour shortage increased competition for labour between employers. As central wage control restricted the role of wages in the competition for labour, performance requirements took its place.

The very high rate of full-time female employment has caused significant social conflicts. The household, as a particular non-commodity-producing unit, is highly labour intensive. The hours worked in the household are on the whole equal to or even more than the total man-hours worked in the whole of the market-oriented economy (Timár, 1988). The greater part of this huge volume of work is done by women, mostly by women who are also employed full time. Although this social division of labour is to a significant extent a legacy of the past, a not insignificant role in it is played by the natural division of labour, which is mainly connected with giving birth and raising children. Nor can it be ignored that while, because of growing productivity and shorter working hours, the weekly, annual and – particularly – the life-time working hours of those employed tend to decline, the work time spent in the household remains stable. This may surprise those who believed that the development of commodity production, the social division of labour and the mechanisation of household work would sooner or later 'liberate' women from the 'slavery of the household'. But household work tends to fill up all available time and its volume remains the same (Hawrylyshyn, 1976; Timár, 1989).

It follows from the foregoing that the high rate of full-time employment of women in Hungary exerts an unfavourable effect on both work performance and household commitments, as well as on the life of families and the upbringing of children.

8.3 MANPOWER UTILISATION AND ITS STRUCTURAL CHANGES

The worsening economic situation in the second half of the 1980s and the reform measures aimed at building up a market economy have led to new phenomena in the structural changes of employment. As a result of the gradual lifting of the legal and economic constraints on the private sector and the legalisation of different types of small private ventures in 1982, the non-agricultural 'complementary business' which had originally worked in the framework of state and cooperative farms merely because of the more favourable conditions there, started to abandon this organisational framework. The growth of state industry and construction became increasingly restricted by the decline in demand of both domestic and external markets. Because of stagnating and then diminishing household incomes, housing construction declined significantly. The competitiveness of Hungarian manufacturing in Western markets did not improve sufficiently, while in East European markets solvent demand diminished. As a result, the deficit in the balance of payments of the country and of the state budget regularly exceeded the estimates.

All this accelerated the changes in the structure of employment by various branches of the economy – as illustrated in Table 8.2.

Table 8.2 Structural employment changes*

	1984	*1989*
Mining and manufacturing	30.8	30.1
Construction	6.8	6.5
Agriculture and related	21.1	18.2
Transport and communications	7.7	7.9
Commerce, hotels and related	11.9	12.4
Water works and supply	1.6	1.6
Services	20.1	23.3
Total	100.0	100.0

* According to the corrected activity rate. See note 4.
Source: See Table 8.1.

The changes in the shape of the Hungarian economy by sectors in the last thirty years gradually brought the structure of employment into line with employment trends in developed industrial countries (see Figure 8.2). This summary, however, may give rise to unjustified satisfaction. A proper structural economic change is indicated by

Figure 8.2 Changes in employment in Hungary and European Economic Community countries

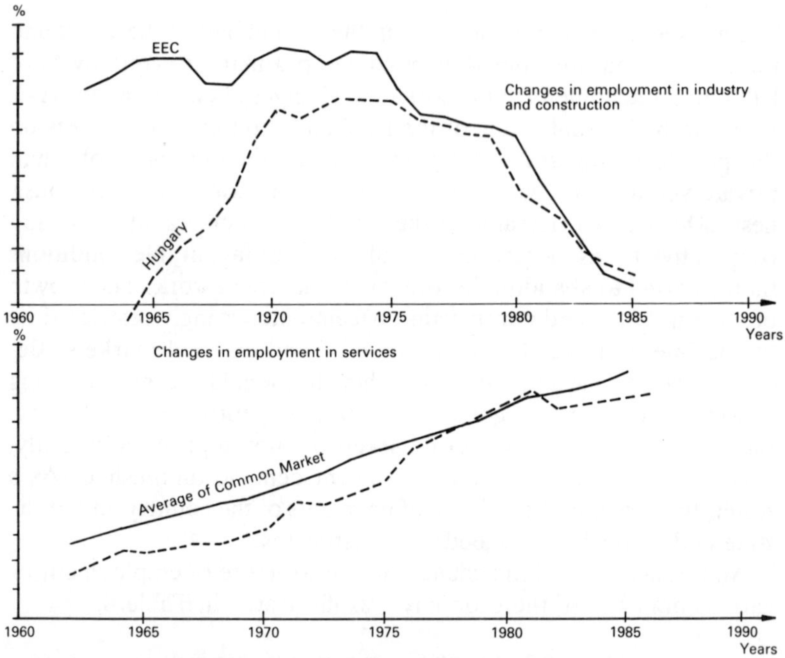

Source: For Hungary *Statistical Yearbooks*, and for EEC countries *Statistiques de la population active, 1965–1985*, OECD.

favourable adjustments in the product pattern (product mix), in export capacity and in foreign economic relations, about which the major employment sectors of the economy do not give information.

It should also be noted that Hungarian statistics, using the statistical system of the CMEA, lists all kinds of repair and fitting activities together with industry and construction, while in market economies these are counted as services. With this correction, the share of those employed in industry and construction would be about 32–33 per cent instead of the 37 per cent to be found in Table 8.2, and the ratio of services would reach 27–28 per cent. If these ratios are compared with the sectors of the European market economies, the Hungarian ratio of industrial employment is somewhat lower than the average, while that of services approximates the South European average, of a development level similar to that of Hungary.

The share of agricultural employment certainly seems to be high, especially if the production of household plots which turn out one-third of Hungarian agricultural output is taken into account. Most of the work performed there is done by the inactive population and the industrial and other non-agricultural employees living in the villages – in their free time (Timár, 1987, p. 110).

The impact of the establishment of a market economy is indicated by changes in the distribution of the economically active population by 'social sectors'. Although the constraints on private, small-scale production and the retail trade had already begun to decrease in the 1960s, essential changes only occurred with the new legal regulations which came into force from 1982. These not only gave the green light to the development of traditional craftsmanship and the retail trade, but also made possible several new forms of small ventures. Although the dislike by government administration, state enterprises and other organisations, remnants of the past, and some government provisions for a short time continued to hinder the development of such ventures, they spread increasingly. In the last two or three years, now that a supporting policy rather than a restrictive one has come to the fore, a growing number of jobs has been created in these organisations as against the stagnating and declining state sector.

These highly important structural changes are hardly shown in the traditional classification system of Hungarian statistics, according to which total employment in 1989 was 183 000 less than in 1982. Within this figure employment in the 'socialist sector', that is, in the state and cooperative enterprises, diminished by 325 000, while employment in the 'private sector' – self-employed, helping family members and employees – increased by 145 000. Thus, according to the official statistics, the share of this private sector increased from 4.1 per cent in 1982 to 7.2 per cent by 1989.

Although this change, pointing to the future, is not negligible, the change in ownership structure, which is of decisive importance for the transformation of the economy, is more noticeable if those small ventures, affiliates, contractual and leased units, as well as small cooperatives and cooperative groups are also listed in the socialist sector which – on the basis of formal ownership criteria – has been statistically classified until 1989 as the socialist sector. But the economic activity of these small ventures is regulated by market relations and not by central rules and instructions relating to state enterprises and big cooperatives.

About 300 000 people, i.e. 6 per cent of all employees, were working in these organisations in 1989. The ratio of this private sector is already great in some industries, about one-third in construction, and in trade and catering more than one-quarter of the employees worked in this sector in 1989. Thus, if the 'official' private sector and small ventures are combined, they represent at least 13 per cent of total non-agricultural employment.

According to these data, which better reflect reality, employment in the 'non-socialist' sector between 1982 and 1989 increased by 440 000, as distinct from the earlier mentioned 145 000. But this is not yet the complete picture. In the second half of the 1980s, the Hungarian government opened the door to foreign investors – both in the form of joint ventures and as autonomous foreign firms. According to information available to date, more than 600 joint and foreign firms were already operating in Hungary at the end of 1989; the value of foreign investment exceeded US$1 billion and is growing very fast. The restrictive regulations, valid for state enterprises, are generally not applicable to these ventures. Thus, it also holds true for these enterprises – as was said about small firms – that they operate according to the rules of a market economy. The number of those employed in such enterprises may be estimated at about 40 000 in early 1990.

Regarding what has been said, the most important phenomenon of structural change in the 1980s, pointing to the future, is the rapid spread of private and joint ventures operating according to the rules of a market economy. In the 1980s, these were the dynamic units of the Hungarian economy, and employment within them exceeded 14 per cent of the economically active population by the end of the decade.

This development tendency corresponds completely with the programme of the last government which led the country till the elections in March and April 1990. Accordingly, the key problem to modernising the Hungarian economy is to bring about a modern market economy by changing ownership relations. Parallel with this process, the technical and organisational modernisation of the economy, as well as structural changes, will be implemented.

8.4 NEW CONDITIONS IN THE LABOUR MARKET AND THE SOCIAL PROBLEMS INVOLVED

The investment restrictions of the 1980s and the growing difficulties of sales began to affect the intensity of demand for labour, though to varying extents in different regions. On the whole, the labour market was characterised – until almost the end of the decade – by asymmetry deriving from excess demand.

Figure 8.3 Changes in employment in the branches of the material sphere

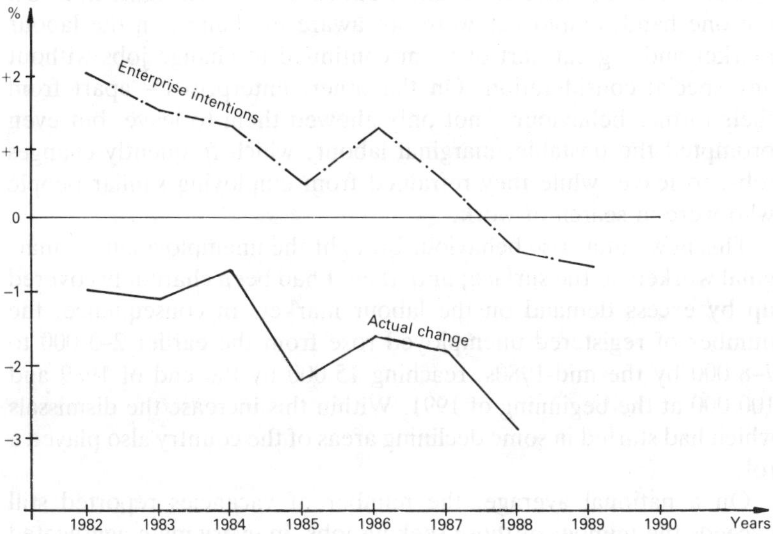

Source: *Munkaerópiaci információk, OMIK.*

The number of vacancies reported by enterprises to labour exchange bureaux – in the early 1980s around 100 000 on average – fell to under 50 000 by the end of 1989 and to 13 000 at the beginning of 1991. A similar picture is shown by the intentions of enterprises for annual changes in the workforce, announced since 1982 at the beginning of each year to the regional labour exchange bureaux. (See Figure 8.3.) In 1982, the enterprises still planned an average 2 per cent growth of employment: in actuality their workforce diminished by 1 per cent. In the following years, too, firms planned increases in employment, though, for well-known demographic reasons, the number of employees continually diminished. In the 1980s, there was still not the heavy pressure on firms which would have prompted them to increase labour intensity and productivity and to mobilise internal labour reserves. And the competition within the labour market was maintained by the significant labour turnover: enterprises competed with each other on the labour market to replace those who left their jobs.

Under the impact of economic difficulties in the second half of the 1980s, enterprise strategies changed somewhat. Although by 1988, they envisaged a decrease in employment (see Figure 8.3), their manpower management practices were still not characterised by realistic and organised rationality, but rather by belt tightening. On the one hand, employees were not aware of changes in the labour market and a great part of them continued to change jobs without any special consideration. On the other, enterprises – apart from their former behaviour – not only allowed them to leave, but even prompted the unstable, marginal labour, which frequently changes jobs, to leave, while they refrained from employing similar people who were in search of work.

This new enterprise behaviour brought the unemployment of marginal workers to the surface; until then it had been charitably covered up by excess demand on the labour market. In consequence, the number of registered unemployed rose from the earlier 2–3 000 to 7–8 000 by the mid-1980s, reaching 15 000 by the end of 1989 and 100 000 at the beginning of 1991. Within this increase the dismissals which had started in some declining areas of the country also played a role.

On a national average, the number of vacancies reported still exceeds the number of those seeking jobs, in every main aggregated group of manpower (see Table 8.3). But excess demand diminished considerably between 1986 and 1989. There is still some shortage of skilled workers, but the job opportunities for those belonging to other occupational groups, particularly unskilled workers, have significantly deteriorated.

But the national averages cover up the structural deviations between demand and supply in respect of individual occupations and geographical areas. In some occupations, there are even now more people seeking jobs than there are vacancies (e.g. porters, guards, office clerks, shop assistants, waiters, livestock attendants, precision mechanics, etc.), while in others, demand continues to exceed supply to a significant extent (e.g. locksmiths, bricklayers, carpenters, water and gas-pipe fitters, welders, textile clothing workers, etc.).

Both the global and structural imbalances appear to accumulate in some geographical areas. There are regions where there are not enough vacancies even in those jobs which are most sought after on the national level (e.g. in the north-eastern part of the country), while in the area round Budapest, there is a shortage even of unskilled labour. Table 8.3 also indicates that in 1989 the unfavourable local labourer markets expanded considerably. These regional deviations are difficult to balance in spite of the small size of the country. Because of established traditions and customs, even the

Table 8.3 Job openings and job seekers (1987–9, 4th quarter)

	Year	*Number of job openings accruing to one job seeker* Total	*of which* skilled	semi-skilled manual workers	unskilled	Non-manual employees
For the whole country	1987	4.3	13.9	6.3	1.2	4.2
	1988	5.1	14.5	6.2	1.1	5.3
	1989	1.6	3.2	2.8	0.5	0.6
Budapest	1987	24.6	59.7	4.8	9.3	365.2
	1988	28.4	66.3	33.8	3.8	32.6
	1989	7.0	12.8	7.6	1.6	10.1
Pest county	1987	7.2	26.6	11.7	1.3	5.3
	1988	20.7	79.8	17.2	5.0	11.5
	1989	8.9	20.7	7.1	2.6	4.1
Komárom county	1987	12.9	55.3	52.0	2.4	5.7
	1988	16.3	79.8	79.6	2.8	13.1
	1989	6.1	12.6	17.5	1.5	1.4
Szabolcs-Szatmár county	1987	1.5	3.6	2.9	0.7	1.2
	1988	1.5	4.1	2.4	0.5	0.9
	1989	0.8	1.1	2.2	0.4	0.2
Hajdu-Bihar county	1987	3.9	35.2	6.9	0.5	3.4
	1988	1.6	3.4	1.2	0.6	2.9
	1989	0.6	0.9	1.1	0.3	0.2
Békés county	1987	1.5	3.7	15.5	0.4	0.8
	1988	3.4	5.1	11.9	0.7	2.6
	1989	0.6	0.8	1.5	0.2	0.8

Source: *Munkaeröpiaci információk*, omik, 1988, nos. 1–14; 1989 nos. 1–14.

young people are reluctant to change domicile, and the general shortage of dwellings, as well as relatively high housing rents and low wages, set limits to the regional mobility of manpower, which is anyway difficult to bridge.

The open unemployment which has appeared in recent years has produced strong social repercussions. The trade unions protested and some of them declared unemployment to be 'unacceptable'. Social researchers, as well as the press and telecommunications media, not infrequently reported about unemployment in a tragic tone. This panic can hardly be explained by the extent of unemployment, which still at the end of 1989 hardly reached 0.3 per cent, while the rate is 10–15 times higher even in the most social market economies of

Europe, and it is 25–40 times higher in other Western countries. But in Hungary – and also in the other East European countries – a large part of the adult population is composed of cohorts grown up in the last forty years. The socialist objectives of society and even their partial implementation deeply influenced the thinking and behaviour of even those people who were dissatisfied with or opposed to the 'existing socialism' as a socio-economic system.[7] The 'real' full employment and security of existence, experienced for decades, seemed to be a natural state of affairs to everyone.

Now, however, the marginal labour force is still changing jobs in the old way, and the residual labour force, which could earlier find work with not much difficulty, is experiencing a shock when the gates of enterprises begin to be closed against them.

Under the shock impact of developing unemployment in recent years, the government has taken rapid measures to modernise the institutional system of the labour market, on the model of Western market economies. The regional labour exchanges, whose main task had earlier been to satisfy the demand for labour of the state enterprises, were put at the service of those seeking jobs. The modern labour market institutions and methods tested in the Western 'social market economies' were introduced one after the other: a system of unemployment benefits, retraining of the unemployed and of those changing jobs, support to those participating in retraining, support for job-creating investment projects, interest-free 'restarting loans' to promote ventures by the unemployed, or severance pay of a considerable amount, transitory 'public works' for those finding jobs with difficulty, organisation of temporary 'probationary' jobs for young graduates not finding jobs, etc. To finance all these the government has created an employment fund (Table 8.4), the sum of which is annually determined in view of the expected outlays. The fund is financed from state revenues. In 1989, the fund amounted to 2255 million forints and for 1990 the amount of 6300 million forints is planned. In 1989, it made up 0.15 per cent of GDP and in 1990 it will amount to 0.4 per cent.

Compared with the labour market institutions of the economically much more developed Western European countries, the Hungarian system may be considered relatively advantageous. In Austria, an economically much more advanced country, the amount of unemployment benefit is 40 per cent of the earlier earnings. In Hungary it moves – depending on the cause of unemployment – between 50–70 per cent of earlier earnings, while in the case of retraining, those

Table 8.4 The utilisation of the employment fund (in percentages)

Title of utilisation	*1989 factual*	*1990 estimate*
Unemployment benefits	11.1	12.7
Development of the labour exchange network	12.3	6.3
Retraining	16.0	14.3
'Public works'	11.1	5.6
Early retirement	1.3	4.8
Refunding of interest on enterprise loans	4.9	10.1
'Stipends' of graduated 'probationaries'	0.2	0.6
Support for the creation of new work places	43.1	27.8
Special support given to crisis areas		17.8

Source: Based on information given by the State Wage and Labour Board.

affected get 75–90 per cent of the average wages of the trade in question during the otherwise free-of-charge training (see: OECD 1988; Schmid, Reissert and Bruche, 1987). By comparison, almost nothing has happened to modernise the personnel management system of enterprises, and only initial steps have been taken to develop industrial relations. However, because of the impact of the social and psychological factors mentioned, criticism is still directed at the prevailing system of benefits and supports, mainly on the restrictions on the payment of unemployment benefits. The criticisms which point out the weaknesses in the administration of the newly created labour exchange bureaux are more to the point. Because adequate expertise and practice are missing, they do not deal adequately with those seeking jobs, and their work is slow and sometimes disorganised.

The 'normal' institutions in the labour market have proved rather ineffective in solving the special problems of residual and marginal unemployment. To quote characteristic example: when the first retraining courses were organised in the north-eastern region of the country, it was surprising that very few of the registered unemployed volunteered to participate, and of those volunteers the majority left the retraining courses in a very short time. This was a natural consequence of the fact that only special social programmes are suitable for handling residual and marginal unemployment, which – going beyond the framework of the labour market – are adjusted to the special requirements and problems of individual groups. The gypsies, living in a subculture different from the national culture, those released from prisons, alcoholics and asocial personalities present problems that are not primarily related to employment, but are dependent on much deeper social factors.

The contradictory relationships of society and the economy, both in the process of transformation, and changing equilibrium relations in the labour market are reflected in a survey (Table 8.5) which explored the actual opinions of some occupational groups about job security and the chances of finding new jobs.[8]

Table 8.5 Public opinion unemployment poll (in percentages)

Occupational group	*Believing they can lose their job*	*Capable of immediately finding a new job*	*Could not find a new job, or only with worse conditions*
Graduates in leading positions	9.4	39.8	18.8
Executives with secondary education	12.2	30.2	25.8
Graduates in subordinated positions	11.9	37.7	15.5
Other white-collar workers	15.2	25.4	22.9
Skilled workers	14.9	34.7	21.3
Semi-skilled workers	18.4	20.9	32.3
Unskilled workers	17.3	21.0	28.6

Source: KSH, 1989.

8.5 CHANGES IN WAGE DIFFERENTIALS

The changes in the political and economic environment in recent years have also started to modify relative earnings. Earnings relative to occupation and job hierarchy in East European countries were for a long time characterised by diminishing differences between manual and non-manual workers. Even smaller earning differences existed between highly skilled non-manual workers in non-managerial positions and manual workers. On the other hand, the wage differentials of manual workers were marked by significant differences within the same occupational group, while the earnings of non-manual workers were characterised rather by levelling.

The differentiation of earnings among manual workers mainly reflected the fact that, under conditions of labour shortage, state enterprises did not enforce strict and uniform requirements of performance, and employees – depending on their individual strategies – varied their standards of performance and accordingly received different earnings. The major variations in performance levels were determined partly by differences in individual faculties, and partly by the fact that those who earned major incomes in the second economy made efforts to minimise their performance in the (full-time) work place and thus did not claim high earnings.

With non-manual workers, the levelling of salaries was helped by the restricted possibilities of measuring performance and thus of paying salaries by results. The higher incomes of those in leading positions are frequently derived from sources other than salaries, from formal and informal bonuses.

These processes greatly restrict the performance-stimulating effect of wages. The government's position has for a long time been that proper wage differentiation is very important. In practice, however, the spontaneous tendency to levelling has continued to prevail.

In recent years, a change in earlier practices has been noticeable. Differences in earnings between various enterprise groups have grown significantly. The earnings in the private sector and of those employed in joint ventures have essentially been growing faster than average, and major differences in earnings have also developed within the state sector, because central wage regulation has become partly liberalised and thus some enterprises have a better chance to raise earnings.

The tendency for relative earnings to shift in favour of non-manual workers, particularly executives, is new. Among subordinated employees (department heads, engineers, economists, accountants, etc.) it is the earnings of those capable of higher performance, and particularly of those speaking foreign languages, that have increased faster – although this has not been a consistent or general tendency. The greatest favourable change has occurred among the managerial staff, since their ability to assert their interests has grown now that they are free from ministerial tutelage.

These changes in relative earnings indicate that efficiency requirements have become more important in the economy than was earlier the case. At the same time, these changes, which are derived from greater opportunities to assert interests or from a monopolistic position, are not properly regulated by a mechanism to reconcile special group interests. The institutional forms of collective bargaining are already in the process of formation, but, for the time being, they have scarcely any influence on the labour market.

8.6 CONCLUDING REMARKS

The labour market processes clearly indicate that the social and economic transformation going on in Hungary also involves several grave social conflicts. In the field of employment policy these mainly stem from unemployment which is expected to grow fast in the future with the marketisation of the economy. Unemployment causes grave problems in every Western country. Its impact, however, is significantly mitigated, on the one hand, by the fact that in market economies economic recessions, the uncertainties of employment and the concomitant unemployment are well-known phenomena to which the population is more or less accustomed. On the other hand, there is an attempt to counterbalance the problems caused for the unemployed and their families with the aid of a diversified 'social network'.

In Hungary, however, the people became used over long decades to employment security, which makes them particularly sensitive to 'unexpected' economic recessions and to the difficulties in keeping their jobs or in finding new ones. Enduring unemployment is made especially difficult by the stagnation and decline in living standards and by the inflation which rapidly reduces the real value – and thus the efficiency – of the old and impending new social care systems. Thus, the key to solving the social problems which are emerging in the field of employment can basically be found in overcoming the economic crisis, in restricting inflation and, in the last resort, in reviving the economy. This will make it possible to provide an active employment policy, and strengthen the 'social network' – so that the social burdens deriving from the socio-economic changes can be effectively mitigated.

NOTES

1. A good survey of the development of Hungarian economic thought is provided by Szamuely (1986), and of the process of economic reform by Révész (1990).
2. In 1989, General Electric bought the 51 per cent majority package of shares in the biggest electric bulb factory in the country for US$ 150 million and has started modernising it. General Motors has begun a joint venture for the creation of a factory with a capacity of 100 000 Opel motors annually, mostly for West European cooperation, and to a lesser extent for a domestic car assembly plant; finally, Suzuki has created an assembly plant capable of producing 100 000 Swift-type cars annually.

German, Canadian and British investment companies have been formed with significant registered capital.

3. The economically rational changes in price level and price structure aggravated the situation of low income groups, particularly that of families with several children and of pensioners. The price level of staple consumer goods increased faster than average and thus the consumer price index for low income families was higher than for high income ones (see: A fogyasztói árszinvonal . . ., 1989). This was only partially counterbalanced in low income families by increases in family allowances and child-care aid, as well as by a higher than average rise in the lowest pensions.
4. In a study summarising changes in the Hungarian employment policy between 1949–84 (Timár, 1987), I have already indicated that the official Hungarian employment statistics essentially deviated in content from international statistics. In the interest of a better understanding of Hungarian conditions I have recomputed the data of official employment statistics according to the ILO system (ILO, 1976). To illustrate the impact of the modification, I repeat here the 1984 data published in the study quoted, according to the new system for those who wish to study more deeply the situation in the Hungarian labour market (Timár, 1987, p. 105).
5. These are official data of the 1980 population census modified according to the ILO conventions.
6. Western Europe means the average of Austria, Belgium, France, the Netherlands, Switzerland. Northern Europe refers to Denmark, Finland, Iceland, Ireland, Norway, Sweden, the United Kingdom (ILO, 1986).
7. This is also indicated by the programmes of the several dozen parties which participated in the elections at the end of March, 1990. The demand for full employment, security of existence and a 'social network' covering the whole population – fundamentally of a socialist nature – can be found even in those programmes which otherwise follow conservative or right-wing political trends.
8. In October–November 1988, the Central Statistical Office conducted a public opinion poll, covering 0.4 per cent of the population between 15 and 69 years of age (KSH, 1989).

REFERENCES

ANTAL, L. (1985) *Gazdaságirányitási és pénzügyi rendszerünk a reform útján* (Budapest: Közgazdasági és Jogi Könyvkiadó).

'A fogyasztói árszinvonal változása az 1988 évben. Fogyasztói árindex.' (1989) *Füzetek 1.* Központi Statisztikai Hivatal (KSH).

GÁBOR, I.R. (1979) *Közgazdasági Szemle*, no. 2, pp. 171–87.

Hawrylyshyn (1976) 'The Value of Household Services: A Survey of Empirical Estimates', *The Review of Income and Wealth*, no. 2.

ILO (1976) *Recommendations on Labour Statistics* (Geneva).

ILO (1986) *Economically Active Population. Estimates: 1950–1980. Projections: 1985–2025*, Vol. V (Geneva).
KORNAI, J. (1980) *The Economics of Shortage* (Amsterdam: North-Holland).
KŐVÁRI, Gy. and Timár, J. (1984) *Közgazdasági Szemle* 5.sz, pp. 528–34.
KSH (1989) *A munkahely biztonsága – kereseti lehetőségek*, p. 59.
Munkaerőpiaci információk (Information about the labour market) 1988, 1–14. sz. es 1989, 1–14. Országos Munkaerőpiaci Központ.
OECD (1988) *Description of Employment Benefit Systems in OECD Countries* (Paris: OECD Employment Outlook), September.
RÉVÉSZ, G. (1990) *Perestroika in Eastern Europe. Hungary's Economic Transformation, 1945–1988* (Westview Press).
SCHMID, G., REISSERT B. and BRUCHE G. (1987) *Arbeitslosenversicherung und aktive Arbeitsmartpolitik* (Berlin: Wissenschaftszentrum für Sozialforschung).
SZAMUELY, L. (ed.) (1986) *A magyar közgazdasági gondolat fejlődése 1954–1978* (Selected studies) (Budapest: Közgazdasági és Jogi Könyvkiadó).
TIMÁR, J. (1987) 'Employment Policy in Hungary', in Adam, J. (ed.) *Employment Policies in the Soviet Union and Eastern Europe* (London: Macmillan).
TIMÁR, J. (1989) *Idő és munkaidő* (Budapest: Közgazdasági és Jogi Könyvkiadó).

Index